Oct.'86

POLITICAL THINKERS

edited by Professor Geraint Parry
University of Manchester

8

JOHN LOCKE

POLITICAL THINKERS

JOHN LOCKE

Geraint Parry
Professor of Government
University of Manchester

London
GEORGE ALLEN & UNWIN
Boston   Sydney

First published in 1978

GEORGE ALLEN & UNWIN LTD
40 Museum Street, London WC1A 1LU

© George Allen & Unwin (Publishers) Ltd, 1978

British Library Cataloguing in Publication Data

Parry, Geraint
    John Locke. – (Political thinkers; 8).
    1. Locke, John – Political science
    I. Title II. Series
    320'.01   JC153.L87

ISBN 0-04-320130-X
ISBN 0–04–320131–8   Pbk.

Typeset in 10 on 11 point Plantin by Trade Linotype Ltd
and printed in Great Britain
by Billing & Sons Limited, Guildford, London and Worcester

For Linda,
Susannah and Daniel

PREFACE

John Locke was a philosopher, a theologian, a doctor, an economist. He wrote at a time when it was still possible for a well-educated man to contribute to advanced thinking in a range of intellectual activities. In this study, I hope to enable the student of Locke's political thought to perceive the relationship in which it stands to his other inquiries. The greatest of political thinkers seek to explain the place of politics within the range of human activities, and Locke is no exception.

A welcome stage in the writing of any book occurs when the author can acknowledge his many debts. The kernel of the argument of this volume, now somewhat modified, appeared in an article in *Political Studies* in 1964, and I am grateful to the editor and to Oxford University Press, the publishers, for permission to use some of the material. The Librarians of the University of Glasgow, and in particular of its remarkable Special Collections, were invariably helpful. I should like to thank also the Keeper of the Western Manuscripts at the Bodleian Library for assistance in consulting the MSS in his care. Scholarly debts are many. To Professor Michael Oakeshott I owe my introduction to political thought and this is an occasion to express my gratitude, whether or not the subject, or its treatment, meet with his approval. I owe much to discussions with my colleagues of the Departments of Government and Philosophy at the University of Manchester. Professor Allen Potter, of the University of Glasgow, and Professor Jack Lively, of the University of Warwick, both read the manuscript and, as ever, both provided me with shrewd criticisms and stimulating suggestions. Naturally, responsibility for what survives remains inescapably mine. The typescript was produced by Mrs Nancy Walsh and Miss Celia Wallace at Glasgow and by Mrs Lynn Dignan at Manchester. My thanks are due to them. Mr Charles Furth and Mr Michael Holdsworth at George Allen & Unwin were discreetly patient whilst I pursued other research. For what my wife, Linda, contributed no thanks can be enough.

Manchester, 1977

CONTENTS

TEXTS AND ABBREVIATIONS

Two Treatises of Government, ed. P. Laslett, Cambridge University Press, 1960; references to the *Second Treatise* are by number in the text, e.g. (110); references to the *First Treatise* are prefixed by I, e.g. (1, 61).

Essay concerning Human Understanding, ed. J. W. Yolton, Everyman, Dent, 1965. Cited as *Essay* followed by book, chapter and section, e.g. *Essay*, II, xxi, 43. The *Essay* has been definitively edited by P. H. Nidditch for the new Clarendon Edition of Locke's Works, Oxford University Press, 1975. The Everyman edition is used here as more readily available to the student reader.

Two Tracts on Government, ed. P. Abrams, Cambridge University Press, 1967. Cited as *Two Tracts*.

Essays on the Law of Nature, ed. W. von Leyden, Oxford University Press, 1954. Cited as *Law of Nature*.

A Letter on Toleration, ed. R. Klibansky and J. W. Gough, Oxford University Press, 1968. Cited as *Toleration*.

The Works of John Locke, 10 vols, London, 1823. Cited as *Works*.

Some Considerations of the Consequences of Lowering the Interest and Raising the Value of Money in *Works*, Vol. V. Cited as *Some Considerations*.

Further Considerations concerning Raising the Value of Money in *Works*, Vol. V. Cited as *Further Considerations*.

The Reasonableness of Christianity, as delivered in the Scriptures in *Works*, Vol. VII. Cited as *Reasonableness*.

Some Thoughts concerning Education, in J. Axtell (ed.), *The Educational Writings of John Locke*, Cambridge University Press, 1968. Cited as *Education*.

Of the Conduct of the Understanding, in *Works*, Vol. III. Cited as *Conduct*.

Manuscripts in the Bodleian Library, Oxford. Cited as MS Locke.

Chapter I

Introduction

Locke's thought is a mixture of the old and the new. Philosophically he was identified with the new movement of ideas in the natural sciences which was developing in the second half of the seventeenth century. Locke worked with the leading figures in this movement, Newton and Boyle. His *Essay concerning Human Understanding* has been interpreted as an account of the extent and limits of the knowledge attainable by the new experimental science and of the means of attaining it.[1] He was acclaimed within a very short time as, along with his friend Newton, the chief intellectual inspiration of the critical spirit of the Enlightenment. Richard I. Aaron in his standard work on Locke has said of him: 'His writings secured for posterity the advances which had been made by the most radical and progressive elements of society in the seventeenth century.'[2]

Yet, in his political writings, Locke's theme is 'restoration'. He is intent in his mature works on re-establishing government upon its original foundations. His objective is to preserve rights which lie at the basis of all government and to restrain political leaders who depart from the principles implicit in the origins of their authority. Locke's attitude to the forms of government in England was more conservative than that of many of his associates and he was concerned to show that they were indeed more conservative than his royalist opponents. He might not be more royalist than the king but he wished to be more constitutionalist. It is absolutism which is condemned as a 'new' policy. Novelty was not then a term of approbation in politics. In this Locke placed himself in a long legalist and constitutionalist tradition going back, perhaps, to those early common lawyers who upheld the 'good, old law'.

Locke's theological writings display a similar concern. Although he was by no means execrated to the degree that Hobbes had been, Locke's writings on Christianity were repeatedly attacked for their alleged unorthodoxy. Yet Locke emphatically reiterated that he was unholding the essentials of Christian doctrine as expounded in the gospels. Certainly his conception of the order of the universe and of the place of mankind in it forms part of the conventional wisdom of the age which in outline he shared with nearly all his theological and political opponents.

What was novel was Locke's manner of defending old beliefs.
Throughout his work Locke opposed authoritarianism in intellectual
life. He sought to dispense with concepts and arguments which he
regarded as resting solely on untested tradition and which led into
error, or obfuscated the truth, or were merely superfluous to its defence.
He was concerned with what could and could not be said in philosophy,
science, politics and theology. There is, of course, a degree of false
modesty in Locke's famous picture of himself in the *Essay*'s Epistle
to the Reader as a mere 'under-labourer' who 'is clearing the ground a
little', yet it does describe something of his enterprise. It is more
immediately apparent in the *Essay* and the *Reasonableness of Christianity* than in the *Two Treatises*, but here also it is as much through
the critique of the language and false analogies of absolutism as through
the positive case that Locke clears the way for an understanding of
what is implied in the idea of civil government. Locke was well aware
that his manner of argument might appear unacceptable. He acknowledges that some arguments are 'new' and that others will seem 'strange',
but his reply in the *Essay* to those who regard him as 'pulling up the
old foundations of knowledge and certainty' might as easily describe
the reply he would make to such challenges to his politics: 'I persuade
myself at least that the way I have pursued, being conformable to
truth, lays those foundations surer.'[3]

The political foundations which Locke wished to lay in a surer
fashion were those of the rule of law whereby rights were protected by
established rules, known to all and obeyed by government and subject
alike. It was a particular mode of ruling which was termed 'civil
government' and which was to be sharply distinguished from certain
other types of power currently being claimed by or for some governments. There were several forms which civil government might take,
but in England it had been at least approximated by the balanced rule
of monarch, nobility and commons. Although civil government had
been seemingly well grounded in the experience of European nations,
it had increasingly been discovered to be a delicate practice endangered
by another conception of government – identified as absolutism – which
saw ruling as a matter not of neutral procedures but of securing certain
substantive goods for its subjects.[4] By the late seventeenth century the
modern sovereign state was rapidly becoming reality. Central governments had freed themselves of many of the limitations imposed by
custom and local and corporate privileges imposed on medieval rulers.
For the sake of the good and safety of the people this new sovereign
government was increasingly able to abolish old privileges, amend or
repeal old laws, grant new rights and make new laws. For the sake of
its subjects' souls it was able to declare what was the true religion and
to take over many of the welfare functions previously performed by
the church. Increasingly refined techniques of administrative and finan-

cial control and greater professionalism amongst public servants enabled such claims to be translated more effectively into action. Setting aside any distinct 'interest' (as Locke would term it) on the part of the ruling elite such government justified itself by its procuring substantive benefits for subjects. This could require regulation of the economy, granting of monopolistic property rights, control of the church, legislation on dress and consumption. Such power was welcome to many groups whose interests had been impeded by ancient privileges, but at the same time the attempted abolition of such privileges or 'liberties' meant the abolition of the rights of old entrenched interests. The state was becoming the fount of liberty and the consequences were set out by Thomas Hobbes in his typically succinct manner:

> [Liberties] depend on the silence of the law . . . And therefore such liberty is in some places more and in some less, and in some times more, and in other times less, according as they that have the sovereignty shall think most convenient.[5]

Everywhere this modern state emerged, from the sixteenth to eighteenth centuries, it was attended by civil unrest as political, economic and religious interests cut across one another: the Fronde, the English Civil War itself, the Thirty Years War, down to the Hungarian resistance to Joseph II at the end of the eighteenth century. The search for stability was an understandable preoccupation of politicians and those who reflected on politics. There was also, however, the question of the political form that stability might take. At what cost to liberty might stability be attained and, since this is inherent in the question, at what cost to whose liberty? To many political thinkers, the mature Locke included, in certain hands this great Leviathan could become a new threat to the liberty not merely of the traditional interests but to the people at large. To make liberty dependent on will and not on standing laws was a threat to the institution of property itself which made liberty actual. At the time Locke was writing the *Two Treatises of Government* political stability in England might have been achieved by following either a direction leading to absolute monarchy on the lines of Louis XIV's France or to parliamentary monarchy. Locke's aim was to show that, in any deep understanding, stability could only occur where liberty and property were made secure by law. To establish this Locke, like most thinkers, turned to the conceptual tools most at hand, which were to be found in the tradition of European constitutionalism. His novelty lay in the extent to which he defended this constitutionalism, not by appeals to legal precedent or by reference to constitutional history, as was customary to the tradition, but by reducing it to rational principles. In this respect the scholastic practice may be justified of comparing Locke's achievement with that of Hobbes in similarly founding absolutism on rational principles.

The ideology of absolutism was not however to be discovered in Hobbes's attempt to derive absolute authority from absolute individualism. It was to be found in the theory of order, according to which the absolute authority of the monarch was analogous to the absolute authority of God over the universe, and had been granted by God to the ruler to secure all the benefits for which God had also ordained political society amongst men. It was in the particular form of the work of Sir Robert Filmer that the ideology presented itself for Locke's attention. Filmer was a contemporary of Hobbes, whose work was republished in the royalist interest from 1679 onward and became 'the backbone of the Tory ideology'.[6] It was therefore incumbent on Locke to establish that absolute monarchy was neither part of the natural order nor directly instituted by God, but that civil government was entirely consistent with what could be discerned about God's plans for mankind. Although civil government was not natural but an artefact of man – a position shared with Hobbes – it could be shown to be the kind of government most compatible with the rational, autonomous men whom God had created. Locke therefore had to fashion his statement on civil government so as to refute absolutist theory in the particular shape given to it by Filmer, showing that absolutism was incompatible with the idea of a civil association of free men and with the institution of private property on which freedom rested and which absolutism boasted it could best defend.

Who better, it is often asked, to accomplish such a task than John Locke, property owner and client or adviser of successive Whig politicians?[7] born in 1632 of a minor Somerset landed family Locke had a Calvinist upbringing from his father who had been a Parliamentary captain in the Civil War. The patronage of a more influential family enabled him to go to Westminster School and on to Christ Church, Oxford, where he graduated as a Bachelor and then Master of Arts, and in 1660 was elected Lecturer in Greek. Whilst fulfilling normal, but not heavy, academic responsibilities Locke became increasingly interested in the study of science and medicine, associating with Robert Boyle who was to be mentioned in the Epistle of the *Essay* as, along with Newton, a master builder of the commonwealth of learning. Necessarily this meant an interest not only in the substantive discoveries in science but in the experimental method practised and proclaimed by his circle. Locke's study of medicine was intensive even though it was not considered to have been extensive enough to warrant the award of a doctorate by the University, as Locke had requested. It was nevertheless his medical skills which were to bring about the greatest turning point in his career.

Locke had been introduced in 1666 in his medical capacity to the Whig politician Lord Ashley, later to be the first Earl of Shaftesbury. Ashley was sufficiently impressed by Locke to invite him to join his

London household as a personal physician which he did in 1667. In the following year Ashley became dangerously ill of a liver disease. Locke directed a remarkable operation which Laslett has described as 'one of the medical miracles of the age', in that the patient not only survived but was cured. From this moment Locke became firmly established as one of Ashley's leading advisers ranging over politics and economics, with medicine a very minor matter. Thus Locke became Shaftesbury's 'assistant pen' or, as he has been called, his 'ideologist in residence'.

This was not, however, Locke's first acquaintance with political reflection. In Oxford he had already written, but not published, on two topics which were to concern him throughout his intellectual life – religious toleration and natural law. In the works on toleration the future libertarian was in 1660–1 an advocate of the absolute authority of government over religion.[8] He opposes the claim that government has no right to legislate on ceremonies and rituals which are not essential to the core of the Christian religion, and which are not themselves good nor evil but 'indifferent', and must leave this to individual conscience. Locke, mindful of the political and religious disputes which had raged since the time he first became aware of his political world, argued that men were constantly inclined to claim that the dictates of their conscience should be the law for others. His argument leans on traditional notions of the sin of intellectual pride. Each if left free will attempt to make his rituals necessary to others, with the result that order becomes impossible, as well as the genuine liberty which depends on order. Whatever theory one may have of the source of government authority, the ruler must be allowed the right to declare and enforce the religious ceremonies which are to be followed in any nation. Locke recognises fully the distinct provinces of churches and governments, but argues that toleration in practice endangers order. The conclusions are similar to those of Hobbes, but in these tracts Locke does not commit himself to Hobbes's derivation of absolute authority from consent but only refers to it as one possible theory, along with that of divine right; nor does he elaborate a theory of natural law as the foundation of either consent – as Hobbes had done – or divine right.

From 1660 to 1664 Locke was, however, writing on the law of nature in essays which he was again not to publish but the contents of which, unlike those of the *Tracts*, show a marked continuity with his later philosophical work.[9] He attempts to show that knowledge of the law of nature – the universal laws of morality – is based on reasoning from experience of the world, but cannot be derived from tradition or from any consensus of mankind.

By 1667 Locke's position on toleration had changed radically in a liberal direction, when he wrote an *Essay on Toleration* as an advisory paper for Shaftesbury. It is not possible to establish how this change came about. It is possible that it reflects the first attempt at resolving tensions implicit in the early writings. There has never been any incompatibility between the theory of natural law as such and absolutism. Nevertheless the intellectual anti-authoritarianism already so apparent in the early *Essays on the Law of Nature* does not sit easily with the absolutism Locke feels in the *Tracts* is required to control the consequences of free-thinking. By 1667 Locke may already have felt that the way to the knowledge of the law of nature and to salvation required individual experiment and that the dangers of religious experimentation were not so great as he had once feared.[10] An alternative explanation that Locke was merely expressing Shaftesbury's policy of religious toleration (though not for Roman Catholics) is also possible and not entirely incompatible. Shaftesbury may have persuaded Locke that toleration would not in fact endanger stability, thus removing the problem which the early *Tract* had discussed and, at the same time, permitting Locke to pursue the intimations of his anti-authoritarianism for religion, the theory of knowledge and for politics.

Locke wrote his first work on economics in 1668, although it was not to be published until 1692 as *Some Considerations on the Lowering of Interest and Raising the Value of Money*. Ashley had been appointed Chancellor of the Exchequer. In 1672, Locke received a minor government post from Shaftesbury, now briefly Lord Chancellor. In 1673, he was appointed Secretary to the Council of Trade and Plantations which advised on foreign and colonial trade. After its disbandment in 1675, Locke left for France for reasons of health and stayed there until 1679. Shaftesbury had been restored for another brief spell of office. At this time Shaftesbury was engaged with the struggle to exclude the Catholic James, Duke of York, from the throne. It was a struggle which raised major constitutional issues concerning the right to determine the royal succession and to delimit royal authority. It necessarily raised questions of religious toleration, including the toleration of Catholics and dissenting Protestants. The political techniques employed on either side were frequently ruthless and unscrupulous, as both parties attempted to control Parliament and elections, ending with the dissolution of the Parliament and a period of non-Parliamentary government from 1681. Finally it produced a vigorous pamphlet war.[11]

By this time Locke had written most of what is now the *Two Treatises of Government*. Although the work did not appear until 1689 and although its Preface declares that the author hopes it will establish the right of William III to the throne of England, it has been established by Peter Laslett that the bulk was written by 1681 and that it was further revised in 1689 to take account of the intervening events leading up to the Revolution. The *Second Treatise* was the first to be written, setting out the general principles of Locke's position, followed by the *First Treatise* in which he dissects the arguments of Filmer whose work had been reproduced for the royalists in the Exclusion

Crisis. The publication of Filmer's *Patriarcha*, containing the foundations of his position, led Locke to write the *First Treatise* and revise the *Second Treatise* to incorporate a more general response to Filmer's work. Laslett suggests a dating of 1679–81 and that the work must be seen as a general and a particular attack on Filmer's defence of absolutism.[12] This dating revised the traditional dating of 1689 startlingly, and changed the significance of the work from a defence of a successful political restorative revolution to an unpublished call for one. The dating has been widely accepted although there have been some suggestions, notably by R. W. K. Hinton, of an even earlier dating.[13] According to this hypothesis Locke may have written his first version of the *Second Treatise* in 1673–5, drawing on the experience of the earlier years of Charles II's reign and on that of Charles I. Around 1679–80, however, the importance of Filmer's work led Locke to revise the *Second Treatise* to incorporate references to Filmer's arguments and to write the *First Treatise*. This case rests on judgements on the continuity of Locke's argument if the acknowledged clear references to Filmer's position are omitted. Its significance would be that the earliest version of the *Second Treatise* would not be a reply to Filmer but an independent treatise or, if a reply to anyone, a reply to Hobbes or 'Hobbists'. There seems to be no firm way of settling the question in the absence of any original manuscript. It will be argued later that certain of Locke's arguments do make sense as responses to a Hobbesian position, particularly on slavery and despotism and on the state of nature which cannot refer to anything in Filmer. This does not, however, depend on the dating, nor necessarily on Locke's direct acquaintance with Hobbes, since he could be as familiar with the Hobbesian position from reviews and criticism as can a modern reader be with a current philosophical notoriety. Nevertheless the reply (if so it is) to some arguments shows a subtle appreciation of the implications of Hobbes's case. In this respect Locke had two absolutist opponents, with the more embarrassing of whom Locke shared assumptions which he would not have cared to acknowledge.[14]

From 1671 onwards Locke had also been working on the *Essay concerning Human Understanding*. Prompted by a discussion of the knowledge of morality and revelation Locke was led on to consider the extent of knowledge as such. The *Essay* went through successive revisions until its appearance in 1689 which established Locke's philosophical reputation.

Locke continued to work on the *Essay* after the great reversal of his fortunes in 1683. Shaftesbury fled to Holland in 1682 after the collapse of an attempted coup to place the Duke of Monmouth on the throne. In January 1683 he died. In June the Rye House Plot was exposed, Whig leaders were arrested, including Algernon Sidney who was accused of writing seditious political treatises, and Locke was under suspicion for some possible treasonable activity. In September Locke left for Holland, not to return until 1689. At some stage a middle section of the *Two Treatises*, which in the Preface Locke says was as long as the rest put together, and which appears to have been a continuation of the discussion of Filmer, was destroyed. The *First Treatise* breaks off in mid-sentence, Locke not having bothered to complete it when he published the full work. Whilst in Holland he completed the *Essay* and wrote finally, in publishable form, his thoughts on toleration in *Epistola de tolerantia*, and wrote to his friend Edward Clarke letters concerning education, which were to be worked up into book form as *Thoughts concerning Education*, published in 1693.

Upon Locke's return his three major works were published in England – the *Essay*, the *Two Treatises* and the translated *Letter concerning Toleration*, the latter two appearing anonymously although Locke's authorship of *Toleration* was rapidly made public, to Locke's annoyance. He also received a minor office as Commissioner of Appeals, after declining diplomatic posts abroad, and in 1696 was appointed to a far more influential place as a Commissioner on the new Board of Trade. Here he resumed his work on developing and protecting England's foreign and colonial trade. It was in this capacity that Locke gave his notorious advice on unemployment and pauperism. Able-bodied men might be forced to labour as naval seamen, women and the infirm put to work in Houses of Correction, and children from 3 to 14 set to work in pauper schools on a minimal diet.[15] This was the limit of his welfare provisions, which were regarded as an incentive to employment rather than as protection. The schooling of course contrasts rather sharply with the civilised sensitivity of his *Thoughts concerning Education* for the children of more gentle birth. Despite continuing ill health – Locke suffered severely from asthma – he exercised considerable authority on the Board and also as adviser to leading Parliamentary figures, of whom Lord Somers, William's Chief Minister from 1697 to 1700, was the most important. He had been previously called in by Somers to advise on the reform of the coinage and in 1695 had published his *Further Considerations concerning Raising the Value of Money*. His advice was taken by the government and Locke's friend Sir Isaac Newton was involved in its implementation as Warden of the Mint. Locke was an intellectual in politics, rather like those modern academics who sit on British Royal Commissions or are called to Washington by a new President. Whereas nowadays Locke's counterparts have an institutional base in the universities and research institutes, Locke and his contemporaries generally could attain positions of influence only through personal patronage. Both then and now, such figures tend to perceive themselves as lending the knowledge of their new science to the community.

During this period of political activity, as well as revising the *Essay* – including writing a chapter, 'Of the conduct of the understanding', which was posthumously published separately – Locke wrote increasingly on religion. Further lengthy *Letters on Toleration* defended the original against criticism and in 1695 he published *The Reasonableness of Christianity*, anonymously like all his controversial religious works. In it Locke seeks to show the compatibility of Christianity with the natural law of reason, but also that the Christian gospel can teach the principles of morality more clearly than even the greatest philosophers who have studied them. Though Locke affirmed its orthodoxy, the work partly established Christianity's reasonableness by paring doctrine down to very few essentials. Its opponents found it Unitarian in tendency and subversive of Christian faith. Locke's *Vindications* of it were clearly necessary, as its approach was increasingly taken up by the advocates of natural religion.

After Somers fell from office in 1700, Locke also retired from public affairs. Religious questions still concerned him. His last major undertaking was a commentary on the Epistles of St Paul, but revisions of both the *Essay* and the *Two Treatises* went on to a late date. Locke died in 1704.

Locke was therefore a political thinker, a philosopher, a theologian, an economist, an educationalist and a doctor. During the greater part of the time he was so intellectually active in writing, he was also deeply involved at the centre of practical politics to a degree seldom, if ever, surpassed by any political thinker. Can any coherence be made of his many intellectual and practical endeavours? Interpretations have diverged widely. Locke's own manner of dealing with his writings has added to the difficulty of forming a conclusion. Some of the writings we now have available were not published by Locke. He clearly changed his position on toleration and would not be expected to have published the *Two Tracts* in his later years. But the early *Essays on the Law of Nature* do concern problems with which he continued to wrestle. Moreover, although he was proud to acknowledge authorship of the *Essay concerning Human Understanding*, his writing on toleration, Christianity and government appeared anonymously and Locke did not acknowledge authorship until his will, although in the case of the *Letters on Toleration* and the *Reasonableness* it was widely known. The lengths he went to to conceal his authorship of the *Two Treatises* are, however, quite extraordinary.[16]

Why was Locke so reluctant to acknowledge these works? The answer will probably never be known, but speculations are many and varied. Was he less confident about the views expressed in the anonymous works? This seems unlikely in that he stoutly defended the *Reasonableness* and he recommended the *Two Treatises* on two separate occasions as among the best books dealing with the principles of politics and of property, writing as if they were by some author unknown to him! Did he recognise a difference in the scientific status of the *Essay* and the other writings? This is possible, but involves distinguishing the writings on religion from the *Treatises*. He may have felt that in writing on toleration and Christianity he was, on some matters, expressing more personal statements of his own faith than would be true of the *Essay*, and that they should not be controverted in the same technically philosophical manner. Though more modern confessional writers such as Rousseau would have wished to acknowledge and personalise such work, Locke was of an obsessively secretive disposition. The *Two Treatises*, however, are clearly statements of political principle to which this hypothesis would not apply. Hans Aarsleff has suggested[17] that Locke did not wish the search for truth to be disturbed by irrelevant personal or partisan controversy – a view he frequently expressed. To identify the *Two Treatises* as the work of a Whig and a former exile might have damaged the work's attempt to provide a rational justification of limited civil government, liberty and property which all men of all but the most absolutist persuasions could wholeheartedly accept.

A further hypothesis is that Locke believed that in discussing religion and politics he was placing himself in considerable personal danger. One version of the hypothesis is that the danger arose because the views he was espousing were basically those of the execrated, atheistical Hobbes.[18] Locke was so accused in his own day on the basis of his *Reasonableness of Christianity*. His denials of any familiarity with Hobbes have, with some justification, been viewed as a case of protesting too much. There are matters which, without so declaring, Locke agreed with Hobbes – in regarding political authority as an artefact founded on individual consent, in some elements of his analyses of language and of the will and in his minimal definition of the requirements for a distinctively Christian belief. The areas of disagreement are however more extensive and more fundamental. His failure to cite Hobbes as an opponent may reasonably be explained in several ways. With a few exceptions, of whom Filmer is the most notable, Locke seldom does cite specific opponents. In this way he is like Hume and like Hobbes himself. The points of disagreement with Hobbes could be at times widely divergent, at others subtle but none the less crucial – their agreement about the dependence of property on law and their disagreement about the significance of this will be cited as one instance – and it would certainly not have assisted Locke's case to have been constantly debating such matters.

There was however a more direct reason for Locke's supposing his writings dangerous, without his trying to secrete his alleged Hobbism. The reason also affects the *Two Treatises* much more than the other works and could explain his much greater obsession with the secrecy of its authorship, even trying to conceal it from his publisher. At any of the supposed dates of their composition the *Treatises* were indeed potentially subversive, as Locke's very concern in the final chapter of the *Second Treatise* to anticipate such a challenge demonstrates. The work may justify a conservative revolution, but governments are not normally much more sympathetic to this than to any other revolution which might topple them. Algernon Sidney was indicted on, amongst others, the count of writing, but not yet publishing, subversive works of political theory which were not dissimilar in some of their themes and contents to those which Locke had written and attempted to file secretly. Locke had to flee the country and was pursued by English intelligence even in Holland. The turmoil of Hobbes's time is regularly cited as helping to explain his political stance, but it is certainly arguable that Locke was in far greater personal danger. Such dangers may seem to have passed after 1688 but the retrospective view of the Revolution as having tipped the political balance irrevocably towards Parliamentary constitutionalism is misleading, and was not shared by contemporaries. Party conflict was intense and the ultimate succession still uncertain. Not until after 1715 did political stability seem assured. Perhaps Locke, as the greatest philosopher of his day, did not have so much to fear but no doubt he would have had little relish for the prospect of exile again at his age. The fact that he did acknowledge authorship in his will suggests that, with the passing of any personal danger, he did not fear for the safety of his posthumous intellectual reputation.

The final hypothesis, however, touches on this very point. Locke may have been sensitive to the possibility that his critics would seize on the inconsistencies between the *Essay* and both the *Treatises* and the *Reasonableness of Christianity*. The alleged inconsistencies have centred on the existence of the law of nature and the method of knowing the moral truths it contains. The problem of the knowledge of the law of nature was put to Locke on several occasions and his replies, even to his friends and associates like James Tyrrell, were notoriously tetchy.[19] This may, however, either reflect Locke's genuine irritation that his questioners had not understood a position he himself believed to be clear, or his unease at being tested on a matter about which he felt uncertain and vulnerable.

The inconsistency between the *Essay* and the *Two Treatises* was most forcefully alleged by Sir James Stephen in essays on Locke in his *Horae Sabbaticae*.[20] Stephen asserted that the 'great singularity' of Locke's political theory was its 'striking incongruity with his metaphysics'. Whereas the *Essay* had destroyed the doctrine of innate ideas and had reduced all knowledge to the generalisation of experience, the *Treatises* had assumed a law of nature and a state of nature which, in Stephen's view, could not possibly be discovered on the basis of experience. C. E. Vaughan argued for a similar inconsistency in what was for a long time a standard textbook in political philosophy,[21] and the more recent textbook of G. H. Sabine[22] suggests that there was a fundamental anomaly between his epistemological empiricism and the rationalism of his political thought.

Other interpretations have found greater consistency in Locke, but in quite different ways. Leo Strauss suggested that it was to be located in a Hobbesian conception of natural law as a law of self-preservation which, although it leads to a theory of constitutional government, grants that government effectively the power of Hobbes's Leviathan. Only by breaking this Hobbesian code in the work can the otherwise patently obvious illogicalities of Locke's position be overcome.[23] The language of traditional natural law can be stripped away to reveal an individualistic theory of natural rights. Strauss expresses sympathy with C. B. Macpherson's notable Marxist interpretation of Locke contained in his *The Political Theory of Possessive Individualism*.[24] Again natural law is viewed as a facade of moral obligations which Locke dismantles, to reveal a defence of individualist property accumulation in an open market society, coupled with a justification of a political society in which power rests with those who, by their supposed rationality and industry, have been most successful in the world of economic competition. Locke's is a theory of natural rights, rather than natural law, in which the rights described as natural are, in reality, the conventional rights of commercial society.

Natural law has been regarded as the key to the coherence of Locke's thought by those who find Locke's political thought rooted in religion. The most extended interpretation so far published along those lines has been by John Dunn in his *Political Thought of John Locke*.[25] It is also advanced in major articles by Hans Aarsleff, Richard Ashcraft and, to the degree that he discusses Locke's politics, by John Yolton.[26] It is also the interpretation to which the present volume is most sympathetic.[27] There remain differences over the success of Locke's enterprise, and perhaps over its political implication. It is argued that Locke's work must be comprehended within a very particular Christian framework in which the nature of men's rights and duties are, in principle, rationally explicable but owe their obligatory character to the will of God. Although this approach lays far more emphasis on men's duties in a divine order than does either the Hobbesian or Marxist interpretation, it by no means necessarily denies a strongly individualist cast to Locke's thought, as it is hoped will be shown. Each man is capable of understanding the duty to his maker to seek salvation and respect others in the performance of their similar duty. But the precise path to salvation is not clearly set out for men and they must find their own way, both in their reflections and in their works. It is not always clear whether there is indeed only one true path which every man must seek without ever being sure that he has taken the right one – the grim, melancholic doctrine to which Dr Johnson seemed to adhere – or whether there are many paths and a man's inner conviction and sincerity could themselves bring some assurance of salvation. In either case an individual's right to pursue his life plan is also to be understood as the performance of his duty, and is consistent with a social life characterised by self-affirmation and competition. The law of nature entails that one respect other persons as equally creatures of God, and desist from injuring them by unfairly denying their right to express their own sense of individuality to the degree of which they are capable. In political societies, as long as established ground rules are observed the respect for individuality is entirely consistent with competition on the open market place of economic or intellectual life, even though Locke does not commit any quasi-Darwinian fallacy of supposing that whatever survives in either 'market' is necessarily in accord with the law of God and reason.[28]

Estimates of Locke's achievement in reconciling his epistemology with his theology and in politics appear to depend on how far one adopts an internal or external view of his endeavours. Sir James Stephen did in fact perceive that Locke's political theories rested on theological arguments but found these permeated by gross fallacy. It will be argued in subsequent chapters that there is a certain internal coherence to Locke's thought provided that the reader is prepared to allow those arguments by which Locke attempted to establish the existence of a divine legislator from experience of the design of the world. There is no doubt that Locke found the argument satisfying and that it is a thread which runs from the early *Essays on the Law of Nature* to the late works. If however one looks at Locke's enterprise with Hume's demolition of such arguments in mind in the *Dialogues of Natural Religion*, it can become difficult to persuade oneself even that Locke could have found his position consistent. The effort of imagination must nevertheless be made if one is to understand how Locke saw the relationship between the realms of morality and politics, and how he perceived the problems he needed to tackle.

Can Locke's political theory be assessed or understood apart from its theological substructure? To a very considerable extent it can be and must be. Neither Locke's theology nor his epistemology entails his political conclusions. Very different political systems have been found compatible with ideas of natural law. Certainly the conception of man and his moral rights and duties, which Locke derives from his theology, is capable of generating political rights other than those Locke defends, often of a much more radical, egalitarian character.[29] More significantly for our secular age, the *Two Treatises* has an existence of its own. It must be remembered that Locke intended it to lead this independent life, at least during his lifetime. The generality of readers of the early editions of the *Treatises* did not know that its assumptions were underpinned in the *Essay concerning Human Under-*

standing and, slightly later, in the *Reasonableness of Christianity*. These assumptions are that no man is naturally subordinate to another, but that all are free and equal and may employ the resources of their minds and bodies in ways conducive to their own freely chosen ends, whilst respecting the equal entitlement of others to do likewise. These are the fundamental moral principles of liberalism, and would also be shared by many socialists as well as by certain conservatives. They are held by many who are totally unsympathetic to the theology which Locke so clearly found rewarding. Other foundations have therefore been provided for such principles or else they, or generally what amount to only slight variations upon them, have been asserted as irreducible moral notions. In total these assumptions identify man as an autonomous, self-directing but not self-sufficient individual. Locke articulated, as clearly as any writer had previously done, the politics implicit in the 'theory of individuality' which had gradually emerged in Western Europe with the decline of feudal society, and in reaction against that society's ideas of a natural hierarchical community. The theory of individuality explained and justified the conduct of persons who proclaimed themselves as self-determining individuals, character-ised by their ability to make choices and regarding this capacity of self-direction as itself a distinguishing virtue of human agents. Locke's concern was with the form of political association which would most effectively permit the cultivation of individuality (which is not to be identified with aggressive individualism, even if it is a frequent accom-paniment) and therefore with the kind of government which could be guaranteed not to menace individuality or reject the virtue of its cultivation.

The foundation of Locke's theory of individuality lay, as the present study will attempt to trace, in a view of man as a being with rights and duties in a divine order of creation. Locke's conception of man and of his political relationships is not, however, totally confined within this theological frame nor bounded by the historical circum-stances of its publication. Divorcing Locke's political and moral assumptions from their theological roots does an injustice to Locke's intentions, but does not rob those assumptions of their significance. They are still recognisable as part of the philosophy of individuality which, since its emergence at the end of the feudal era, has as Oakeshott put it 'remained the strongest strand in the moral convictions of the inhabitants of modern Europe' and, one must add, of Europe's intellectual offspring. It has been a philosophical theme with in-numerable variations and there has been perennial contestation of its central concepts, but the notion of individuality has been the focal point of moral reflection ever since its clear emergence around the fifteenth century. It is an undeniable fact of human experience. And once such a notion enters moral consciousness it remains part of the subject of moral discussion even if the original social situations which encouraged its first emergence have themselves been transformed. The nature of individuality, its character as a virtue, the political association which is appropriate to it, remain subjects of our current political discourse. To all of these subjects Locke made a major contribution.

Notes Chapter I

1 See particularly the work of John W. Yolton, notably *Locke and the Compass of Human Understanding*, Cambridge, Cambridge University Press, 1970 and on the religious controversies *John Locke and the Way of Ideas*, Oxford, Oxford University Press, 1968 edition.

2 *John Locke*, Oxford, Oxford University Press, 2nd edition, 1955, p. 302.

3 *Essay*, I, iv, 24.

4 See the brilliant survey by Michael Oakeshott, 'On the Character of the Modern European State', in his *On Human Conduct*, Oxford, Oxford University Press, 1975.

5 *Leviathan*, ed. Oakeshott, Oxford, Blackwell, 1955, ch. 21, p. 143.

6 Gordon J. Schochet, *Patriarchalism in Political Thought*, Oxford, Blackwell, 1975, p. 120.

7 Maurice Cranston, *John Locke, a Biography*, London, Longmans, 1957, is an admirably full and clear guide to Locke's political and intellectual career. Laslett provides a concise summary and interpretation of Locke's life in the second chapter of the Introduction to his edition of the *Two Treatises*.

8 Published with an excellent introduction by P. Abrams as *Two Tracts on Government*, Cambridge, Cambridge University Press, 1967.

9 Published with a magisterial introductory essay on these works and on Locke's attitude to natural law by W. von Leyden, *John Locke: Essays on the Law of Nature*, Oxford, Oxford University Press, 1954.

10 Esmond S. de Beer has suggested that Locke's experience on a short embassy in 1665–6 to Cleves may be responsible for the change. Locke noted that despite religious differences people there lived peaceably together. 'Locke and English Liberalism' in J. Yolton (ed.), *John Locke: Problems and Perspectives*, Cambridge, Cambridge University Press, 1969, p. 36.

11 See O. W. Furley, 'The Whig Exclusionists: Pamphlet Literature in the Exclusion Campaign, 1679–81', *Cambridge Historical Journal*, XIII, 1, 1957, pp. 19–36.

12 See ch. III of Laslett's Introduction.

13 'A Note on the Dating of Locke's *Second Treatise*', *Political Studies*, XXII, 4, 1974, pp. 471–8. It receives some support from K. Olivecrona, 'A Note on Locke and Filmer', *Locke Newsletter*, no. 7, summer 1976, pp. 83–93, who also sees the references to Filmer in the *Second Treatise* as an insertion but does not commit himself to the earlier date.

14 This is not of course a return to the old textbook assumption of some necessary clash between the two great 'masters of political thought' but rests on a sense of the differing relevance of different sections of Locke's argument. The contrary view is expressed by Laslett and with the greatest subtlety by John Dunn, *The Political Thought of John Locke*, ch. 7, who very rightly sees the menace of Hobbes to Locke's theology and epistemology but who finds it irrelevant to the *Second Treatise*.

15 See Cranston, *John Locke*, pp. 424–6 for the details.

16 Laslett opens his Introduction with a clear account.

17 'Some observations on recent Locke Scholarship' in J. W. Yolton (ed.), *John Locke: Problems and Perspectives*, Cambridge, Cambridge University Press, 1969, p. 269. Aarsleff extends his suggestion more broadly to Locke's other anonymous works but this makes it more difficult to see why the *Essay* should have been excepted.

18 The 'Hobbesian interpretation' of Locke has been advanced by Leo Strauss, *Natural Right and History*, Chicago, University of Chicago Press, 1953, and Richard H. Cox, *Locke on War and Peace*, Oxford, Oxford University Press, 1960.

19 See Cranston, *John Locke*, p. 334.

20 London, Macmillan, 1892, Second Series Essays VII–X. Essay IX on Government emphasises the incompatibility. All the essays are forthright, critical and shrewd.

21 *Studies in the History of Political Philosophy before and after Rousseau*, Manchester, 1925, Vol. 1, p. 163.

22 *A History of Political Theory*, London, Harrap, 3rd edition, 1963, p. 530.

23 *Natural Right and History*, pp. 202–51, especially pp. 220–1.

24 Oxford, Oxford University Press, 1962.

25 Cambridge, Cambridge University Press, 1969.

26 Hans Aarsleff, 'The State of Nature and the Nature of Man in Locke', in J. Yolton (ed.), *John Locke: Problems and Perspectives*, pp. 99–136; Richard Ashcraft, 'Faith and Knowledge in Locke's Philosophy', in J. Yolton, op. cit., pp. 194–223; J. Yolton, *Locke and the Compass of Human Understanding*, ch. 7, and 'Locke on the Law of Nature', *The Philosophical Review*, LCII, 4, 1958, pp. 477–98.

27 The outline argument was suggested in the article 'Individuality, Politics and the Critique of Paternalism in John Locke', *Political Studies*, XII, 2, 1964, pp. 163–77.

28 It appears to be the tendency of Macpherson's analysis to attribute such a view to Locke.

29 The point has been neatly made by D. J. Manning in a discussion of Locke's theological argument in *Liberalism*, London, Dent, 1976, pp. 121–5.

Chapter II

Man in the Order of Nature

Locke opens the *Essay concerning Human Understanding* by stating that it is 'the *understanding* that sets man above the rest of sensible beings, and gives him all the advantage and dominion which he has over them'. Underlying Locke's moral and political theory is a conception of man as a rational agent, capable of choice and, hence, of acting responsibly. Fundamental to any such conception is a view of the role of human reason, its capacities and its limitations. To act responsibly implies that the actor knows what he is doing or, at least, is capable of knowing. In turn this means that he is capable of understanding the facts and circumstances that are relevant to his decision. 'Ought implies can' and praise or blame for a person's actions are only appropriate where those actions are freely undertaken by actors who can be presumed capable of reflecting on their situation and prospects.

A major task of political theorising is to examine what kind of society a rational man would choose to live in. It is true that not all political theories pose the question explicitly in these terms. Many writers, impressed by the complex evolutionary character of human societies, have argued that the 'choice' of a society is not a choice that the individual is normally called upon to make. Particularly since the rise of the inter-related studies of history, sociology and comparative politics in the middle of the eighteenth century, theorists such as Montesquieu, Burke, Hegel and Marx have stressed in their different ways that men are born into a set of social and political arrangements which can therefore never be entirely of their own choosing. To approach the questions of political theory by considering how a rational individual would choose from, as it were, a range of possible political worlds is then readily dismissed as involving a superfluous and misleading hypothesis. Nevertheless even these critics are concerned to show how the society into which men are born can be justified to them. This they attempt to do, in conservative versions, by displaying the rationality which pervades the existing condition of affairs and indicating how that rationality might be maintained and extended. The radical response is to show how the society men inherit can be reformed or reconstructed so that it might properly claim the allegiance of a rational man. Whether the world is merely interpreted in various ways or changed, this is theoretically on rational grounds. Implicitly or explicitly, then, political theory explains the rationality of possible oᴄ actual political systems to men presumed to be capable of being reconciled or exhorted by the reasons offered.

The arguments which are expected to satisfy these rational men vary considerably. This is largely what the disputes between political philosophers are about. Not only are the arguments disputed, however. So are the accounts of what is meant by a rational man. Is he a man 'of reason' or a man 'capable of reason'? Is he the 'reasonable man' of English law who is not expected to act as if he were able to contemplate in a quiet hour all the consequences of his conduct but, rather, to consider his actions in the light of the information available to the average man in the circumstances, and to respond to his situation with average speed displaying the attitudes normally expected from a member of his society? Burke warned that politics should be adjusted to human nature rather than to human reason, pointing out that reason was but part of human nature and by no means the preponderant part. It is certainly doubtful how far the rationality of political action can be considered in abstraction from the society to which it is supposed to refer. Yet it has proved a standing temptation for political thinkers to attempt to set out what kind of political arrangements might satisfy some posited irreducibly rational man. It is a mode of political argument most associated with those individualist theorists who have employed the image of a social contract to illustrate the terms on which rational men will enter into political society with one another. Individuals capable of rational choice are envisaged in a pre-political condition – termed a 'state of nature' – in which they are faced with the task of selecting the most suitable form of government to remedy various defects which they find to be inherent in a world without rules. One of the most recent exemplars in this long tradition of political argument is *A Theory of Justice* by John Rawls.[1] In this work rational individuals are concerned, not directly to establish a rational form of government, but to decide on rules of just treatment which all might agree to as fair in advance of knowing what roles they will play in society, or even what capacities they might have, or what styles of life they might eventually want to adopt. But since the thoroughgoing analysis of a concept – and an ideal – such as justice must give rise to the further analysis of equality, liberty, community and the whole gamut of political concepts, Rawls's individuals are faced with the problem of working out the most rational form of society for such rational, though supposedly ignorant, individuals. Though the substantive conclusions Rawls reaches need not concern us immediately, it is worth noting that the criticisms levelled against his version of contract theory echo those directed against such a 'classical' contractualist as John Locke. Is this the way, the critics ask, that a rational individual would act? Just as it is asked whether 'Lockean man' would create Lockean society, so the same question has been asked about 'Rawlsian man'. How far is it proper to portray rational man as self-interested and what does this in fact imply? How far does Rawls's picture of rational individuals in a state of nature rely for its per-suasiveness on its being modelled on 'rational' behaviour in Rawls's state of modern America? This question has been raised about Locke in one of the most celebrated and most controversial analyses of his work.[2] C. B. Macpherson has suggested that Locke's state of nature is but a thinly disguised version of Locke's seventeenth-century English society with its burgeoning capitalist values. Locke thus presents us with a picture of seventeenth-century Englishmen 'rationally' selecting seven-teenth-century English society. Rousseau had made much the same criticism of Hobbes's contractualism. Hobbes's competitive self-interested individual was not natural man but a brilliant picture of modern so-called civilised man with his concern for wealth and status.[3]

   There is a distinct element of truth in these sorts of criticisms. The Lockean polity resembles English political institutions of the seventeenth century with certain reforms and modifications. Indeed, David Hume was to regard it as a serious criticism of Locke that his theory led to the conclusion that the only legitimate government in the world was the English one. This, Hume suggested, flew in the face of all ordinary usage and understanding.[4] Such criticisms are not, however, entirely conclusive against the legitimacy of Locke's enterprise. Locke sought to outline the kind of political and social arrangements which would be acceptable to men who were identified as being free, responsible and self-reliant. This conception of human individuality had gradually emerged in Western Europe from around the fourteenth century. It challenged a theory of society in which a person's way of living was largely determined by his status as a member of a group – whether a guild, a church, a locality or a family – and where his range of choices, his rights and privileges belonged to him not as an individual but as a member, with a known standing, of a community. During the seventeenth century a political theory of individuality developed which explained and justified the conduct of persons who proclaimed them-selves as self-determining individuals, as masters of their own situation, as natural sovereigns, and who could only justify their subordination to others in a system of government as being the outcome of their own choice, represented by a contract. Individual freedom, responsibility and self-reliance may have become recognised as virtues during this period but they are not moral and political ideals confined to the seventeenth century. The notion of individuality, like other moral and political ideas, can take on an independent life not determinable by those who first expounded them nor by the social conditions of their origin. Any attempt such as Locke's to show what kind of political institutions seem to follow from a belief in such values must therefore raise issues which are not confined to the concerns of seventeenth-century England. Whilst it is true that Locke considered these values realisable in and through the political system and certain of the social and economic relationships of his day it is also true that these values may be transcribable into other institutions or, indeed, be far more compatible with other social arrangements of which Locke could perhaps not have conceived. This in part explains the recurrent interest in Locke and in the potentialities of Lockean or 'neo-Lockean' doctrine.

The theoretical problem with which Locke's *Two Treatises of Government* deals is, therefore, to discover how men with the attributes of freedom and reason can preserve themselves as free and rational agents whilst living in a community, with the apparent restrictions that entails. Locke's conception of human nature is not fully expounded in the *Two Treatises* but may be pieced together from his work on epistemology, religion, education as well as from his overtly political writings. Freedom, reason and self-reliance together constitute the 'Ariadne's thread' which permits one to trace the connections of Locke's ideas. And if Locke's work does not display the obvious systemic quality of a Hobbes, yet an overall disposition or way of looking at the world is discernible. Locke once said that politics was a 'part of moral philosophy'.[5] His own political thinking is certainly the pursuit of what is politically intimated in the moral disposition he believes to be necessary to human life.

The pre-eminence Locke ascribes to reason and the understanding in man is attributable to his overall conception of man's standing in the universe. Locke shared the widespread conception of the world as ordered in a hierarchy of beings and species. This belief in a 'Great Chain of Being' was, in one or other of its varied forms, central to the world view of most philosophers, theologians and men of learning and imagination until the late eighteenth century[6]. The world was conceived as comprised of a myriad of beings which effectively filled all the available space in nature. The beings of the universe were arranged in a hierarchy stretching from God through the various ranks of angels down to man, and from man through the animals down to the smallest of creatures whose existence was scarcely perceptible. Alexander Pope, whose *Essay on Man* is the greatest eighteenth-century expression of this view of nature, presented this hierarchy in eloquent fashion:

> Vast chain of being, which from God began,
> Natures aethereal, human, angel, man,
> Beast, bird, fish, insect! what no eye can see,
> No glass can reach! from Infinite to thee
> From thee to nothing! . . .[7]

Though this order stretches in an unbroken chain from highest to lowest, two main ranks of creatures may be distinguished – those having intelligence and those lacking it. Thus God and the angels form the ranks of the purely intelligible species. The lower ranks of animals form the ranks of sentient beings. Man is in a curious position, belonging to both parts of the order. He is, as Pope put it, on an 'isthmus of a middle state'. He is the sole earthly creature to share intelligence with God and the angels and is, hence, the lowest of the beings with reason. On the other hand, unlike God and the angels, he shares the physical character of the animals and is, hence, the highest of the order of sentient beings. The idea that man was in a middle state did not mean necessarily that there were equal members of orders above and below him. In fact, man was more often thought to be fairly low in the scale of existence. Locke sets out the general picture of this ordered creation in which there are 'no chasms or gaps'.[8] The descent is 'by easy steps' such that it is difficult to discern differences between animals on one step and those on another. There are animals which are so like both birds and beasts that they fall in between, amphibious animals that link 'the terrestrial and the aquatic', fish that have wings, 'not to mention what is confidently reported of mermaids, or sea-men'. All this was designed by God so that the ranks of beings will ascend upwards from man to Him just as they descend from men down to the scarcely distinguishable line between the organic and inorganic. This apparent pattern of the world suggests to Locke that 'there are far more *species* of creatures above us than there are beneath; we being, in degrees of perfection, much more remote from the infinite being of GOD than we are from the lowest state of being, and that which approaches nearest to nothing'.[9]

The ordered world is itself evidence of a designer. Anyone who seriously seeks a rational account of the world is necessarily led to conclude that there is a God who 'presides over the world'.[10] God makes his presence felt in the ordinary operations of the world as much as he had done through the performance of miracles in times past. It is God who has created the universe, who sets the planets in rotation, who determines the boundaries of earth and sea. God lays down the way in which plants will germinate and grow and determines the life-cycle of every being on earth. The most apparently irregular conduct in the universe is ultimately subject to the fixed laws of God. In these ways 'the visible marks of extraordinary wisdom and power appear so plainly in all the works of the creation . . .'.[11]

God is both the creator and the ruler of the ordered hierarchy. He rules by means of fixed law – the law of nature. The law lays down the mode of operation for every being in the scale of existence. This mode of operation is always appropriate to the nature of each being. Citing Aquinas in support, Locke asserts that every thing in the universe fulfils the task which destiny has set it.[12] Just as it is evident that the whole order of nature must be the creation of a divine being, so that creation implies a purpose. It is inconceivable that such creative activity could be without aim.[13] God has accorded each rank in the universe its specific purpose or destiny. God's law ordains that each is to move in the manner appropriate to its reaching the end arranged for it. Each in achieving its purpose contributes, by its teleological movement, to the fulfilment of God's purposes for the universe as a whole. As Pope was to put it:

> All are but parts of one stupendous whole,
> Whose body Nature is, and God the soul.

To each rank God has granted the capacities necessary to the attainment of its pre-ordained end. Each has the level of mental and physical abilities appropriate to its contribution to the plan which lies behind the 'mighty maze' of the universe. Each being is thus differentiated from every other by its possession of unique characteristics, which are suited to its needs – whether its particular sense of smell or hearing, its distinctive coat or its individual turn of speed. Not only are these distinguishing marks, however. It is by displaying these unique qualities that each being plays its role in the universal drama. The roles they play are already written down for them. Even the drawbacks to the role are part of the overall scheme. Greater animals prey on lesser, but all is part of the universal design, the ultimate purpose of which men cannot know – Pope's *Essay on Man*, like Locke's *Essay concerning Human Understanding*, concerns the limits of human reason.

Is it then to be expected, Locke asks, that man alone should be exempted from the operation of the laws of this regular universe? Clearly not. Man is but part of this whole. He is, equally with the other beings, part of God's creation and subject to his laws. God who lays down the laws for the movements of the heavenly bodies, lays down, too, the laws for the movement of man. And, as Pope insisted, the purposes behind these movements are God's and not men's. He is given the capacities appropriate to his station in the ranking of the universe. They are the capacities which enable him to perform the duties which are joined to that station. He is as well equipped for his tasks as the other animals are for theirs. The constant theme of Pope's *Essay* is once again to pacify man's complaints against the limitations of his nature. Every other being in the order is content with the powers assigned to him:

> Is Heav'n unkind to Man, and Man alone?
> Shall he alone, whom rational we call,
> Be pleas'd with nothing, if not bless'd with all?

> The bliss of Man (could Pride that blessing find)
> Is not to act or think beyond mankind;
> No pow'rs of body or of soul to share,
> But what his nature and his state can bear.[14]

And in the ensuing lines Pope puts elegantly what Locke argues altogether more prosaically in Book II of his *Essay*.[15] The 'all-wise Architect', as Locke describes him, has suited our sense organs to the conditions of 'this globe of earth allotted for our mansion' and, in turn, has suited these conditions to our senses. If men had been given more sensitive hearing they would never have found rest, their senses invaded by the sounds of nature (stunned by 'the music of the spheres' in Pope's version). And if men had eyes like microscopes, though they might see further into the texture of bodies they would lose all perspective and never (Locke's practical business sense revealing itself) see their way to the 'market and exchange'. Locke and Pope are at one in holding that men have been given by their 'infinite wise Contriver' those senses and faculties which are suited to the particular business of human life. Men are able, with the faculties they are given, to attend to their ordinary tasks of making a living. They are also enabled to worship and admire God, even if they are not fully enabled to understand all his purposes or his workings.

Men thus share with other beings in the pattern of God's universe. This means that, like other species, they possess certain unique faculties which differentiate them from all other ranks in creation and, more particularly, from those ranks immediately above and immediately below. What are these distinguishing features of the human species? First and foremost it is man's reason which marks him off from all other species on earth. This sets him above the other terrestrial ranks, even if man's physical and emotional qualities keep him below the spiritual realms.

God has uniquely granted to man amongst the beings of this world the capacity of reason. In line with his ordinance for the rest of creation it is the proper employment of this reason which will further distinguish and differentiate man, and enable him to play his part in God's design for the world. It is by his use of this God-given faculty that man can raise himself above the animals, above what Locke often called the 'brute beasts'. God has also provided man with one further distinguishing characteristic. Alone amongst the beings of this world man possesses the faculty of freedom of choice. Locke believes it to be strictly misleading to describe this faculty as the 'freedom of the will'. A man is not able to refrain from willing or choosing. In his deliberations he must come down on one side or the other. If a man is trying to decide whether to walk or not to walk he must make some decision. He is not free to make no decision whatsoever.[16]

Nevertheless, it makes sense, Locke says, to speak of a man being free. He is, normally, free to act or not to act in a particular way. Though he must decide either to walk or not to walk he is free to decide which it shall be. Freedom consists, firstly, in being able to make his choice and, secondly, in being able to convert this choice into action. A man would not be free if he were tied hand and foot and, therefore, prevented from walking as he had chosen. As Locke puts it:

> He that is a close prisoner in a room twenty feet square, being at the north side of his chamber, is at liberty to walk twenty feet southward, because he can walk or not walk it; but is not, at the same time, at liberty to do the contrary, i.e. to walk twenty feet northward.[17]

For the moment, however, what needs concern us is the freedom of choice.

Man is provided with the power of suspending the execution of his desires. A man can stop and deliberate before making his decision. This power of delay and deliberation is, in Locke's belief, the 'source of all liberty'.[18] It is a paramount task for man to use this power to the full. From its mismanagement 'comes all that variety of mistakes, errors, and faults which we run into in the conduct of our lives, and our endeavours after happiness'. This mismanagement consists in being careless and over-hasty in concluding one's deliberations. Since this is the God-given capacity which permits man the 'opportunity to examine, view and judge of the good or evil of what we are going to do', it follows that man has a duty to God to employ it to the full. This capacity is 'the great privilege of finite intellectual beings'.[19] It uniquely permits them to assess each proposed action to discover whether it will lead to true happiness. Men are thus able to employ their faculty of reason to seek out any relevant information which will enable them to make a correct decision as to their ultimate happiness. 'The principal exercise of freedom is to stand still, open the eyes, look about and take a view of the consequence of what we are going to do, as much as the weight of the matter requires.'[20] The delaying power of liberty enables the individual to look around, to check the range of actions open to him, to search out the remoter and less obvious consequences of his proposals. It enables him to trace the likely impact of his conduct on others as well as on himself. By this means he has less chance of acting in ignorance or acting inadvertently. To a considerable extent ignorance and inadvertence must be considered culpable. The power of suspending a decision gives a man the time in which to rectify his ignorance and act with due consideration instead of inadvertently. He has the opportunity to discover the facts of the case and it is incumbent on him to take the opportunity. Acting responsibly, knowing what it is that one is doing, is the mark of a human being. To act unthinkingly, to take unnecessary risks, to guess as to what is right when it is possible to act with greater certainty – these are 'wrong and irrational' ways of proceeding.[21]

This process of delay and deliberation comes to an end once the individual has determined which course of action will lead to the achievement of happiness. More strictly still, as Locke rectified his argument in the second edition of the *Essay*, what prompts the individual to choose a particular course of action is the hope that it will remove the 'uneasiness' he feels at the absence of something he acknowledges to be good.[22] Locke says that he came round to the view that the mere contemplation of something that is good is not sufficient to prompt a man into desiring that thing. He must, firstly, feel uneasy about his lack of the good before he will choose to alter his conduct. Locke suggests that the fact that a poor man will acknowledge wealth to be a good will not, of itself, prompt him to desire it and seek it. He may be content in his poverty or, at least, not feel it pressing upon him. Only when he becomes conscious of wealth as something he lacks will he be moved to desire it. Locke's argument, here, is not dissimilar to that of modern sociologists who suggest that it is the sense of relative deprivation which prompts the poor to complain, rather than the pure contemplation of wealth itself. A life of contentment would therefore be inert. No motivation to action and industry would exist. God has ensured that man will be sufficiently motivated, by building 'uneasiness' into his constitution. Men are led to their own preservation and the preservation of the species by their desire to obtain what they lack. Hunger, thirst, sexual drives are all to be seen as types of 'uneasiness'. Pain is therefore a necessary part of the human condition and of the structure of the world. It is the removal of this pain which prompts all our actions.[23]

Uneasiness determines the will because it is immediately felt. This, Locke argues, helps explain why a man may still fail to pursue an acknowledged good when he sees it. An absent good impinges less forcefully on a man than a present uneasiness or pain. This may be true of the most important benefits that can ultimately come to a man and which accrue from living a life of virtue. Locke says that most men's lives are occupied with removing the ordinary pains and uneasinesses which are part of day-to-day existence. They seek to overcome cold, hunger, thirst, tiredness rather than turn their attention to some greater but more remote good.[24] Even when men do lift their heads above the routine uneasinesses of life they still do not positively pursue some absolute good. Rather, they seek to remove pain incrementally, so as gradually to leave them with a moderate degree of pleasure in a number of ordinary and even trivial activities. Lockean man does not aim at maximising pleasure but at living a life of moderate ease, keeping pain to a minimum. The absence of good does not itself contribute to misery. If this were so, Locke says, human life would be infinitely miserable since the amount of absent good is infinite. Only when its absence is perceived as a lack does it become a pain and a spring to action. It is in these ways that 'absent good' is 'justled out' and attention is directed to the cure of immediate uneasiness.

The will is, then, always activated by uneasiness at the lack of an absent good. Men differ very greatly as to which lacks they feel uneasy about. More significantly men are able to reassess the importance of what pleases or displeases them. Habits, fashions and customs frequently lead men to feel the absence of things which otherwise would not matter to them. It is here that the faculty of deliberation plays so important a part in man's moral life. By suspending judgement a man is able to bring to the forefront of his mind those absent goods which ought to be of greatest concern to him. He can bring evidence to bear on his situation. He can in his mind pursue the consequences of undertaking one course of action rather than another. He can bring himself to see that what he once might have considered only a remote absent good is of immediate interest and value to himself. In this way an absent good is transformed into an immediately felt uneasiness which can prompt action. The 'due and repeated contemplation' of the good has given the individual some 'relish' for it, and it competes for his attention with the other sources of uneasiness.[25] This is the purpose of having liberty. Liberty exists to allow one to frame action according to one's judgement of what is good. In turn, what is good determines the will when its absence has become the most pressing source of uneasiness. Locke denies that such determinism negates liberty. God is no less free to deliberate even though He cannot choose what is not good. For a human being the freedom consists in being able to deliberate with the object of being determined by what he judges to be best for him. This is 'the end and use of our *liberty*; and the further we are removed from such a determination, the nearer we are to misery and slavery'.[26]

This power of deliberation is something the individual can cultivate. The power of suspension means that, within limits which it might be difficult to specify, the individual has time to think matters over. Clearly, this is time which may be well spent or ill spent. Having the liberty to decide does not necessarily mean that the decision taken will be the right one, even though it will always be that which appears to be correct at the time to the individual in question. Nevertheless, it remains possible that he should have taken longer to consider the matter. He may have been impetuous. Or he may have been insufficiently assiduous or industrious in searching out the issues involved – particularly over the long term. If this is so he may properly be blamed for failure to make the utmost use of his liberty and of his power of understanding. This basic failure will then morally taint the actions which are consequential on his misuse of his God-given powers:

> And here we may see how it comes to pass that a man may justly incur punishment, though it be certain that, in all the particular actions that he *wills*, he does, and necessarily does, will that which he then judges to be good. For, though his *will* be always determined by that which is judged good by his understanding, yet it excuses him not; because, by a too hasty choice of his own making, he has imposed on himself wrong measures of good and evil; which, however false and fallacious, have the same influence on all his future conduct as if they were true and right. He has vitiated his own palate, and must be answerable to himself for the sickness and death that follows from it. The eternal law and nature of things must not be altered to comply with his ill-ordered choice. If the neglect or abuse of the liberty he had, to examine what would really and truly make for his happiness misleads him, the miscarriages that follow on it must be imputed to his own election. He had a power to suspend his determination; it was given him that he might examine, and take care of his own happiness, and look that he were not deceived.[27]

This passionately worded passage was worth quoting at length because it emphasises the awesome responsibility Locke placed on man to make good use of the capacities with which he had been endowed. It also emphasises that this is a matter of moral responsibility. Man is a choice-making animal. He is not impelled to live a good and righteous life. But he is obligated to do so. He has a duty.

The duty is owed to God. It is demanded of man by the law of nature and it is through a knowledge of the law of nature that man can come to some understanding of what it is that God asks of him. Though Locke was accused of holding heterodox views in religion his protestations that he held to the basic tenets of Christianity should be regarded as sincere. Locke's views of morality and responsibility operate within a theological world view. John Dunn has argued most persuasively that this conception of the world is fundamentally Calvinist and that the key to Locke's understanding of man's duty lies in the Calvinist notion of the religious character of a man's calling in life. There is much that is convincing about this interpretation. Locke's upbringing was Calvinist. His life and thought manifest a Calvinist sobriety and deep sense of religious commitment. Nevertheless, it seems certain that Locke also abandoned some elements of Calvinism and greatly moderated others. In this he may have been influenced by the natural law teachings of Robert Sanderson and by the liberal theology of the Cambridge Platonists. Calvinist notions of election are absent and Locke's emphasis

on man's 'uneasiness' and on his need for a constant search for the
right path to salvation may reflect the consequent lack of certainty.
Locke's conception of individuality might then seem more burdensome
and more liberating than that of Calvin. The 'calling' is that of being
a man, endowed with reason and with liberty and under an obligation
to make his way in the world with all the joys and the risks which
that involves. This sense of individuality is coupled with his religious
toleration which made the all-embracing political community of Calvin's
Geneva as distasteful to Locke as were the similarly wide-ranging
aspirations of Catholicism. In his theology Locke was an eclectic,
attempting a singular fusion of Calvinist commitment, traditional
Thomist rationalism and of moderate Anglicanism whilst exposing all
to a searching examination of their intellectual foundations. Yet the
balance between the elements is open to dispute and dogmatism is
unwise. A profound study of Locke's theology is a striking gap in the
literature.

The law of nature is integral to Locke's conception of the universe
and of man's duties within it. At the same time, his characterisation of
this law has been seen as one of the least clear parts of his moral and
political thought, In outlining the law of nature, Locke has to establish
three things. Firstly, he must show how it is that men can know and
understand the law of nature. Secondly, he has to show how the law
obliges men to carry out its instructions. Thirdly, Locke must indicate
what the content of the law is – what it is that men are instructed to
do. Ideally he must explain who is obliged, to do what, by whom,
when and how. There is reason to think that Locke found considerable
difficulty throughout his philosophical career in providing satisfactory
answers to the first two questions about man's knowledge of the law and
the manner of the law's obligatoriness. On the other hand, Locke
remained consistent in what he believed to be the content of the law
of nature.

Locke held that the law of nature was willed by God. All laws are
commanded by rightful legislators, and the law of nature is no exception. The law of nature is law, and binding on its subjects, because
God has commanded it. To this extent Locke is what is variously
termed a 'nominalist' or a 'voluntarist' in his conception of natural law.
The traditional difficulty with this position is that it seems to make
the law of nature an arbitrary ruling by God. It is analogous to the
arbitrariness implicit in asserting that it is the command of the
government that makes the positive law of a state a law and, hence,
obligatory. The ruler could, it would follow, command one thing today
and another tomorrow, and each would, in turn, be equally law and
equally obligatory. The traditional alternative to the nominalist view of
natural law was the 'realist' view, which declared that the law of nature
was law and was binding because it laid down that which was rational

and morally right. Men, by the use of reason, could discover the rationality of the law and this rationality would render it obligatory. The natural law would, therefore, be valid independently of its being promulgated by God who was himself unable to alter the law. God could no more declare that to be wrong which was naturally right, than he could declare that two plus two be not four. Indeed, God was a hypothesis with which such a theory of natural law might even be able to dispense. Instead the rules of morality might be rationally deduced from self-evident first principles, much as the propositions of geometry could be deduced from its axioms.

Locke, whilst holding with the nominalists that the law of nature is willed by God, nevertheless also believes that the rules of morality can be discovered by reason. At various times he asserts that moral propositions are demonstrable in much the same way as those of mathematics. It is probable that Locke believed he could reconcile the tensions between these two positions within his theological world view. On the other hand his reluctance to publish his thoughts on the law of nature may have reflected lingering doubts about his success, and also about his account of how men could come to a knowledge of the law.

For Locke the foundation of all knowledge is sense perception. This is true of our knowledge of the law of nature, as it is true of our knowledge of material objects. He enunciates this in the early *Essays on the Law of Nature* and it was, of course, to be the theme of the *Essay concerning Human Understanding*. Locke rejects the widely held view of his day that men are born with ideas already printed on the mind. Men do not possess any impressions 'stamped upon the mind of man; which the soul receives in its very first being, and brings into the world with it'.[28]

The ideas which Locke cites are ideas – in the sense of propositions – about logic and morality. They included mathematical principles, rules of logic, moral laws and ideas about God. Locke's arguments aroused considerable opposition since they appeared to threaten the bases of the most fundamental propositions about God and morality. It was felt that to assert the innateness of the rules of morality and of the idea of God would best safeguard morality and religion against the challenges of atheism and deism. As Yolton says:

> In every case, it is invoked as a means of stabilizing morality and religion, of providing men with certain and sure foundations for the virtuous life. The principles which are listed as innate are always formulations of the existing values of the society.[29]

Locke protested that it was far from his intention to subvert morality and religion. Rather, he expected that by replacing old weak arguments he would be able to rest traditional beliefs on stronger intellectual foundations.[30]

Locke offers a number of criticisms of the innateness of ideas. There seem to be three chief objections.

Firstly Locke suggests that the doctrine of innate ideas implies that these innate ideas must be known to and accepted by everyone. But this, Locke says, is untrue. Locke, from his earliest writings to his mature masterpieces, consistently rejects any argument for moral principles based on an alleged consensus of mankind. This rejection of consensus is impressively honest in that Locke might have argued that the moral rules contained in the law of nature were discovered as a result of the common experience of all mankind. They would then be those rules which all men had discovered by experience were necessary to their own preservation. But Locke insists that this flies in the face of the evidence. Men do not agree in fact on what would be regarded in modern European nations as the fundamental principles of morality. Nothing could be more striking than the diversity of rules about sexual practices, suicide, and self-preservation, treatment of the old and infirm, theft and homicide, which are revealed by the study of history and by the reports of travellers.[31] There are even nations who, 'as is reported by those who have considered it worth while to go to these places', have denied the existence of God which is a necessary proposition if natural law is to exist at all. And even if the mere existence of a God were universally acknowledged, the belief in polytheism amongst the Greeks and Romans would itself be an argument against a consensus on this vital matter. Locke concludes:

> . . . there is almost no vice, no infringement of natural law, no moral wrong, which anyone who consults the history of the world and observes the affairs of men will not readily perceive to have been not only privately committed somewhere on earth, but also approved by public authority and custom. Nor has there been anything so shameful in its nature that it has not been either sanctified somewhere by religion, or put in the place of virtue and abundantly rewarded with praise.[32]

Even if there were a consensus on moral matters this would not, Locke adds, establish that this consensus represents the law of nature. Each individual has to derive the law from the principles of nature not from the opinions of others.[33] If one were to establish for oneself the principles of the law of nature it would in no way magnify the truth of such principles if one were subsequently to discover that everyone else consented to them. Neither the breadth of support for any opinions in morality nor the strength of conviction behind them can of itself establish that these opinions do indeed coincide with natural law.[34]

Secondly, Locke argues that if ideas were innate they would be immediately obvious to the most untrained minds. The most natural mental condition is to be found amongst the young, the illiterate and the primitive.[35] They have not been exposed to the influence of prejudice and custom which might have diverted them from the natural condition. Yet primitive societies do not display any standards of morality. Locke discovers in them largely dishonesty, treachery, cruelty and debauchery.[36] It is equally apparent that children are unaware of the truths of morality but have to grow to an awareness of them, which they do through education and experience. It is education which is largely responsible for the degree of consensus on moral matters which has developed amongst the more civilised nations. There is a tendency to think that these ideas must have been instilled by nature since they are so fervently held. But they are inculcated from earliest infancy by all the souces of instruction in society – parents, teachers and friends. The daily course of moral lessons renders men unaware of the educative process. They come to defend stubbornly as natural morality what in fact has been acquired from society in the shape of public opinion or, as Locke called it 'the law of opinion'.

Thirdly, Locke turns to a weaker formulation of the theory of innate ideas. This argued that men had the rational capacity to know certain propositions. This theory seems to require, however, that reason is needed to discover ideas that are self-evident. There seems to be an inconsistency in holding that reasoning, which for Locke is an arduous and painful labour of searching, is needed in order to reveal principles such as rules of logic imprinted by nature which are supposed to be the foundation of reason itself.

Having dismissed the case for regarding the knowledge of the law of nature as innate, Locke has cleared the way for his own account of how men may arrive at moral truths. Reason has a role to play in the discovery of the law of nature, but it cannot be the ultimate basis of the law. For Locke, reason consists in reasoning. It is the faculty by which men can proceed in ordered fashion from things known to things unknown.[37] Reason establishes the connections between ideas. It is a matter of inferring either certain or probable truths from more basic ideas. The ideas themselves are derived from sense-experience and by reflection on that experience.

Reason . . . I take to be the discovery of the certainty or probability of such propositions or truths, which the mind arrives at by deduction from such *ideas*, which it has got by the use of its natural faculties, viz. by sensation or reflection.[38]

Reason and the senses are both necessary to man. Without reason men would scarcely be at the level of 'brute beasts', many of whom surpass men in the sharpness of their senses. But without the senses reason would lack its raw material.

Unless the ideas of objects penetrate the mind there will be no subject-matter of reasoning, nor could the mind do more towards the construction of knowledge than an architect can towards the building of houses if he falls short of stones, timber, sand, and the rest of building material.[39]

What reason cannot consist in is a body of moral principles stored in the mind and termed 'right reason'. This is to confuse the truths which reason seeks with the faculty by which such truth is sought.

Locke's next task is to show in what way discovery of moral principles is derivable from sense-experience. Clearly, one cannot perceive moral rules in the way one perceives a table, a chair or a river. Yet it is from the perception of stars and rivers that Locke sets out in his argument for the existence of a law of nature. Through our senses we learn of the order of nature. We learn of the revolution of the planets and the regular changes of the seasons. The beauty, order and motion of the world revealed by the senses lead men to inquire into the origin and the creator of this work. There can be no doubt that such a world could not have emerged by chance. The inference must be that it was made by a being surpassing all others in wisdom and power. The creator can bring life into being and bring it to an end.

It is this power which renders it obligatory for the created to obey the creator's commands. The power of creation not only implies the power to destroy, but also the right to destroy and, it would appear, the right to mould the lives of those he creates. The creator is of course God, to whom men are rightly subject. This conclusion, Locke believes, is one to which reason is necessarily led on the basis of the evidence provided by the senses. In this indirect way the moral principles known as the law of nature which, we have seen, are the commands of God, are ultimately ascertained through sense-experience.

As well as possessing the authority of a creator, God, like other law-givers, attaches sanctions to any breach of the law. Unlike other laws, however, the sanctions of the law of nature are only fully effective in the life after death. Men are moved to do that which is right by the prospect that, by doing so, they will remove a sense of uneasiness that they will feel in wrong-doing. God has in his hands the power of rewarding and punishing. The severity of these punishments or the wealth of these rewards are entirely at his discretion.[40] In a future life either can be infinite in duration. The right-thinking man will so frame his conduct that it conforms with God's law, and will thus be likely to 'procure them happiness or misery from the hands of the ALMIGHTY'. Moral conduct consists in such voluntary conformity which will, in Locke's calculating language, be 'useful' to the individual.[41] Since this is a matter of free choice, it is clear that some men –

Locke even says most men – may fail to bring their actions into line with God's law. The sanctions of a future life are remote from men's thoughts.[42] Nevertheless, this only further emphasises the responsibility that falls on the individual to consider his situation and his prospects. He will be expected to reflect before acting. There can be little excuse for a failure to do so. Punishment will be his just desert if his conduct does not correspond to the moral law. The prospect of pleasure and pain is thus the motive for men's conformity to natural law. Nevertheless, his hedonism is a qualified one, which Locke believes fits into his theological framework. It is God who has so made man that he is moved by the prospect of pleasure and pain and that he is notwithstanding a free, reflective being. God has 'by an inseparable connexion, joined *virtue* and *public happiness* together'.[43]

More importantly, although it is the anticipation of pain and pleasure (or more properly the absence of ease) which moves man to act rightly, it is not that which makes it a duty. It is a duty because it is the will of God as a rightful superior. It is also a duty because it is inherently right. Here Locke incorporates elements of the rationalist position on natural law. He suggests in the *Essay* that moral principles could be shown to be demonstrably certain and could have the same status as the truths of mathematics. In an earlier Journal entry (15 July 1678, MS Locke/f3/fo/201) Locke had suggested that moral rules were deducible from what was logically necessary to the fulfilment of God's intentions for mankind. But in the *Essay* Locke appears to take the project of demonstrable ethics much further. Men are able to construct complex ideas which are products of the mind and which do not refer to any real existence. Locke terms these complex ideas 'mixed modes'. Men construct these complex ideas largely in order to arrange, categorise and communicate thoughts. In this way men have evolved the concept of 'murder' to distinguish the killing of men from the killing of sheep and the concept of 'parricide' to distinguish the murder of a father from the murder of any other aged man. Such concepts are constructed according to social need which may vary from time to time and place to place. Concepts common to one era or society may not be found in another, and there are many possible 'mixed modes' which have never been thought of.[44]

As constructs of the mind these concepts are in many cases logically interconnected. Mathematical ideas are such concepts and could be shown to be connected with one another even if there were no circles or triangles in the real world. The truths of mathematics are what follow from the more basic definitions.

Locke's claim is that the truths of morality are similarly demonstrable. Moral concepts are likewise the creation of the mind. Moral truths are derivable from these concepts just as propositions about triangles are deducible from the concept of an angle. Some of the instances Locke offers are of negative correlations – cases where one concept is logically incompatible with another: 'No government allows absolute liberty.'[45] Here the idea of government implies the existence of laws which are backed by sanctions to ensure obedience. The idea of absolute liberty (which Locke elsewhere terms 'licence') implies that a man can do as he pleases. The proposition that government and absolute liberty are mutually incompatible is then as certain as any in 'the mathematics'. Locke offers a further example drawn from politics: 'Where there is no property there is no injustice.' This, he says, is 'a proposition as certain as any demonstration in Euclid'. The name 'property' is the label for the idea of a 'right to anything'. The name 'injustice' is similarly a label for the idea of an invasion of such a right. Hence if there were no rights there could be no invasions of rights. This is as reliably true as the proposition that a triangle has three angles equal to two right angles. The reservations Locke expresses in the *Essay* about the demonstrability of ethical propositions arise out of the tendency towards inexactitude in the use of moral language. Mathematicians were more fortunate than moralists in that they could all employ a constant public language of exact numbers or geometrical figures. Moralists were too likely to make mistakes, to forget elements of the argument or to be careless about their terms. But morality cannot be a mere construction of the logical consequences of names. This would be altogether Hobbesian in its nominalism and relativism, since there seems no guarantee that the moral definitions correspond to 'reality'. Locke, therefore, makes his way back around the circle to try to discover the bases of these definitions in God's presumed intentions for man.

Locke's examples of demonstration are in fact highly formal and fall well short of establishing a demonstrative ethics. He does not attempt to demonstrate in the same way more particular propositions about what property laws are just or why government ought to be obeyed. The instances of demonstration Locke gives are of alleged logical interconnections between moral concepts and do not, and cannot, establish the obligatoriness of any particular proposition concerning them.[46] Locke also recognises that there is considerable scope for interpretation when it comes to the application of the law of nature by individuals or by government. In the 1667 *Essay on Toleration* he allows government to set aside the strict law of nature in certain instances.[47]

Several of Locke's friends were excited by the prospect of a systematic account of ethics on these lines and urged him to attempt it. Locke, however, declined. One reason was the great difficulty of the enterprise. Another reason refers back to the theological foundations of morality. Locke refused to see the urgency of the need to formulate an ethical system since the content of such a system had already been given man in the teachings of Christianity. All the past attempts to construct a rational system of morality had failed to establish moral teachings as comprehensive as those contained in the gospels. The revelations of Christ constitute 'a full and sufficient rule for our direction',[48] and one which is entirely compatible with the conclusions of reason. The great heathen philosophers had not been able to make out 'an entire body of the law of nature' but had led themselves into 'a wild wood of uncertainty' or an 'endless maze'. There was nowhere a Brutus or a Cassius could have turned to discover a clear guide to their duties.

There was still less urgent need for such a demonstration when one considered the effectiveness of Christ's revelations as compared with the effectiveness of any lessons in mathematical ethics. Christ came to earth with the power of God and was able to put morality in plain terms, understandable to the ordinary man or woman. To assist him in communicating with the body of mankind Christ made use of disciples who were themselves 'illiterate men', and his instructions were made still more vivid by being accompanied by the miraculous curing of the sick or healing of the lame. The alternative route to ethical certainty would require proofs deduced from first principles in such a way as would be convincing to all. 'And you may as soon hope to have all the day-labourers and tradesmen, the spinsters and dairy-maids, perfect mathematicians as to have them perfect in ethics this way.'[49]

Some scholars[50] have interpreted this and similar passages to mean that Locke was primarily concerned to advocate a form of religion which would satisfy and placate the poor, ill-educated classes. The classes were differentiated by, amongst other things, their levels of rationality. The poor had developed their understanding to a lesser extent than the more substantial orders of people. This might be due to moral laziness – a lack of endeavour – or to the fact that the poor were too preoccupied with grinding out a bare subsistence to afford the leisure to develop more scholarly activities. Hence a rational religion could have little impact on their understandings and on their moral conduct. This view of Locke's theology must be accorded some weight. The final pages of Locke's *Reasonableness of Christianity* are devoted to defending the simplicity of the Christian gospel as a religion suited to 'vulgar capacities' and to the man who wields the plough and spade, whose 'head is seldom elevated to sublime notions'.[51] Locke feels that God has 'consulted the poor of this world' in so fashioning Christianity. And it is not at all unlikely that Locke might believe that a by-product of such a religion would be to instil respect both for the order of the universe and for a well-ordered political society.

Nevertheless, Locke's stated concern went beyond providing the people with an opiate. He worried that if religion were intellectualised the mass of mankind would be excluded from what he saw as its joys and benefits. God scarcely intended that only the intellectuals and scholars should be saved. Rather, it was the believers who would be rewarded.[52] Belief, moreover, was the underpinning of Locke's whole moral system, not merely a substitute for those unable to arrive at the law of nature with the help of reason. For it was not only the poor of the world who lacked the rational capacities necessary to this endeavour, but the Platos and the Aristotles as well. And the poor would have needed to be 'perfect' mathematicians, rather than very good ones, to be convinced of their obligations.

There is in the end a certain circularity to Locke's argument, but one which, as Gough has remarked, would not in all likelihood have disturbed Locke.[53] The demonstration of moral truths occurs within a theological framework in which belief plays as important a part as reason. Moral conduct is only made obligatory by its being the command of a law-maker with the power to punish or reward. It is the assurance of the existence of such a law-maker which has made virtue not merely commendable but requisite. It is this which, in Locke's remarkably mercantile language,[54] has made virtue 'the most enriching purchase, and by much the best bargain'. Previously virtue could only be said to be its own reward, or to bring one fame and respect in future generations. Now it could be shown to be in one's long-term private interest. Though, as has been seen, Locke held that the argument from design served as a rational case for the existence of the divine legislator, yet it would also seem from the *Reasonableness* that faith completed the argument in almost Thomist fashion when he suggests that 'some parts of . . . truth lie too deep for our natural powers easily to reach, and make plain and visible to mankind; without some light from above to direct them'.[55] Reason cannot bring full knowledge of the truth of religion. No human may claim certainty, and no man's faith can be such as to appear equally convincing to another. All that may be expected is that each person should reflect as much as he is capable about his beliefs and what they imply for conduct. If certainty about religion is not to be discovered, then to enforce religious conformity must be misplaced. In the *Reasonableness of Christianity*, Locke offers what he believes to be the central core of Christian faith whilst reminding his readers of how much may rightly be open to reasonable doubt and tolerant dispute. The dispute may properly be conducted by Biblical criticism – of which Locke was an early practitioner – but it cannot be settled in this, or any other, way. In the last resort, though he may call upon all the help of the civilisation of which he is a part, the individual must seek his own path to such truth as he may find.

For Locke, then, sense-experience, reason and faith combined to give the reasonable Christian confidence in the existence of a creator and law-maker. The creator's purposes were embodied in the divine and natural law to which man as his creation and dependant is obligated. What prompts man – or should prompt him – to obedience is the prospect of pain or pleasure which will ensue as a result of the overwhelming punishments and rewards which await him at the hand of God in a future life.

Notes Chapter II

1 Cambridge, Mass., Harvard University Press, 1971.
2 C. B. Macpherson, *The Political Theory of Possessive Individualism*, Oxford, Oxford University Press, 1962.
3 *A Discourse on the Origin of Inequality*, ed. G. D. H. Cole, London, Dent, 1952, p. 181.
4 'Of the Original Contract', *Essays Moral, Political and Literary*, Oxford, Oxford University Press edition, 1963, p. 473.
5 Cited in Lord King, *Life of John Locke*, London, 1830, Vol. 1, p. 9.
6 The classic study is A. O. Lovejoy, *The Great Chain of Being*, Cambridge, Mass., Harvard University Press, 1936. For one treatment of the political implications of the theory see W. H. Greenleaf, *Order, Empiricism and Politics*, London, 1964.
7 *Essay on Man*, Epistle I, VIII, lines 237–41. Twickenham edition of *Works*, Vol. III (i), ed. Maynard Mack, London, Methuen, 1950.
8 *Essay* III, vi, 12.
9 *Essay* III, vi, 12. Also IV, xvi, 12.
10 *Law of Nature*, I, p. 109.
11 *Essay*, I, iv, 9.
12 *Law of Nature*, I, p. 117.
13 *Law of Nature*, IV, p. 157.
14 *Essay on Man*, I, lines 186–92.
15 Pope had many other sources at his disposal but it is perhaps striking that lines 193–204 do take up precisely the examples Locke discusses in *Essay*, II, xxiii, 12.
16 *Essay*, II, xxi, 21–30.
17 *Essay*, II, xxi, 27.
18 *Essay*, II, xxi, 47.
19 *Essay*, II, xxi, 52.
20 *Essay*, II, xxi, 67.
21 *Essay*, II, xxi, 66.
22 *Essay*, II, xxi, 34–47. In an interesting study Ellen Wood argues that this power of suspension must itself be a determined act of volition and that Locke cannot evade a position close to Hobbes. *Mind and Politics*, Berkeley, University of California Press, 1972, p. 37.
23 *Essay*, II, xxi, 36.
24 *Essay*, II, xxi, 45.
25 *Essay*, II, xxi, 45. Also 69.
26 *Essay*, II, xxi, 48.
27 *Essay*, II, xxi, 56.
28 *Essay*, I, ii, 1.
29 J. W. Yolton, *John Locke and the Way of Ideas*, Oxford, Oxford University Press, 1968, p. 29.
30 *Essay*, I, iv, 24.
31 *Law of Nature*, Essays III and V.

32 *Law of Nature*, Essay V, p. 167.
33 *Law of Nature*, V, p. 177.
34 *Essay*, IV, xix, 12.
35 *Essay*, I, ii, 5.
36 *Law of Nature*, III, 141.
37 *Law of Nature*, IV, 149; *Essay*, IV, xvii, 2.
38 *Essay*, IV, xviii, 2.
39 *Law of Nature*, IV, p. 149.
40 *Essay*, II, xxviii, 8.
41 *A Letter on Toleration*, ed. Klibansky, p. 101. Translated by both Popple and, recently, Gough in temptingly mercantile terms as 'profitable'.
42 *Essay*, II, xxviii, 12.
43 *Essay*, I, iii, 6.
44 *Essay*, III, v, *passim*.
45 *Essay*, IV, iii, 18.
46 See the discussion by J. Yolton, *Locke and the Compass of Human Understanding*, ch. 7.
47 H. R. Fox Bourne, *Life of John Locke*, London, 1876, Vol. I, pp. 182–3.
48 *The Reasonableness of Christianity*, *Works*, VII, p. 143.
49 *Reasonableness*, *Works*, VII, 146.
50 Notably C. B. Macpherson, *Possessive Individualism*, pp. 224–6.
51 *Works*, VII, 157.
52 *Works*, VII, 158.
53 J. W. Gough, *John Locke's Political Philosophy*, Oxford, Oxford University Press, 2nd edition, 1973, p. 19.
54 *Works*, VII, 150–1. Rightly noted by Macpherson, *Possessive Individualism*, p. 225.
55 *Works*, VII, 144.

Chapter III

The Condition of Man and the State of Nature

> The Freedom then of Man and Liberty of acting according to his own Will, is *grounded on* his having *Reason,* which is able to instruct him in that Law he is to govern himself by, and make him Know how far he is left to the freedom of his own will. (63)

Freedom and reason go together throughout Locke's thought. Freedom exists to make possible the rational pursuit of human purposes. 'Without liberty, the understanding would be to no purpose: and without understanding, liberty . . . would signify nothing.'[1] Men have onerous duties placed upon them but they have also been equipped with the faculties which enable them to direct themselves towards the performance of these duties. Some parts of the law of nature are clear to all who 'will but consult it' (6), others require some study (12, 124). In either case, it is reason which, whatever its limits, must be employed in discovering and clarifying the law. Freedom is what permits this investigation into one's duties to continue.

The broad nature of these duties is reasonably clear. They are to fulfil the mission given to the human species and to each member of it by God, the maker. Each and every human being has a duty to preserve himself, to honour God in the manner he believes appropriate and to develop to the full his distinctively human attribute of reason. If Locke may have doubts about how precisely the law of nature is to be known and about how it obliges, he is confident about its content. Much more is, of course, needed to make these duties more precise and, indeed, this is to be the reason for the institution of political society. None the less where men acknowledge these broad duties it is enough for them to be able to recognise one another as members of one moral community. Each recognises the other as similarly human and equally subject to the law of nature. Each acknowledges himself, and others like him, to be rational creatures and capable of adjudicating disputes in a rational manner. Though this is not enough to guarantee peace amongst men, what follows from this common subjection to the law of nature is far from being morally negligible.

The first duty is self-preservation. It may seem more appropriate to regard self-preservation as a right but, as is usually the case in Locke, what a man has a right to do he also has a duty to do and Locke varies the stress according to the particular argument he is expounding.

For the desire, strong desire of Preserving his Life and Being having been Planted in him, as a Principle of Action by God himself, Reason, *which was the Voice of God in him*, could not but teach him and assure him, that pursuing that natural Inclination he had to preserve his Being, he followed the Will of his Maker . . . (I,86)

Although Locke in various places speaks of men having a property in their own persons and an unlimited liberty of disposing both person and possessions, he nevertheless always qualifies this property right by reference to the superior right of God. This right derives from God as creator. No human property right can exclude the prior property right of God.[2] Divine creation is of a different order from any other creative act. God fashions man in ways only He fully comprehends, and equips him to fulfil the divine purpose. It is not for the subject, in this instance, to determine that such divine objectives are no longer to be pursued by bringing his own life to a premature end. Since a man's life is God's property the individual cannot destroy what is not entirely his (6). The individual has certain property rights in his own person which exclude the rights of other individuals but in his property relations with God he enjoys rights as if from a feudal superior who may lay down conditions for the management of what is ultimately the superior's property. One of these conditions is that the property be preserved so far as is humanly possible.

From God's creation and His property in men certain moral duties follow in what Locke might have regarded as a deductive manner. It is along these lines that Locke appears to connect demonstrable ethics with religious faith. If a man has a duty under natural law to preserve himself, that law must grant him a right to preserve himself. If each man has a right to preserve himself it must equally follow that other men have a duty to respect that right. There would be no value in a right to preserve oneself that was constantly frustrated because others did not acknowledge the legitimacy of acts to ensure such preservation. A universal duty of self-preservation entails a universal right of self-preservation. If one man believes he has a duty and a right to safeguard himself, he must recognise the similar right and duty under the law of nature of each and every other human being who finds himself in like circumstances.

Each man consequently has a duty not to harm another who is going about his legitimate business. All men are equally members of the human species, equally shaped by God. In matters of rights and duties there can be no relevant differences between them. They are all

> ... the Servants of one Sovereign Master, sent into the World by his order and about his business, they are his Property, whose Workmanship they are, made to last during his, not one anothers Pleasure. And being furnished with like Faculties, sharing all in one Community of Nature, there cannot be supposed any such Subordination among us, that may Authorize us to destroy one another, as if we were made for one anothers uses ... (6)

Murder is wrong, as suicide is wrong. If a man may not justly terminate his own life, he may not terminate the life of another nor, of course, may his own life be arbitrarily terminated by another's act. The law of nature is universal and equal. Where others have found in Locke signs of aggressive individualism, Locke himself discovers a notion of community.

Respect for others thus follows from one's right that others respect oneself. But Locke goes further and suggests that the law of nature imposes a more positive duty to come to the assistance of others when their preservation is threatened. The duty to safeguard oneself as God's workmanship cannot be divorced from a duty to preserve the rest of those of God's creations which are in all essentials similar to oneself. Locke admits one qualification to this duty. The obligation to protect others does not require that one's own life be put seriously at risk. Whether this is chiefly because each individual can be expected to be more capable of self-protection than of protecting others or because there is an 'inward instinct'[3] of self-preference in men Locke does not say. This limit on natural mutual assistance is however to be one of the factors which will make a collective political system of protection essential.

The preservation of God-given life is, therefore, the first duty of man. The next duty is the pursuit of a good life. The individual is to use to the full the distinctively human capacities which he possesses – his liberty and his rationality. These capacities in the first place distinguish the human species from the other ranks of creation, whose lower capacities and physical constitution make them in Locke's eyes suitable objects for human consumption, placed in the world by God so that they may be instruments of human preservation (6).

'Reason' is a name which 'stands for a faculty in man, that faculty whereby man is supposed to be distinguished from beasts, and wherein it is evident he much surpasses them'.[4] 'Reason' as Locke understands it in these contexts is not 'right reason' but, rather, 'reasoning'.[5] Men are born rational in the sense that they are all born with the capacity to calculate and to draw proper inferences. Failure to use this unique capacity would mean that a man scarcely differentiated himself from a beast. He would be failing to attend, to the utmost of his abilities, to the matters which concerned him as a man. This Locke counts as a breach of the law of nature and as morally reprehensible.[6]

The assiduous use of reason and reflection not only distinguishes men from the 'brute beasts'. It also distinguishes men from one another. Their duty to God requires that each person pursue a life which he believes will most effectively develop his capacities. God's law requires that an individual stretch himself to the full. As choice-making animals men have the ability to seek their salvation in a variety of ways. Although not all will find the path to salvation and many will go astray in their attempts to perform their duty, in all such cases there is great merit in the pursuit. It is only through the industrious exercise of the reasoning faculty that goodness and salvation may be approached. The individual's salvation can only come through his own industry and his own choices. The development of indivduality is part of God's law. The man who only acts after due reflection about how he ought to conduct himself is acting in a manner 'suitable to the dignity and excellency of a rational creature'.[7] He has 'a Mind free, and Master of itself and all its Actions'.[8] Such self-determining individuals are 'free and at their own disposal'.[9] All men being equally endowed by God with the capacity of reason, they must all be supposed equally capable, 'by nature', of making reasoned choices and of directing their activities sensibly towards their ends in life – the honour of God and their own preservation. Each individual is entitled to be left to take his own decisions as to the ways in which he will act in pursuit of these ends. He should be left to explore his freedom. The obligation to develop the reasoning capacities, on which a successful exploration of freedom depends, falls on every individual. It is one which he may not, as a man, renounce and which, moreover, he has no reason to renounce since no man can, by nature, be better informed than he of the directions he should pursue or of the choices he is to make.

There is no natural authority among men. By developing the powers of reason, men cultivate self-reliance. The rejection of authoritarianism is essential to the ethics of individuality. Truth and virtue may be discovered if the individual is prepared to strive for it.

> . . . by saying that something can be known by the light of nature, we mean nothing else but that there is some sort of truth to the knowledge of which a man can attain by himself and without the help of another, if he makes proper use of the faculties he is endowed with by nature.[10]

'Proper use' implies consistency and industry. Locke regularly couples 'rationality' with 'industry'.

Concealed in the bowels of the earth lie veins richly provided with gold and silver; human beings besides are possessed of arms and hands with which they can dig these out, and of reason which invents machines. Yet from this we do not conclude that all men are wealthy. First they have to equip themselves; and it is with great labour that those resources which lie hidden in darkness are to be brought to the light of day. They do not present themselves to idle and listless people . . .[11]

It is only the rational and industrious who receive a final reward. Locke interprets 'For whosoever hath, to him shall be given' to mean that rewards will go to whoever 'improves' the 'talents' he has.[12] The only way such improvement can come about is by regular practice. Men must train themselves to make choices, to use their freedom to suspend decision until they can become better informed as to what their right course of conduct should be. This is the lesson Locke drives home throughout his educational writings: '. . . we are born to be, if we please, rational creatures, but it is use and exercise only that makes us so, and we are indeed no further than industry and application has carried us.'[13] A sound educational programme will be one which gradually extends the range of decisions which the child can make in accordance with his developing experience of the world. Locke advises parents 'always to carry this in their Minds, that Children are to be treated as rational creatures'[14] by which he means that they are capable of giving, and being given, reasons for action, but only those reasons which their experience and past training permit them to grasp. It must be reasoning suited to the 'Capacity and Apprehension' of the child of 3 or of 7 or whatever and not to the understanding of an adult.[15] Freedom and reason are the product of age and effort: 'Thus we are *born Free*, as we are born Rational; not that we have actually the Exercise of either; Age that brings one, brings with it the other too' (61). And although there may be an arbitrary age when the child ceases and the adult begins, there is no point at which a man may cease to exercise his freedom of reasoned choice nor cease to extend his experience thereby.

It is a strenuous and unremitting task that Locke is saying is required of men. It is therefore not surprising that there are many who either do not recognise their obligations or who find them too demanding. They 'neglect' their understanding despite both the rewards of virtue and the severe retribution which may befall them at least after death. Instead of deciding for themselves they prefer to be guided by

. . . the example of others, or by traditional customs and the fashion of the country, or finally by the authority of those whom they consider good and wise. They want no other rule of life and conduct, being satisfied with that second-hand rule which other people's conduct, opinions and advice, without any serious thinking or application, easily supply to the unwary.[16]

Locke returns again and again to this central theme from these early writings to his most mature works.

It is commonly suggested that Lockean man is not only self-directing but self-sufficient, owing nothing to society for the development of his person or capacities.[17] This is, however, in certain important respects misleading. No being in the great scale can be properly understood apart from its relations to others[18] and this is clearly true of man himself. Locke's natural man is a social animal. He is neither physically nor intellectually isolated. Far from owing nothing to others, Locke constantly reiterates that ordinarily the bulk of men's ideas and attitudes are derived from others. It is true that Locke regrets this, that he urges men to resist the pressures of social habits and intellectual tradition. But his object is to insist that men come to understand for themselves, rather than accept ideas on trust or simply because they have been received opinion. It is a basic tenet of Locke's thought that for knowledge to be true, or belief to be profitable, or for laws to be authoritative, they must be understood and assimilated by the individual thereby making them in a sense his 'property'.

This does not mean therefore that the individual is entirely abstracted from the social pressures upon him. Human beings are like chameleons that always 'take a Tincture from things near us'.[19] The greatest part of mankind govern themselves 'chiefly, if not solely, by this law of fashion'.[20] They find it easier to rely on others '. . . whether parents, neighbours, or ministers, or who else they are pleased to make choice of to have an implicit faith in, for the saving of themselves of the pains and trouble of thinking and examining for themselves'.[21]

Such people have several sources of alleged authority on which to rely – parents and teachers, public opinion (*vox populi*) represented by current fashion or by tradition, priests and religious sects or parties, booklearning and the veneration of antiquity. Some men may be excused to a degree from not seeking truth because they lack the means or the leisure, but for the most part it is attributable to mental and physical laziness. Locke never ceases to emphasise that the search for truth is arduous and that many who could undertake it shrink from it. It involves an investment they are not prepared to make. They will spend their income on new clothes and

. . . would think themselves miserable in coarse clothes, or a patched coat, and yet contentedly suffer their minds to appear in a piebald livery of coarse patches and borrowed shreds, such as it has pleased chance, or their country tailor (I mean the common opinion of those they have conversed with) to clothe them in.[22]

Others fail to use their own judgement less out of laziness than out of a fear that they would discover things which did not suit their prejudices, their education or their current mode of life. Again they 'content themselves without examination to take upon trust what they find convenient and in fashion'.[23]

Those who in this way neglect to use their understanding and show such fear of freedom can, nevertheless, be passionate in defence of the prejudices which they find so comforting. As children they imbibe propositions, especially about religion, from parents and teachers, and when adults they come to regard these propositions as 'sacred things' which not only may not be questioned, but serve themselves as the standards of truth. They will obstinately adhere to the greatest absurdities as long as they are consistent with their fundamental beliefs, and reject the evidence of their eyes if it does not fit their preconceptions.[24] Fanaticism, or 'enthusiasm' as it was then called, results in the acceptance of 'local truths' which are fiercely defended, even though the evidence in support of them has never been examined. This is a 'short and easy way of being in the right'.[25]

But the chances of being in the right are substantially diminished the more derivative the reasoning which is employed. The acceptance of traditional authority involves 'an inverted rule of probability' whereby an opinion gains in credency the more remote it is from its original source, and so

. . . what a thousand years since would not, to a rational man contemporary with the first voucher have appeared at all probable, is now urged as certain beyond all question, only because several have since from him, said it one after another . . . and those [propositions] which found or deserved little credit from the mouths of their first authors, are thought to grow venerable by age, and are urged as undeniable.[26]

Such propositions, as Hobbes put it, pass 'like gaping from mouth to mouth'.

At the same time the pressures on each individual to conform with tradition or fashion are all but overwhelming. The love of 'reputation' is what moves most men. They desire to stand well in the opinion of others, which they are most likely to do if they conduct themselves as others do. Locke compares society with a club which enforces its sanctions by the pressure of opinion, which few will or can resist.[27] It is effective in a way which neither the laws of the state nor even the law of nature commonly are. It is therefore from laziness, fear of the consequences of free speculation, conservatism or horror of a loss of reputation that men incline to fanaticism and sectarianism. But there is another factor at work – the self-interest of those groups who benefit from the lack of autonomy on the part of others. Priests 'to secure their empire' have kept reason out of religion and have not dared permit it to 'speak' to the people.[28] Status plays its part here too. Professors do not like to see what they have taught for decades challenged and their 'authority of forty years' standing, wrought out of hard rock, Greek and Latin, with no small expense of time and candle' undermined by some 'upstart'.[29]

Locke's plea to men to 'dare to know' and 'to have the courage to use their own understandings', to borrow Kant's characterisation of the Enlightenment, must therefore be seen in the context of his awareness of the pressures of public opinion, tradition and the interests of established authorities. Locke may have had little awareness that the conceptual tools of criticism were themselves historical, social products, but he did not abstract his individual entirely from the world around him. Whilst assimilating knowledge until it appears a private possession, the individual should still remember what he owes to the 'whole stock of human knowledge' and how far he can travel along the road to truth only because of those who have already 'cleared the woods, drained the bogs, built the bridges, and made the ways passable'.[30] At the same time the debt is a moral one which each individual must repay in his own way. Society as such cannot enforce any claim on him in respect of some collective effort in providing his education. It may merely demand the taxes which pay for the establishment of the secure conditions in which the individual may acquire his knowledge.

The Lockean individual is one who can stand up against the pressures of authority and think his own thoughts, who is prepared to withstand the social consequences that heterodoxy might bring. He must see for himself, think for himself, believe for himself and assent for himself:

> Knowing is seeing, and if it be so, it is madness to persuade ourselves that we do so by another man's eyes . . . Till we ourselves see it with our own eyes and perceive it by our own understandings, we are as much in the dark and as void of knowledge as before, let us believe any learned author as much as we will.[31]

In this respect Locke's *Of the Conduct of the Understanding* (1697) is a bridge between his epistemology and his social and political thinking. In it he expounds the habits and dispositions necessary to a rational individual who is to use his faculties to think for himself and make his own way in the world. The concern is, of course, similar to that found in the educational writings, but here Locke is directing his attention to adult moral agents not to children. The nature and limits of knowledge are those examined in the *Essay*. The *Conduct* is an intelligent, and industrious, man's guide to clear thinking. It is a manual for the man who wants to make a success of his own life and stamp his identity on it. It outlines the branches of learning in which the individual should be competent. It warns against the dangers of partiality, prejudice, haste and inattention. Consistently with the *Essay* Locke cautions his reader about the limits of analogy and simile and the abuse of words. But the leitmotiv is self-reliance.

This is something of which all men are capable, however their natural faculties may differ. Most of the differences between men whether in the schools of Athens or the woods of America arise from a 'neglect of their understandings'. What is required is not so much rules of logic as the rectification of certain bad habits of study.[32] With this, even men in the meanest walks of life can be expected to raise their powers of reasoning sufficiently to understand their own jobs. In the same way, even the poorest men can and must apply their minds to matters of religion. Their one day of rest affords them sufficient leisure and all this requires is some encouragement, since 'the original make of their minds is like that of other men'.[33] To assume men incapable of at least this minimal understanding would be levelling them 'with the brutes, and charging them with a stupidity below the rank of rational creatures'.[34]

Each individual can improve himself to the extent that his opportunities for reflection permit. No man need merely cite authority (even though Locke himself invokes that of Bacon). Each can seek the appropriate evidence or proofs for the claims of the learned or the beliefs of the multitude. Though the multitude is seldom to be relied upon, the intellectual who strays too far from ordinary usage is also to be suspected: 'It would be madness to refuse to breathe the common air, or quench one's thirst with water, because the rabble use them to these purposes.' Neither the ancients nor the moderns are to be given automatic deference.[35] Instead, the individual is to attempt, as far as he can, to examine the foundations of all doctrines. The instance he offers near the close of the work is the seigneurial political theory of Filmer which he had challenged in the *Two Treatises*:

. . . if it be demanded, whether the grand seignior can lawfully take what he will from any of his people? This question cannot be resolved without coming to a certainty, whether all men are naturally equal; for upon that it turns; and that truth well settled in the understanding, and carried in the mind through the various debates concerning the various rights of men in society, will go a great way in putting an end to them, and showing on which side the truth is.[36]

The issue is one which for Locke is central not only to politics but to all activity involving human understanding: 'In the whole conduct of the understanding there is nothing of more moment than to know when and where, and how far to give assent; and possibly there is nothing harder.'[37]

The *Conduct* unites the concerns of the *Essay* and the *Two Treatises*. It guides the Lockean individual as to how he should employ his liberty of suspending judgement as he considers when, where and how far he should consent to join a civil society or assent to the proposition that a government has or has not kept its trust. At the same time it proclaims Locke's suspicion of authoritarianism which runs from the earliest to the most mature works. Already in the *Essays on the Law of Nature* he insists that someone who defers unthinkingly to authority is 'yielding to the morality of others'.[38] Not even the prophet should be accepted without reservation since 'God when he makes the prophet does not unmake the man'.[39] It always remains the task of the individual to examine the evidence for any assertion whatever its source.

> He that believes without having any reason for believing may be in love with his own fancies; but neither seeks truth as he ought, nor pays the obedience due to his Maker, who would have him use those discerning faculties he has given him, to keep him out of mistake and error.[40]

There is a corresponding implicit obligation on theologians, mathematicians and writers to set down their evidence and proofs. It is not by the bare reading of an author that his knowledge is 'transfused into the reader's understanding', but by understanding the grounds of the argument.[41] The modern reader owes a debt to those past authors who have made it possible to test and criticise their conclusions.

Self-help does not, therefore, imply that the individual is intellectually self-sufficient, any more than he could be economically self-sufficient. At the same time as he rejects arguments from authority, Locke recommends his readers to keep their minds open to the greatest variety of ideas. In this respect he resembled Mill in his eclecticism.[42] One reason why men differ from one another in their understandings is the different range of ideas and situations they experience. The day-labourer and the country gentleman devoted to hunting and drinking are, in their different ways, so narrow in their experiences of life that they cannot be expected to attain high levels of reflection in matters of politics. Showing a contempt for the 'idiocy of rural life' Locke ranks a city porter higher in understanding than a country town mechanic, and him in turn higher than the village labourer, just as he places the 'coffee-house gleaner' ahead of the country gentleman by virtue of the range of experiences available to the city-dweller. Similarly, the intellectual is limited who keeps himself to a sect or who corresponds only with those who share his views instead of going 'abroad' and venturing out into 'the great ocean of knowledge'.[43]

Locke's is an 'open society', one in which the individual may be exposed to the 'variety and stock of knowledge' as instances of the 'variety and freedom of *thinking*'. In this way he will 'increase the powers and activity of the mind'.[44] In this way also he fulfils God's purposes. Out of this should emerge, given sufficient security, a community of men ready and eager to stretch themselves to the full. Each seeks truth, but does so in his own way by contributing to the variety of human ideas and experience. Ideally, each must consider whether to give or withhold assent to the ideas he encounters and none will defer naturally to the mere unsupported authority of another for 'They who are blind will always be led by those that see, or else fall into the ditch; and he is certainly the most subjected, the most enslaved, who is so in his understanding.'[45]

Property

Every individual has an obligation to preserve himself and to attempt to play such a part in the world as will most adequately develop his God-given capacities. 'Ought' implies 'can', and 'can', in turn, implies for Locke something more than capacity, important though that is. It implies that a man is free to act, that his life is sufficiently secure for him to pursue his goals with reasonable hopes of success and that he can sustain himself physically throughout. Locke encapsulates this in his theory of property. It is a man's property in his life, liberty and possessions which enables him to perform the duties attaching to his station. At the same time, the way in which he uses his property displays the direction and industriousness of his self-chosen life. Property plays both an instrumental and an expressive role.

Commentators on Locke point out that he uses the word 'property' with a wider and a narrower connotation. It is, perhaps, less frequently emphasised that the two usages are intimately connected.[46] The wider notion covers what we would tend to refer to as 'rights' – 'Lives, Liberties and Estates, which I call by the general Name, Property'. (123).[47] The narrower notion refers only to possessions and, in particular, to land. Locke asserts at one point that he always employs the term in the wider sense: 'By *Property*, I must be understood here, as in other places, to mean that Property which Men have in their Persons as well as Goods' (173). Nevertheless, it is clear that in chapter V entitled 'Of Property' the topic is the narrower one of goods and land. C. B. Macpherson, in his notable interpretation of Locke, has argued that this ambiguity is crucial to Locke's justification of unequal political rights.[48] Macpherson's textual exegesis, particularly of chapter V, is extraordinarily illuminating. As will become apparent, his interpretation of the text may be questioned in certain respects, while in others it will be suggested that he has reached the right conclusions by the wrong route. The ambiguity to which Macpherson refers should not conceal a fundamental unity in Locke's approach to property. To own property means to have the right to decide what uses may be made of a thing or in what ways an activity may be performed. It means that the owner can direct the exploitation of certain specifiable resources. For Locke these resources could include one's bodily activities or one's liberty as well as one's physical possessions. The way in which a person exploits these resources reveals his qualities as a rational agent. Private property – the exclusive individual right of exploitation – is necessary to individuality.

For liberals such as Locke property has a moral dimension. It marks off a private realm in which men may show their distinctive qualities. One person may squander his property, whether this comprises the resources of his body, or the liberty of suspending judgement and of considering one's conduct, or one's goods. Another may improve or develop his resources. But the ways in which a man may develop – or ruin – his life, liberty and possessions may be extremely varied. A man may be a rational, experimenting farmer, a merchant, a churchman or merely a day-labourer. He may be a philosopher or an administrator, an economist, a doctor, a theologian or, as in Locke's case, a bit of each. Whatever the career, Locke believes that success or failure represents the outcome of choices. The individual has chosen how to use the rights he has by nature. He displays his character by the way he uses his property. If he had no property – no private arena – he could not display this individual character. He would be undifferentiated – like a slave who had no opportunity for choice because he had no resources under his own direction.

Both reason and revelation demonstrate the necessity of property if men are to survive (25). Locke founds private property on the property someone has in his own person (27). This view was far from original to Locke. It was to be found in the writings of some of the Levellers, such as Richard Overton's *An Arrow against all Tyrants* of 1646, although Locke develops the idea differently.[49] Yet it now seems odd to speak of property in this sense.[50] One can understand what is meant by owning a hat or a piece of land. One can see how one might first acquire such property and how one might get rid of it. But can we own our person in a similar way? Is our person something we can acquire or dispose of? Who exactly owns what? How does one distinguish what is owned from the owner? By tracing Locke's arguments from the origin of property it becomes apparent that Locke is ready to exploit a number of different incompatible images to justify the privacy of property.

God as creator is the first proprietor and retains a right in everything he has made (I, 39). He did not, however, directly institute private property. God gave the world to man in common (25–6). This does not mean that mankind, as a community, owned and managed the world.[51] It means that the resources of the world – the land, its products and the animals – were made available to each and every individual to use and enjoy. Locke's great precursors among natural law theorists, Grotius and Pufendorf, had argued in different ways that property was owned by mankind communally and that universal consent was required for this collective ownership to be divided into private portions. For Locke, however, property could only be private. In this he was in unacknowledged agreement with his avowed opponent Sir Robert Filmer. But whereas Filmer had held that property was a direct grant from God, Locke's case is that men must turn objects in common into property by the God-given capacity of labour. However, labour is itself property but of a different kind. Unlike external goods it is property from the outset and can never be common to all men (27). Thus an original property in person and labour is used to create a secondary type of property in physical objects.

J. P. Day has shown the confusions inherent in speaking of property or ownership in either one's person or one's labour. Nevertheless, Locke's intentions are clear. Each individual has the sole right by nature to direct his bodily resources to ensure his own survival. Conversely, no other person has any natural authority to direct an individual's resources in a different manner. The individual employs his resources of reason and recognises that, unless he labours, he will starve, since the goods in common will be inert unless fruit is gathered, animals reared, killed or milked or vegetables sown or harvested. Man is born to penury. Only labour can lift him out of it. It is this labour which creates property. Consent is not necessary since no person or group has any prior property to relinquish. In a famous phrase Locke describes this process as one in which the individual 'hath mixed his Labour' with whatever he removes from the common natural condition (27). Roman and natural law had recognised 'occupancy' as a criterion of property and Locke provides a test of what occupancy consists in. Locke's language suggests a kind of chemical interaction between the labour and the object on which the labour is expended. In turn, since labouring cannot be divorced from the labourer, the object is chemically mixed with the labourer. The object takes on an element of the person. It becomes an extension of himself. In this way, as Hannah Arendt points out, Locke founded private property on the most privately owned thing there could be, the property a man has in his own body.[52] The defence of property can then be linked to the defence of one's person. A threat to property, from any quarter, can be construed to be a threat to life and may be resisted as such. The 'mixing' metaphor is therefore a brilliant polemical stroke. Philosophically it is more dubious. It succeeds by exploiting another sense of 'his body' and 'his labour' where it is like 'his skin'. Locke is persuading his reader that a piece of property is not merely a resource which the individual may direct or exploit, but is a property in the different sense of an attribute of the owner, much like the colour of his eyes. Just as a person cannot share another's skin or the colour of his eyes, so he cannot share an object with which the labour of another person has been mixed (27). The object has become part of that person. It is, however, an illegitimate shift of meaning. It is unclear why mixing one's labour with an object necessarily creates an exclusive property in it, such that one may dispose of it as one wishes – destroy it, sell it, bequeath it. Instead one might have acquired merely a right of usufruct, without the right to transfer it at all or to transfer it only under certain conditions. Nor is it clear that mixing labour with land creates a permanent property in the land as distinct from the 'value-added' content resultant from its cultivation. Property would seem only to arise as long as the land is kept in constant employment. Locke's theory of the origin of property carries conviction if the reader is already committed to the modern theory of exclusive property right which Locke advances, which contradicted certain earlier customary law, and later socialist views. Moreover, even if we may speak of a person having property in his labour – the right to direct his personal resources – it does not follow that he establishes a property in any direction in which he employs such resources. To have a property in something must imply some form of recognition by others. This in turn must derive from some publicly recognised rule.

Locke acknowledges this, at least in part. Firstly, he accepts that one man's property right is limited by the equal property right of another. Secondly, he accepts that property necessarily implies the existence of rules constituting it. At the same time, he wishes to steer a hazardous course between the rocks of Grotius, Pufendorf, Filmer and Hobbes. Grotius and Pufendorf had founded property on a supposed constitutive act of consent, which Locke rejects on the grounds that men would have starved before consent could be given and that consent is superfluous where acquisition of property does not harm others. Filmer and Hobbes had founded property on a constitutive legal enactment by a human sovereign who, in Filmer's case, acted on an authority derived from God. Property outside civil society was hence impossible. Locke wishes to reject this because he believes that property constituted by sovereign enactment cannot be safe from a similar sovereign act of annulment or redistribution. Hobbes had stated that the doctrine that 'every private man has an absolute propriety in his goods; such as excludeth the right of the sovereign' was one which was destructive of the state[53], yet this was the very doctrine which Locke sought to uphold. If he was to make the world safe for private property he had to base it neither on consent, nor on positive law, but on some pre-political law, and, hence, on the law of nature and of God.

The law establishes the right of every individual to remove from the common stock enough to satisfy the needs of himself and his family. Men were at first hunters and gatherers and fishermen (e.g. 28–30) or nomadic herdsmen (38). They picked fruit or killed deer or drove their flocks where and when they pleased, and their labour established their right to the pickings, the kill or to the land temporarily grazed. Farming was at first on a very small scale but as population increased more land was enclosed and made private by the labour of each family. But it was only with the establishment by consent of civil societies that the boundaries of property were established by law, which also laid down the conditions according to which still vacant land was to be settled. Although this could seem a dangerous concession to the Hobbesian position[54] Locke appears to construe such enactments as regulative rather than constitutive of property as such.

Whether the property consists of acorns which have been gathered, fish from the sea, water drawn from a well or land which has been enclosed and tilled, the law of nature imposes certain limitations on the amount which may be legitimately acquired. As Locke points out, an obvious objection to his labour theory of appropriation is that there seems nothing to stop a person grabbing ('ingrossing') as much as he likes and leaving insufficient for others (31). This would, however, be an invasion of another person's equal right and contrary to one's obligations under the law of nature. The law therefore imposes limits to acquisition. No person may, firstly, acquire so much that there is not 'enough and as good' over for others (33) – not, be it noted, 'enough and *as much*'. Secondly, no person may acquire so much more than he needs that the produce wastes and spoils (31). This, too, would be prejudicial to the rights of others though, as Plamenatz has argued, it is only in conditions where resources are finely balanced that one man's waste results in another person's deprivation.[55] Macpherson, who first subjected this section of the *Second Treatise* to detailed analysis, raises the question whether implicitly each person is further limited to that which he may acquire with his own labour.[56] This seems not so much a natural law limitation however as part of what Locke understands by property in a person's labour. A man is not entitled to call upon the resources of another's labour without that person's consent.

The effect of such limitations would be that each person would have only a 'very moderate Proportion' (36). However, the proportions would not necessarily be equal.[57] In the first place, individual needs and capacities vary. Those with a larger family to support could right-fully enclose larger tracts of land. Secondly, even in a primitive barter economy there is an opportunity for the rational and industrious man to accumulate and invest so as to place himself at an advantage. For although natural law banned the useless hoarding of perishable goods, it permitted the accumulation of durable goods which might be consumed at leisure or might serve as the basis of barter for perishables at a later more opportune time (46).

Nevertheless, it is the invention of money which accelerates the movement towards unequal holdings, even though it does not create inequality (48). Money whittles away the limitations on the accumulation of property or, more strictly, since the law of nature is eternal and universal, changes the significance of the limitations by changing the circumstances of the state of nature. Men consented to put a value to something durable which was not itself of great use and which would serve as a pledge that in return for it the giver would receive goods equal to the agreed value. Other objects could be used, but gold and silver were established as currency. Being durable, they could be hoarded without perishing. It therefore became possible for the industrious man to produce more than his immediate needs and sell the surplus in return for durable money. He could then store his money until he required it for further purchases of perishables, or he could use it to purchase further land to produce a larger marketable surplus. He could additionally buy the machinery and materials to improve the productivity of his existing land in order, once again, to increase his profit. Wherever money comes into use private property begins to increase in size (49).

The invention of money also modifies the meaning of the rule laying down that enough and as good be left to others. The open spaces are gradually inhabited. The expansion of population results in the enclosure of more land and the invention of money results in the concentration of such enclosures in the hands of the industrious and provident, those who have employed their faculties as God intended. The right to appropriate belongs only to those who first mixed their labour with the land or the raw materials. Those who come later upon the scene can only acquire property by transfer, with the consent of the original proprietor. In effect this means by inheritance or by purchase. Inheritance will normally be within the family of the original proprietor, purchase will be by those more enterprising proprietors who have accumulated enough surplus to buy out the moderate proportion of another proprietor. The effect is to create a category of landless persons. Some may set up as merchants and manufacturers but a larger number will not have the financial resources and are left with only one possible means of making a living. They must mix their labour with land or raw materials owned by others.

On the one hand, therefore, is a class of persons who own land and material but who lack sufficient labour to extend it further or improve its efficiency, there being a limit to what one can mix one's personal labour with. On the other hand, is the class of persons who possess the natural right to dispose of the resources of their person and their labour but have no property in the material with which it has to be mixed if life is to be sustained and personality is to be developed. The logical conclusion for rational Lockean men is to make a contract by which the owner of labour sells his property in his labour on specifiable terms to the owner of land and materials. The labour is purchased at a certain wage, for certain hours and for a certain period of appointment. It is true, as J. P. Day had argued, that strictly speaking the only labour that is owned by another person is that of the slave which Locke specifically does not have in mind here.[58] What Locke wishes to say is that the employer has the right to dictate the use of the employee's labour resources within the periods laid down and that no other person (including the labourer himself) can have a similar right. In that sense the employer can say that the employee's labour is 'his'. It then follows that those things produced by 'mixing' this labour with the land must also belong to the employer. There is, therefore, no natural law labour limitation to overcome. Every man has the right and duty to employ his labour to the utmost benefit, but what counts as a man's labour is extended to include the labouring activity of his employees.

It is quite clear that in such a society there cannot be enough land or materials for every inhabitant. But is there a substitute which is 'as good', the provision of which would satisfy the natural right of every man to subsistence? Locke's answer is affirmative. The person who encloses land and who purchases labour to improve the land increases productivity a hundredfold (37). Labour adds value to raw materials. Goods owe their value to the labour which has gone into them, and which has transformed barren materials into products which consumers wish to purchase and which sustain life and comfort (40–3). Improved land will support a population much larger than unimproved common land and the wages paid to the labourer will enable him to maintain a standard of living far higher than if each man had been left to make his living by gathering his modest proportion from unimproved, unenclosed common land. This is apparently true, even though Locke frequently acknowledges that the wages of the labouring class enable labourers as a whole to live only a hand-to-mouth existence.[59] The level of pay will depend on supply and demand and scarcity of a particular skill or of labour in a specific area may raise wages. In such circumstances, Locke says, the labour force needs to be 'humoured' or it will not work.[60] There is no suggestion that the labourer is owed a recompense in some way commensurate with the value added to the product by his particular labour. The entrepreneur hires labour at the going rate and then mixes 'his' labour with 'his' raw materials to produce a commodity which is 'his' until the moment of sale, the profits or loss on which are similarly 'his'.

The wage level of a labourer in cultivated Devonshire is 'enough' to maintain his subsistence and offers not only 'as good' a standard of living but better, Locke asserts, than that enjoyed by a king of an Indian tribe in the unimproved lands of America. It is not surprising that Locke did not consider the more appropriate comparison between the living standards of a Devonshire labourer and those he might have enjoyed as a peasant farmer, or as an equal partner in the communal farming and improvement of those same Devonshire lands. Despite his explicit awareness of the fruitfulness of land as a means of production, Locke appears to ignore it for purposes of comparison between an owner and a labourer. The labourer may have 'enough' by some minimal criterion, but his labour is not 'as good' for the purposes of creating future wealth for himself and his descendants. Locke's argument that productivity varies with the extent of occupancy manages, by its loaded comparison, to imply that productivity will also vary with the type of occupancy. The more radical comparisons would occur in the seventeenth century only to Diggers. Locke does not switch to a purely utilitarian defence of private property as contributing to the greater good. Rather, he claims that the natural right to enough and as good is in fact satisfied, and more than satisfied, by unequal private appropriation. Indeed, he is suggesting that unequal appropriation is a necessary condition for satisfying the equal right of subsistence.

Unequal property holding does not deny the equal right to property although it does show that this right becomes a very formal one. The equal right to property does not imply the right to equal property. Men, as men, have the status of property owners. The equal right to acquire and own property is inalienable although particular properties may be alienated by being sold for profit or let for wages. Once alienated, the previous owner ceases, of course, to have a property right in the particular property, but he cannot cease to have a right to acquire other property and, in the case of the property in his labour, he resumes his complete right upon cessation of the contract. However, in the commercial society which Locke considers natural, the right to acquire property is mediated by money. Every man has the right to acquire property according to the rules of the commercial community, at the price determined by supply and demand. The unskilled labourer who has hired out his labour has little opportunity, given prevailing wages for the unskilled, to transform his right to acquire property into actual acquisition of anything durable.[61] A Carnegie may rise from labourer or office boy to entrepreneur in Locke's 'open' society. A man can never lose his right to raise himself by developing his native faculties through the acquisition of property. Whether his chances of doing so are substantially greater than his turning out, as in fairy stories, to be the long-lost heir to the estate is another matter. There is reason to think that Locke was torn between his emphasis on the moral duty of improvement and his awareness of the actual restrictions on social mobility. He could show an awareness that even amongst those who would improve themselves, there were 'some also who are toiling in vain'.[62] But it did follow that the duty of self-improvement required the right of self-improvement and, consequently, at least the absence of legal restriction in natural and civil society on the mobility of the meritorious. The task of law is to assist each individual to perform his duty by protecting his right to property which was, in both its wider and narrower usages, the means to such performance. Without law each individual would be left to enforce his property right himself. The ineffectiveness of such private enforcement would limit individual self-development and consequently make it impossible to assure all men at least their right of subsistence.

The defence of property

Locke's state of nature is, therefore, much like an idealised version of the contract-based, commercial society of Locke's own day but with government absent. This conclusion, though much discussed by recent commentators, would surely not have surprised Locke himself. Locke is not unmindful of the moral defects in the operations of his own society.[63] It did however, when civilised by law, come closer to maximising the opportunities for each person to realise his individuality than previous epochs darkened by privilege and superstition. This natural condition was never intended to be confined to primitive societies. It is a conjecture to show how far men – passionate and rational, distrustful yet social – might be able to secure for themselves the conditions in which each could develop his human capacities without the help of governmental institutions. Market society is not graven on the hearts of men nor is it a consensus of mankind's experience, but it does represent the kind of arrangements which respect the equal rights of men to life, liberty and possessions, and which men might have arrived at by reason and practical judgement, undistorted by the sectional interests of party and religion, or by the historical accidents of war and conquest. As a methodological device, natural market society is not unlike the 'natural' or 'conjectural' histories which were to be favoured in the eighteenth century by historians and sociologists. The state of nature is conjectural because historically it would become rapidly clear to any who might be in such a society that to perfect such arrangements would require the stability which could only be provided by government (101). Hence (the relations between states apart), the records of such natural societies are few (14) and are to be presumed lost in remote antiquity. Yet the conjecture remains a reminder of what might be logically possible without government.

To the extent that market society was unrealisable without government this would indicate the necessary functions of political institutions. To the extent that market society was realisable without government this would indicate the areas in which government was superfluous. The shortcomings of the state of nature thus reveal both the minimum and maximum roles of civil government.

Though the state of nature is, by definition, without government, it nevertheless is, according to Locke, subject to law. The law of nature defines a moral community amongst all men who, sharing the capacity for reason, are capable of working out some of the law's requirements. The law accords to all such men certain rights and duties which each must respect. But as well as the duty of respecting the rights of others, men have a more positive duty of coming to the assistance of others when their rights are threatened. Provided a person does not place his own life in peril, he has a duty to do as much as he can to preserve any other member of the human species (6). Someone who ignores the equal right of another human being and destroys him steps outside the boundaries of this moral community. He is degenerate. He 'declares himself to quit the Principles of Human Nature, and to be a noxious Creature' (10). Such a person ceases to belong to the ranks of human beings and falls to the lower level of creation, to the 'brute beasts'. Accordingly he may be 'destroyed as a Lyon or a Tyger, one of those wild Savage Beasts, with whom Men can have no Society nor Security' (11; also 16).

Though every man is capable of appreciating the broad requirements of natural law, few understand it in all its detail, and many do not take the trouble to study it. Locke is not discussing a Golden Age where every person follows the law in its entirety. He is a Christian writer who has in mind man as portrayed in Christian theology, capable of reason but sinful, swayed by passions. Only a few may seriously infringe the law of nature, but this is a propensity in all men. Infringements of the law are therefore all too likely. But who is to enforce the law? God's sanctions are only inflicted after death and though fear of them can be expected to inhibit many, there is also a need to deal with crimes here and now. In the state of nature no person has greater authority than any other. Locke therefore draws the original conclusion that by nature each individual has an equal right to enforce the law of nature and punish offenders (8). This 'executive Power of the law of Nature' (13) is to be central to Locke's explanation of the origin of the state. In the state of nature, where public authority is absent, each individual has the right, when his life and possessions are attacked, to catch and punish his assailant. Moreover each has the right and duty to catch and punish someone who has attacked a third party. The offender has injured the whole species and in apprehending him the individual is restoring the natural moral community.

The natural law at the same time lays down limits to the right of private punishment. The object of punishment is to restore things as nearly as possible to what they were before the crime. No one is entitled to use more force than is necessary. If he did it would itself be an offence. The limits are set by what is required for 'restraint' and 'reparation' (11). Every person has the right to restrain an offender, but only the person whose property has been stolen or damaged may claim reparation. He may seize the property of the offender or even demand his service to an extent that will recompense the damage. Others may help him in obtaining his compensation.

Private law-enforcement suffers from severe inconveniences. It imposes strains on the most self-reliant and devout individual. The tendencies of human nature which make policing necessary also make the policing itself unreliable. The effect of private policing is to make each individual prosecutor, judge and executioner. He judges whether the law of nature is broken, apprehends the person he claims to be the culprit and punishes him. If additionally he is the injured party then he takes the law into his own hands. There is no impartial person or body to (a) clarify the law of nature where it is disputed, (b) determine whether the law has been broken and whether the accused is guilty, and (c) decide what punishment is commensurate with the crime and see that it is duly inflicted. The problems appear at their most acute where two parties dispute the issue. Each may claim the right to the same property. In such circumstances no one has authority to decide the issue and neither party is under an obligation to renounce his claim. It cannot be self-evident which party deserves the assistance of outsiders. Instead of acting so as to restore natural justice, each disputant will be partial to his own interests and even if the rightful owner could be established, his desire for revenge might well lead him to exceed what was required by justice. Force beyond what justice demands is then itself an act of violence, which may in turn call forth resistance leading to vendettas rather than to peace.

The dangers of excess are great, since Locke regards proper restraint as including the use of such power as will make the transgressor repent and deter both him and others from repeating the offence (8). In the absence of established impartial procedures of justice, any invasion of property may be construed by the injured party as a threat to his life and thus he is entitled to kill a thief who has not yet harmed him on the grounds that the thief is just as likely to enslave or kill him as steal from him (18–19). At the other extreme, the injured party may lack the strength to enforce judgement against an aggressor who will always have an incentive to resist and, in such cases, the assistance of others is not to be relied upon. Similar problems arise over reparation as over restraint. What is a naturally just recompense? Suppose the offender to have destroyed a vase worth on the open market £5, but that the injured party insists that it has a sentimental value and that, if a price had to be put on this, it would need £250 to recompense him for the loss (in addition to punishment for the crime itself). How is such a dispute to be settled? Is the injured party to be free to stipulate any sum as the appropriate recompense? Can the law of nature lay down the just price for the sentimental associations of a piece of property?

When such matters cannot be resolved authoritatively, a state of war rapidly ensues. A state of war occurs when one person deliberately violates the rights of another in such a manner as to give him grounds to believe his life and liberty to be at risk. Such war can occur at any time. Under government, however, the war ceases when the violence ceases and the dispute is then resolved by established judicial procedures. Where, as in the state of nature, there is no impartial judicial procedure, the war will continue until the injured party obtains satisfaction which will include deterring any future violations (20). Because of the lack of law and of certain deterrent punishments in the state of nature, there is a greater likelihood of war breaking out and, just as significantly, where it does break out it will continue for much longer than in civil society. It is, therefore, in order to avoid the state of nature degenerating into a state of war that men institute government (21).

To readers of Hobbes this may seem a very similar argument. Government is instituted to escape from the state of war. But in a clear reference to the Hobbesian position Locke insists that the state of nature and the state of war are to be firmly distinguished 'however some Men have confounded' the two (19).[64] In the state of nature men can suppress isolated acts of war and can draw on the help of others. The moral authority of natural law is acknowledged even though its imprecision makes it an insecure basis for order. The state of nature is inconvenient and the sum of the inconveniences is that when war breaks out it is difficult to bring it to an end. It is not, however, an unremitting condition of 'Enmity, Malice, Violence, and Mutual Destruction'. As such it is preferable to a state of war, and no rational man would abandon the state of nature, with all its inconveniences and dangers of war, and place himself under a form of government where war was the inevitable outcome. The real purpose of Locke's distinction between nature and war is then made apparent for, in contrast to Hobbes, war may occur within civil society. The use of illegitimate violence is war 'both where there is, and is not, a common Judge' (19). In a civil society war is ended by judicial proceedings but under a regime where the government invades the rights of the subjects, and where the judges are themselves biased, the government is at war with its innocent subjects until such a time as it can be defeated (20). To abandon the state of nature for a form of government which provided no guarantee against such a state of war would be contrary to all reason. It would be to abandon the possibility of war for its certainty. Even if the state of nature had already degenerated into war, it would still make no sense to exchange a war between individuals for one where the enemy was the organised power of the state. None of these arguments could have been acceptable to Hobbes.

The state of nature is, therefore, a conjectural condition in which men seek to defend their property in life, liberty and physical goods in the absence of a public authority. For this, natural men are both well equipped and ill equipped. They are born capable of reason and of liberty. They are able to use their understanding to sift, criticise and expand communal experience concerning the management of property, which is the instrument by which both life and the good life are promoted. Each is able to reason that his rights and his duties entail respect for the equal rights and duties of others. Each is to be presumed an adult moral agent capable of reasoned choices, of knowing what his rights and duties are and of developing a plan of life which will develop his character whilst acknowledging the legitimacy of the different plans of his fellow men and, indeed, defending these plans where they are illegitimately hindered. On the other side, these same individuals are, after the Fall, tainted by sin. They are partial to themselves, often unmindful of their obligations, competitive and aggressive.

These failings call into question the very real achievements of which natural, rational man is capable. Specifically property, the instrument of such achievements, is rendered insecure by the self-policing of individuals liable to error and self-love. Rational men are, however, able to understand what it is in themselves that needs to be guarded against. They appreciate that this requires more than self-control, important though that is. It requires common action to establish those institutions of law, justice and administration, the absence of which frustrates men in the performance of their duties under natural law. Conversely, the presence of such properly founded and reliable institutions should suffice to provide the secure framework within which rational men can pursue their individual paths to salvation. The right path can never be certain but each must choose for himself the one he considers correct. No other person or body may legitimately force another along any particular path. Government enables each to go further along his particular path than would be likely in a state of nature.

Realising this, each individual is to consider what form of government a rational man would choose to place himself under in order to protect his rights. Locke's answer is 'civil government'. One way, however, to appreciate the specific character of 'civil government' is to consider what forms of power he did *not* believe that any Lockean rational man could accept – what we might term 'uncivil government'.

Notes Chapter III

1 *Essay*, II, xxi, 67.
2 *Law of Nature*, VII, p. 203.
3 *The Reasonableness of Christianity*, *Works*, VII, p. 159.
4 *Essay*, IV, xvii, 1.
5 *Law of Nature*, V, p. 149; *Essay*, IV, xviii, 2.
6 See above, ch. II.
7 *Education*, sect. 31.
8 *Education*, sect. 66.
9 *A Third Letter for Toleration*, *Works*, VI, p. 211.
10 *Law of Nature*, II, p. 123.
11 *Law of Nature*, II, p. 135.
12 *The Reasonableness of Christianity*, *Works*, VII, p. 50.
13 *Of the Conduct of the Understanding*, *Works*, III, p. 201.
14 *Education*, sect. 54.
15 *Education*, sect. 81.
16 *Law of Nature*, II, p. 135.
17 E.g. Macpherson, *Possessive Individualism*, p. 255 and the discussion of Lockean man as an exemplar of the 'abstract individual in Steven Lukes, *Individualism*, Oxford, Blackwell, 1973, ch. 11, ch. 19 and p. 150.
18 See J. Yolton, *John Locke and the Compass of Human Understanding*, pp. 17ff.
19 *Education*, sect. 67.
20 *Essay*, II, xxviii, 12.
21 *Of the Conduct of the Understanding*, *Works*, III, sect. 3.
22 *Essay*, IV, xx, 6.
23 *Essay*, IV, xx, 6.
24 *Essay*, IV, xx, 9–10.
25 *Of the Conduct of the Understanding*, *Works*, III, sect. 34.
26 *Essay*, IV, xvi, 10.
27 *Essay*, II, xxviii, 12. A history of the idea of 'public opinion' in this period would be a fascinating study. It was to play a central role in eighteenth-century English and Scottish thought.
28 *The Reasonableness of Christianity*, *Works*, VII, p. 135.
29 *Essay*, IV, xx, 11.
30 *The Reasonableness of Christianity*, *Works*, VII, p. 145.
31 *Of the Conduct of the Understanding*, sect. 24, *Works*, III, pp. 251–2.
32 *Of the Conduct of the Understanding*, *Works*, III, sect. 2.
33 *Conduct*, *Works*, III, sect. 8.
34 *Conduct*, *Works*, III, sect. 7.
35 *Conduct*, *Works*, III, sect. 24.
36 *Conduct*, *Works*, III, sect. 44.
37 *Conduct*, *Works*, III, sect. 33.
38 *Law of Nature*, VII, p. 203.
39 *Essay*, IV, xix, 14.
40 *Essay*, IV, xvii, 24.
41 *Conduct*, *Works*, III, sect. 24.
42 See *John Stuart Mill* in this series by John Halliday, London, Allen & Unwin, 1976.
43 *Conduct*, *Works*, III, sect. 3.

44 *Conduct, Works,* III, sect. 19. My italics. This is in fact Locke's definition of the business of education but it serves equally as an account of the objectives of all intellectual activity.

45 *Essay,* IV, xx, 6.

46 An interesting discussion appears in Hannah Arendt, *The Human Condition,* Chicago, University of Chicago Press, 1958, ch. 11.

47 See also 57, 59, 87, 173.

48 *The Political Theory of Possessive Individualism,* ch. V. Macpherson suggests that in Locke's discussion of the limits of supreme power (138–9) he employs only the narrower meaning. However either meaning would fit the context and the reference to 'estates' may be merely an illustration of a more general point.

49 For an excellent discussion, see I. Hampsher-Monk, 'The Political Theory of the Levellers: Putney, Property and Professor Macpherson', *Political Studies,* XXIV, 4, 1976, pp. 397–422.

50 For a sharp criticism of Locke, see J. P. Day, 'Locke on Property', *Philosophical Quarterly,* XVI, 64, 1966, pp. 207–20. David Hume had already recognised the problems. *Treatise of Human Nature,* Bk III, Pt II, sect. III.

51 See the excellent discussion by M. Seliger, *The Liberal Politics of John Locke,* London, Allen & Unwin, 1968, pp. 188–90.

52 *The Human Condition,* p. 111.

53 *Leviathan,* ch. 29, Oakeshott edition, Oxford, Blackwell, 1955, p. 213.

54 Willmoore Kendall regards such arguments as instances of Locke's collectivism. The public determines property by law in Kendall's interpretation whereas the present suggestion is that Locke means that the law regulates the transfer and sale of 'natural' property rights within civil society. See *John Locke and the Doctrine of Majority Rule,* ch. IV.

55 J. Plamenatz, *Man and Society,* London, Longmans, 1963, Vol. I, pp. 242–3. Although Plamenatz regarded such situations as rare it could be noted that since the state of nature also represents international society Locke's injunction would apply to any waste in developed countries which could be said to deprive underdeveloped societies.

56 *Possessive Individualism,* p. 201. The detail of Macpherson's analysis obviates the need for repetition here where it will suffice to indicate differences of emphasis.

57 Seliger has made this point most effectively. *The Liberal Politics of John Locke,* ch. V, especially pp. 149–59.

58 J. P. Day, 'Locke on Property', loc. cit. p. 212.

59 E.g. *Some Considerations, Works,* V, p. 24.

60 *Some Considerations, Works,* V, p. 25.

61 See *Some Considerations, Works,* V, p. 24 for Locke's assumptions about the necessarily high propensity to consume on the part of the day-labourers.

62 *Law of Nature,* II, p. 135.

63 John Dunn rightly emphasises this in his comments on Macpherson: *The Political Thought of John Locke,* e.g. p. 217 and ch. 16 in general.

64 A 'confounding' repeated by Richard H. Cox in his *Locke on War and Peace,* ch. 2. Cox attributes a Hobbesian position to Locke which makes nonsense of a careful distinction Locke wished to draw and to exploit in his condemnation of absolutism. See below, ch. VI.

Chapter IV

Uncivil Government

> The great and *chief end* therefore, of Mens uniting into Commonwealths, and putting themselves under Government, is the Preservation *of their Property* (124).

By 'property' Locke here means the rights to life, liberties and estates. It is in the way that a man makes use of his rights that he marks himself off from other men, that he displays his individuality. A man's liberty consists in his having some guaranteed space within which he can tend this property. In a state of nature there is no such guaranteed space and, hence, rational men are forced to consider what kinds of arrangements between themselves can establish the requisite guarantees. It is only within the context of government that an individual can strive effectively to follow his chosen plan of life. The first problem of government arises, however, from its very character, namely, that it is contradictory to absolute liberty. In the *Essay* Locke cites 'No government allows absolute liberty' as one of those propositions in morality about which one can be as certain as about any demonstration in mathematics.[1] The paradox of government for the political theorist of individuality is that it invades the condition it is intended to preserve. The second – and crucial – problem of government then becomes what character of government conforms most closely to the needs of rational self-determining moral agents. The kind of government which will provide the looked-for guarantee of property and will most closely satisfy the need to recognise liberty is the subject matter of the *Second Treatise* – 'civil government'.

The term 'civil government' refers, therefore, to a particular mode of governing. Not all governments are 'civil'. At the very outset of the *Second Treatise* Locke establishes a distinction between three types of power in terms of the ways in which the power is exercised. 'Civil' government is distinguished by its exercising 'political' power rather than one of the other two forms of power. One of these is of restricted legitimacy and the other is almost wholly illegitimate. The centrality of property to Locke's theory of morality and of government may be gauged from the fact that these three forms of power are differentiated by the ways in which they relate to the distribution of property.

The three types of power are 'political power', 'paternal power' and 'despotic power'. Political power is the kind of power a ruler exercises over a subject. Paternal power is the sort of power a father exercises over his children. Despotic power is the power a lord exercises over a slave. Each of these powers therefore reflects a particular property relationship. Paternal power is exercised over those who are not yet mature or experienced enough to manage property, i.e. over children. Despotic power is exercised over those who have no property rights whatsoever, i.e. slaves. But political power is over those who have property and manage it for themselves, i.e. adult responsible men. As Locke puts it: *'Paternal Power* is only where Minority makes the Child incapable to manage his property; *Political* where Men have Property in their own disposal; and *Despotical* over such as have no property at all' (174).

It is these different relationships between power and property – natural rights – that make it essential to distinguish between them. Locke held it to be of paramount importance to establish 'the difference betwixt a Ruler of a Common-wealth, a Father of a Family, and a Captain of a Galley' (3). The confusion between them arises in part because the same person may play all these parts. He may, as Locke points out (2), be at one and the same time a ruler, a father and a lord over slaves. This does not mean, however, that these powers can be run together. There are fundamental differences between them. A man's power as a father or as a slave-owner is quite different from the power he wields as a ruler.

There is, however, a far more important source of confusion than this simultaneous playing of roles. Locke believed that political thinkers and politicians had deliberately interpreted political power as being the same as either the power of a father or the power of a slave-owner. Like Hobbes, Locke offers an intellectualist account of the civil unrest that had disturbed the country during the seventeenth century. Hobbes had suggested that civil disturbance had been occasioned by what he believed was the growing tendency of every private man to dispute the definitions of good and evil, of justice and injustice laid down by the sovereign ruler. Locke's view is that 'the great mistakes of late about Government' arose from 'confounding' the three distinct forms of power. The political and constitutional struggle had been between those who had claimed for government the power of a father or of a slave-owner and those who would restrict government to a civil, 'political' role (169). It is only by clearly delineating the three powers that it can be shown what kind of power is at all compatible with individual self-determination, and which forms of power constitute a major threat to liberty.

Locke is, therefore, using 'political' and related words like 'civil' in a special, restricted sense. He wishes to deny the claims of paternal or despotic power to be political. The word is to be used only for power employed by rulers in the protection of the property of subjects. States which do not guarantee such protection of rights are not worthy of the name of 'civil society'. Locke is attempting something to be found in many political philosophers. He is endowing a word with an evaluative as well as a descriptive meaning. David Hume was later to complain about Locke's procedure, saying that it flew in the face of ordinary usage of such words. But there is much to be said for Sheldon Wolin's view that

> The designation of certain activities and arrangements as political, the characteristic way we think about them and the concepts we employ to communicate our observations and reactions – none of these are written into the nature of things but are the legacy accruing from the historical activity of political philosophers.[2]

Locke is doing what Aristotle had done when he distinguished as political the Greek city states from the government of great empires and from that of small households. And when a modern writer declared that there could be no politics in totalitarian regimes he was arguing in a similar manner to that of Locke.[3] All were trying to establish that the powers exercised by, or claimed for, certain governments were simply not political, but belonged to some other universe of discourse.

This chapter will be considering what forms of power Locke thought were not political, but it is necessary to begin, as Locke did, with his definition of political power.

> *Political Power* then I take to be *a Right* of making Laws with Penalties of Death, and consequently all less Penalties, for the Regulating and Preserving of Property, and of employing the force of the Community, in the execution of such Laws, and in the defence of the Common-wealth from Foreign Injury, and all this only for the Publick Good. (3).

This definition partly describes and partly prescribes. It describes a situation where there is a body which is authorised as the only one within a territory which can employ violence – the death penalty and imprisonment – to enforce the rules it makes. It employs this power in the name of the community and employs it against foreign attacks. This is very similar to the conventional modern definitions of the state as an organisation with the monopoly of authorising legitimate coercion in a given territory. Such a definition incorporates the essentials of 'legal sovereignty'. There is an independent law-making body which does not acknowledge any other human organisation as its superior and which has no competitors in its territorial area. It does not, however, define who is to exercise this power, whether a king or an assembly – a point which will require further elaboration later.[4]

The prescriptive part of the definition is, of course, contained in the reference to the preservation of property as the purpose of political power. Power is only political so long as it has this purpose. Only for this reason can there be a right to make laws and impose imprisonment or the death penalty. There is no right to do this for any other purpose. So although Locke seems to speak of power as a right which is, as Laslett points out, somewhat strange, in fact the power is only rightful so long as it is political. Where power is employed by government other than to safeguard the subject in his care of his property, it is not political but either despotic or paternal, and in neither case rightful.

This distinction between political, paternal and despotic power was not original to Locke but traditional to political thought since Aristotle. It was the manner of distinction and the use made of it which was so significant in Locke's thought. Whilst Hobbes paid lip-service to the traditional distinction in chapter 20 of *Leviathan*, he nevertheless concluded that the 'rights and consequences of both paternal and despotical dominion' were very much the same as those of a civil government. 'Speculation', 'deduction' and the Scriptures taught that there was little essential difference between ruling a state and ruling over a family or over slaves. When Locke suggested that the disorder of the time arose in large part from 'confounding' these different powers it remains very probable that he had in mind not only his avowed opponent Sir Robert Filmer, but Hobbes as well.

Despotism

It is indeed tempting to suggest that Locke's attack on despotism is directed against Hobbes, just as his attack on paternalism is against Filmer. Locke's attitude to Hobbes is, however, so complex and shifty that it is difficult to be certain. But, as Oscar Wilde said, the only way to get rid of a temptation is to yield to it and it may be worthwhile to follow this speculation a little. Locke seemed to see the Hobbesian system as a kind of self-chosen slavery, based on a contract by which each individual placed himself under the absolute power of a master.

Traditionally despotism, like all other words for forms of government, had a specific meaning. From its Greek origins the term referred to the absolute power of a master over slaves. A despot exercised dominion by virtue of his owning the land or the people under him. Those under his rule had no rights against him. They were all part of his estate. Such despotism was not normally thought of as a European institution but, rather, as typically oriental or Turkish. Locke's own examples include Ceylon, the Tsar, Turkey and Egypt. As well as this technical meaning, 'despotism' acquired a currency as a term of abuse to which Locke may have contributed. Any government which seemed to treat its subjects as if they had no rights might be deemed despotic in fact or in tendency. Such governments turned subjects, as Locke

said, into 'so many Herds of Cattle, only for the Service, Use and
Pleasure of their Princes' (I, 156). Under despotism there would be no
legal constraint on the ruler, who might employ his subjects entirely
for his own benefit (173). Having no property they had no legal right
to prevent any use the ruler might make of them. One could not speak
of their right being invaded. They had none – not even over their own
bodies.

Locke may well have conceived of Hobbes's political system as
tantamount to a despotism. The crucial issue was, of course, property.
Hobbes had argued that property was the product of the sovereign's
law. Law created and defined a person's property. By legislation the
sovereign ruler could make or unmake a property owner. Moreover, no
person's property right could exclude the right of the sovereign state.
To assert that a subject had such a right was one of the most insurrec-
tionary doctrines imaginable. But such a right is basic to Locke's
political thinking, and to the whole liberal–constitutionalist position.
Locke means by property a right which excludes everyone else. The
state has no more right to a subject's property than has any other
individual. This is the whole point of his theory. To be entitled to
property which can be invaded or abolished at will by the ruler is, for
Locke, tantamount to having no title to property, to being in the
position of a slave: 'For I have truly no Property in that, which another
can by right take from me, when he pleases against my consent' (138).
There is in fact little reason to think that Hobbes saw the sovereign as
constantly appropriating the property of his subjects. The degree of
liberty he envisaged would probably have been little different from that
allowed by Locke. Nevertheless, it was the idea of property as the
creation of the sovereign and dependent on his will that Locke rejected
(see also 193–4). Furthermore, there can be little doubt that such
passages as that in chapter 20 of *Leviathan*, where Hobbes cites I
Samuel, viii, in support of the sovereign power to treat subjects as
servants, taking their fields, their vineyards, their sons and daughters at
will, invited Locke's reply. Admittedly, Filmer, and others, also cited
this biblical passage, but even Filmer allowed that it could be taken
for a description of a tyrant. Some guarantee against government
encroachment on property is therefore essential. Locke does not deny
that such a ruler would make laws which protected one slave–subject
from another. But this would be no more than the arrangements a cattle
owner would make to prevent his animals from harming one another, so
that they would continue to work for his profit (93). Such arrangements
serve merely the interest of the ruler. They do not incorporate laws
which would limit the power of the ruler and protect subjects from his
excesses. In clear, albeit polemical, references to Hobbes he suggests
that under such systems it is regarded as the 'Voice of Faction and
Rebellion' even to suggest limits to the power of a ruler whose very

absolutism is used as an argument to justify his right. It would, Locke suggests, be inconceivable that rational men should choose to surrender the admittedly precarious freedom and property of the state of nature for this so-called security (93–4). In a Hobbesian state of nature – the state of war, of every man against every man, men were at least equal. If they now lay down their right of defence and agree, as Hobbes suggests, that one man alone should retain natural liberty, they would have 'disarmed themselves, and armed him, to make a prey of them when he pleases' (137), and this would be worse than the original natural state. They would make themselves subject to the most sudden whim of the ruler – the traditional situation of the slave. To cite one of Locke's most memorable analogies,

> This is to think that Men are so foolish that they take care to avoid what Mischiefs may be done them by *Pole-Cats*, or *Foxes*, but are content, nay think it Safety, to be devoured by *Lions*' (93).

But not only is it crazy for men to make this choice, they have no right to do so. The natural right to one's own person does not extend so far as to permit a man the liberty to sell himself into slavery. Property rights never exclude the prior right of God and no man is entitled to surrender the liberty of judgement with which God has endowed him. This would constitute rejection of the divine plan (23). No man can exercise an absolute power over his own life and, therefore, no man has any unlimited title to his life which he can transfer to any other man. If men cannot enslave themselves, despotism cannot be legitimised by contract, as Hobbes might be interpreted as maintaining. The master-slave relationship is, therefore, neither prudentially nor morally justified.

That might seem to be the end of the matter. The sceptics, however, might recall that Locke had investments in the slave trade and was experienced in the administration of slave-owning colonies. He had also some hand in the authorship of the *Fundamental Constitutions of Carolina* which explicitly grants citizens 'absolute power' over their 'negro slaves'. This work presents many puzzles to the interpreter of Locke but its references to slavery cannot be dismissed as the ideas of a 'right-wing' early Locke since the *Treatises* do, despite everything, allow for slavery. If men could not rightfully make themselves slaves, if slavery is so demeaning, how could the master–slave relationship be explained and justified? Locke's answer was within a traditional frame-work, employing arguments which can in part be traced back to Greek and Roman discussions of slavery. Where a man who engaged in an unjust war – an act of aggression contrary to natural law – is captured, he becomes liable to be destroyed like a 'noxious beast'. However, his captor may instead choose to employ him as a slave subject to his absolute, despotic power (23, 172).

Locke is careful to insist that there can be no element of contract in such a situation. In this he again marks his differences with Hobbes, for whom sovereignty by conquest arose from a compact whereby the subject agreed to serve his new master and for whom this was the normal manner in which a civil government arose. Locke is at least consistent with his own general position in regarding slavery as being but a continuation of a state of war under another form. Either party may resort to violence, whether to resist enslavement or to execute the death penalty which had merely been delayed. Slavery could only cease to be a condition of war if the lord decided to free his slave by recognising him as a man with a property in his own life (as master of himself) and enter into a contractual relationship with him.

But whatever Locke's internal consistency, his explanation of slavery could not serve as a justification of Negro slavery. Whether this was Locke's intention, as Laslett suggests (footnote to 24), cannot be known for certain. As John Dunn says, it could be a case of 'immoral evasion'.[5] Locke sets some limits to the despotic power of even a just conqueror which he would have known did not apply to Negro slavery. A conqueror acquires absolute despotic power over those adult males who have actively waged unjust war against him, who have thereby forfeited their lives. The conqueror cannot, however, claim such power over the wives and children of the conquered. They have not committed aggression and no action of a husband or a father can make their lives forfeit (178–83). Even if Locke had believed those African males captured in raiding parties to be guilty of waging unjust, offensive wars and thereby liable to slavery, he could not have justified the enslavement of wives or children upon this argument. Dunn's allegation of 'immoral evasion' seems correct. It would not, moreover, be original to Locke. Double standards have been characteristic of arguments about slavery throughout Western intellectual history. Greeks and Romans restricted the enslavement of fellow Greek and Roman captives whilst permitting it in the case of barbarians and Locke would appear to accept treatment of Negroes which he would not find acceptable in the case of Europeans.

Locke's attack on despotism is sustained further in his criticisms of those who derived sovereign government from conquest. Here again, Locke may have had the Hobbesian position in mind. Locke maintains that a just conqueror has no right to the property of his captives and consequently no right as such to the land he has conquered. He acknowledges that this is contrary to much practice, but this position is entirely consistent. The conqueror may claim reparation just as any man can who, in the state of nature (which is the state of international affairs), has been the victim of aggression. But the law of nature which accords him the right of reparation cannot accord him more than the appropriate compensation. To exact more would be to commit a new act of war. The law of nature's direction that enough and as good be left for others also means that the conqueror must not deprive the aggressor's wife and children of what is needed for their subsistence which they had been entitled to expect from the defeated husband. If their right to subsistence conflicts with the conqueror's right to reparation, then the fundamental natural law indicates that it is the right of subsistence which should prevail (183).

The right to reparation could never in any case justify the conqueror's claiming any entitlement to the country itself. It cannot turn him into a despotic proprietor. He is entitled to reparations – war damages – at most amounting to five years' production from the land (184). He is not entitled to dispossess subsequent generations. Conquest cannot, with justice, therefore cancel hereditary property right. Should a conqueror attempt such dispossession, he would place himself in a continuing state of war with the people, who would be entitled under the law of God and nature to throw off the despot or his heirs, as the Greek Christians might still overthrow their Turkish overlords (192). A conqueror could only claim a genuine title as a civil ruler over subjects if the people, by some explicit act, consent to acknowledge him as such. The political situation is then transformed, since the civil society, dissolved by conquest, reconstitutes itself through a new contract which establishes the legitimacy of the new regime. This contract cannot, however, be extorted by fear. Such promises are void, and those who attempt to base the rights of government on the supposed contract, implicit in surrender to the conqueror, at one and the same time admit that right does fundamentally derive from consent and make a mockery of that consent. No contract can be made valid merely by some verbal utterance of a promise when it is made with a sword held to the breast (186). Locke may be alluding here to Hobbes who had described sovereignty by conquest in precisely this way as based on the inferred consent of the conquered.[6] If so, this would indicate a subtle reading of Hobbes since most of Hobbes's contemporaries, like many of his subsequent interpreters, made the understandable mistake of attributing to him the view that the very act of conquest established a right of government.[7]

However, other pamphlet writers had combined some form of consent with conquest by taking the act of submission to the conqueror to be a source of authority. Moreover, Martyn Thompson has pointed out that conquest theories which similarly combined the act of force with what Locke dismissed as pseudo-consent were revived from 1688 to justify the right of William III, and Locke may have had these writings in mind.[8] Locke was prepared to allow that a conquest might be put on a proper footing by some subsequent and genuinely free act of consent, but not by one extracted by force and particularly when also subversive of the ends of civil government. The Norman Conquest was the English precedent cited on all sides. Parliamentarian and Whig ideologies succeeded, despite, as Quentin Skinner shows, ever increasing historical implausibility, in accommodating 1066 by variously interpreting it as a reaffirmation of still earlier constitutional rights. Implicitly or explicitly they frequently denied that a conquest had indeed occurred. Algernon Sidney argued that 'William the Norman' had accepted the throne voluntarily, and conditionally on governing according to the ancient laws of Edward the Confessor. Neither force nor fraud was involved and when William subsequently attempted to rule by mere will he was forced by the people to desist and to reaffirm his constitutional oath.[9] Locke's sole reference in the *Second Treatise* (177) is tantalisingly, if understandably, brief. Locke appears to regard William I as an unjust conqueror who thereby gained despotic dominion over the Saxons and Britons, but whose rule over his Norman followers rested on consent. Subsequently conquerors and conquered merged and incorporated into one people, and later generations may all claim descent from this free people or else from the originally free Norman invaders. The later history of England was to include successive attempts to regularise and civilise government to restrain despotic tendencies.[10] Nevertheless the Norman Conquest did present particular difficulties for Locke's theory which were not encountered by other denials of the right of conquest, since the Conqueror's disposal of Saxon property is totally inconsistent with any right Locke accorded a conqueror. A radical could as easily derive from Locke the right claimed by Levellers and Diggers to overthrow the 'Norman Yoke' of despotism.[11] However Locke's concern, here and right up to his late unpublished comments on William Sherlock's *The Case of Allegiance due to Sovereign Powers, Stated and Resolved* of 1691, remains the same. He insists that acquiescence cannot be taken for consent and that it is not a sufficient assurance of civil government for any government to claim an unconditional authority to rule on the basis of divine intervention or force of arms, and then claim to subject itself to voluntary limitations. Constitutional guarantees can only be founded on what can reasonably be construed as a free act of consent by those whose rights are to be regulated.

Locke's strictures on conquest did not apply to colonial adventures. Countries without their own direct sources of wealth in gold and silver could only acquire them by either conquest or commerce. Interestingly, Locke assumes that the prospects of England enriching itself by conquest are negligible. 'Commerce, therefore, is the only way left to us.'[12] The major countries of the Western world had, Locke believes, basically recognised the boundaries of their European territories (45).[13] This negotiated balance precluded conquest but made commercial competition, especially by control of the seas, all the more essential. Colonisation was not, however, ruled out. People outside the European commercial system commonly had a surplus of land which might be appropriated and put to more profitable use. Here Locke's argument does approximate Hobbes's euphemism about constraining the original inhabitants to live 'closer together'. For Locke, as for other writers of his age and of the following century, limited civil government at home was not incompatible with a very different proprietorial policy for the colonies. This was, however, found to be a contradiction by Americans in 1776, revolting to establish Lockean civil government for themselves instead of despotic government from Britain.

Despotism was therefore incompatible with the civil government which alone was appropriate for the rational property owners of Europe who were the subject of Locke's treatise. Whatever its relevance elsewhere, the attempted introduction of despotism by the Stuarts and its defence by the Hobbesians was a major foreign imposition to be resisted by the defenders of the constitutional tradition.

Paternal power

The other form of power with which political power had been 'confounded' was paternal power. Here Locke's philosophical opponent was Sir Robert Filmer and whereas Locke's criticism of what he took to be Hobbes's despotism was covert, the reply to Filmer is quite open. The title page declares that in the *First Treatise* the 'False Principles and Foundation of Sir Robert Filmer and his Followers, are Detected and Overthrown', and the same enterprise runs through sections of the *Second Treatise*.

Filmer's works, of which the most substantial is *Patriarcha*, had been written around the middle of the century and had then lapsed into obscurity. The author died in 1669. In 1679 and 1680, however, they were republished in the royalist cause during the constitutional crisis occasioned by the Whigs' attempt to exclude the Catholic heir, James, Duke of York, from the throne. Filmer's work was reprinted several times, reflecting the success with which it was seen as encapsulating the royalist case. Its success called forth a number of replies from Whig theorists of distinction, who recognised that the range of Filmer's argument and its skilful employment of popular symbols of authority demanded a refutation.[14]

Filmer's work presents a curious mixture. It contains absurd arguments fully deserving the scorn and ridicule poured on them by Locke and his Whig contemporaries. But it also contains shrewd criticisms of the populist theories of consent, which would not be elaborated and surpassed until the genius of David Hume was turned on them a century later. Locke countered some of these criticisms and evaded others.

Basically, Filmer argued that the state was a family and that the power of a ruler was that of a father over his family, which Filmer believed was an absolute power such as a Roman *paterfamilias* had exercised. This in itself is not as strange a notion as it might appear.

It should be remembered that in the mid-seventeenth century the
sovereign nation state was still relatively new. Just as one tries to
explain something new by comparing it with something familiar, so
the seventeenth-century political theorists sought analogies for the state.
Much political thinking is by analogy whether with the traditional 'body
politic' or with modern 'systems'. In the seventeenth century the family
was an obvious institution with which to draw such an analogy. In the
language of the time it referred to a whole household, including servants
and labourers who lived in. Locke at one time was referred to as a
member of Shaftesbury's 'family'. The family was an economic and
social unit as well as a kinship group.[15] Political rights were held by
the heads, and adult potential heads, of these households. These were
'the people' in Locke's political vocabulary. So when Filmer appealed
to the image of the family and of the father as the supreme pattern of
social and political authority he was, in defending monarchy, speaking
a language much more familiar to his readers than was Hobbes's
defence of absolute monarchy, based on natural rights and contract.
Schochet has, however, persuasively argued that Filmer saw the
authority patterns of ruler and father as more than analogous but as
identical. Locke certainly seems to have treated Filmer's argument in
this way, complaining that he had 'confounded' the two authorities and
appealing in turn to a long philosophical tradition which had argued
that the two institutions and authorities must be kept distinct.

Filmer's mode of reasoning was also familiar. He appealed to history,
mainly as supposedly written down in the scriptures. Hobbes's defence
of absolutism had been couched in terms of reason and logic but this,
however convincing to philosophers, was rather less persuasive than the
scriptural 'evidence' which so many seventeenth-century readers
recognised and understood. It was a commonly accepted mode of
argument that if the origins of an institution could be discovered, this
would establish the nature of that institution. If government could be
shown to be absolute in origin, it should follow that it should be
absolute now. Historical, developmental notions were yet to become
prevalent. Hence the concern for origin. The search for the 'original'
of government should not therefore be understood as a historical
investigation but as part of a political argument.

The point is apparent in Filmer's opening comments in his critique
of Hobbes, where he expresses his admiration for the Hobbesian
description of absolute sovereignty but complains that Hobbes's account
of how sovereign authority arises is inadequate and dangerous.[16] He
objects to the suggestion that government authority arises from the
consent of free individuals – an objection which although directed
against Hobbes would apply equally to anti-absolutists like Locke. As
suggested earlier, one difficulty Locke may have felt in openly
challenging Hobbes was that on certain crucial issues they could be

in agreement.[17] Filmer throws down a challenge to both the idea of consent and that of natural liberty. Men are not born free. Men are born into societies which are governed by rules. In particular they are born into families which, Filmer says, are governed by the head – the father or patriarch.

The authority of such a father descends, in Filmer's view, from God who originally granted absolute power to Adam. The power was lordly and total – all other persons and things were part of Adam's domain. This was the foundation of royal authority. After the flood Adam's authority over the whole world passed to the heads of families, each of whom was called a king, wielded absolute power and was normally succeeded by his natural heir. Every man is born subordinate to one of these God-given rulers. Filmer does not, as is sometimes alleged, try to show that the Stuarts were descended by primogeniture from Noah but he does get himself into other tangles. Larger monarchies grew out of the aggression of one lesser patriarch against another – Nimrod being the first biblical instance. So monarchies grew by conquest and usurpation as well as by family alliances. In each case, however, what was acquired was the accumulated fatherly rights of the conquered lords, who now became subordinate to the greater father – the king. The king's power came not directly from conquest but through acquisition of the fatherly power which was of the same absolute extent as that originally donated by God to Adam. The upshot was that all Filmer can claim is that 'Kings are either fathers of their people, or heirs of such fathers, or the usurpers of the rights of such fathers'.[18] If the kingdom is so confused that no heir can be discerned, Filmer even allows that the selection of a new king falls on the heads of families. This is not to be construed as the free consent of the people, however. The patriarchial power of the new king comes from God and those choosing him are mere intermediaries. Their power of selection does not, crucially, permit them to set conditions or limits to the exercise of royal power which is inherently absolute.

So every way Filmer proves his case. He is an arch-'verificationist'; every counter-example is turned into a confirmation of the theory. At this point Locke's polemical claim to have discovered in Filmer's text, or logically entailed by it, fourteen possible claimants to sovereignty from usurpers to all mankind is not unjustified (I, 71).

Filmer has, nevertheless, posed Locke some formidable questions along the way concerning freedom, consent and property. Firstly, if men are born into family relations, into some kind of subordination, in what sense can they be born free? Secondly, if these families are themselves subordinate to government, how can the individual be free to choose his form of government? Filmer insisted that the decisions of fathers are binding on the heirs. Filmer asks of those, who, like Locke, still believe in the natural freedom of men how, if fathers cannot in this way bind their children, the continuity of government is to be maintained. Will each child choose afresh the terms under which he is to be governed? Can this be consistent with a permanent political society? This issue of inter-generational continuity has always been a difficulty for consent theorists and, whatever his other eccentricities, Filmer placed his finger unerringly upon the problem.

Filmer's third set of questions concerned property. How did property originate and on what terms is it inherited? Writers on natural law, such as Grotius, had argued that God had given the world to mankind in common. Private property had arisen later from the consent of men. Filmer argued that this human convention would seem to contradict God's supposed original community.[19] Scripture taught, according to Filmer, that property had from the very beginning been private. Adam had been granted a property in the world, as he had been granted its government. After the Flood property had similarly been given to Noah, and all lesser property portions were traceable to Noah's exercising his fatherly power to bequeath his property to his various heirs or to some subsequent usurpation of his fatherly power. Since the supreme father in a country is the king, all property is to be understood as vouchsafed by him and dependent on his will. The authority of the ruler stems from his ownership of all the property in a country. The king (or his ancestors) donates portions of his property to individuals for their private exploitation, on terms which he lays down. It is the exact relationship between the property rights of king and subjects which is at issue between Filmer and Locke.

The authority of government, then, descends from God to the earthly father–king. It does not ascend from the people. The powers of government are always the absolute dominion granted by God to Adam. The sovereign is supreme law-maker. The prince is, in the classic phrase of Roman law, 'above the law'. He cannot be bound by any constitutional laws. All laws and customs are the command of the sovereign who is also their only interpreter.[20] Parliaments similarly originated at the will of the monarch to assist him in the royal administration. The origin of Parliament had been a matter of great dispute, with Parliamentarians claiming the ancient existence of parliaments with elective power over the king and, hence, the primacy or at least legitimate independent status of the institution. The monarchists' claim for the historical priority of the English monarchy was historically accurate and was employed as justification for Filmer's argument that Parliament's role was confined to the subordinate one of advising and humbly petitioning the king.[21]

The sovereign was subject only to God's law, which enjoined on him all the duties of a father. The sovereign should take a paternal care of his subjects, i.e. of his family. This would include their health and welfare, their defence and their education. In language typical of the patriarchal theory and of what W. H. Greenleaf has termed the tradition of 'order',[22] Filmer describes the duties of kingship: 'As the Father over one family, so the King, as Father over many families, extends his care to preserve, feed, clothe, instruct and defend the whole commonwealth . . . so that all the duties of a King are summed up in an universal fatherly care of his people.'[23]

This paternalist responsibility would justify the growing intervention of the state in matters of health and welfare which had been characteristic of the Tudors and Stuarts. It would also justify state control of religion, although Filmer, unlike either Hobbes or Locke, is remarkably silent on this crucial point. The subject's duties are summed up in the instruction of the Fifth Commandment, 'Honour thy father'.[24]

Fatherly care rather than individual responsibility is the picture we have of Filmer's society. Locke had to destroy Filmer. He had to destroy the patriarchal view of the origin of authority if he was to replace it by authority stemming from the consent of free men and to safeguard his theory from the charge of anarchy. He had to destroy the paternalist view of the role of government if he was to replace it by a belief in individual self-reliance and toleration. Filmer thus set many of the terms for Locke's political thought and, strangely, for the first exposition of modern liberalism – a fate he could scarcely have imagined for himself.

Locke's critique of patriarchalism and paternalism[25]

(a) *The critique of patriarchalism.* Locke's attack on patriarchalism and paternalism raises issues at the centre of his thought not only about politics, but about education, religion, economics and about knowledge itself. All these concerns come together in his rejection of the paternalist notion that it is the task of government to look after its subjects in the same protective way as fathers look after their children. In the case of Locke's chief opponent, Sir Robert Filmer, this paternalism was underpinned by a patriarchal theory of how governments acquired authority. Locke's refutation of patriarchalism may be outlined fairly briefly since many of its salient points should be apparent from Locke's own treatment of property and of the origins of government, and are indicated in the relevant chapters.

Locke launches an attack in the *First Treatise* on the substance and the method of Filmer's argument, describing *Patriarcha* as having been brought back into the world in order to drive liberty out of it. He finds Filmer's definitions of central terms imprecise and hurls himself against Filmer's appeal to scriptural precedent without exposing such precedent to rational assessment. Precedents can be found in the scriptures for all sorts of acts which can be no justification of right:

Be it then as Sir Robert says, that *Anciently*, it was *usual* for Men
to sell and Castrate their Children . . . Let it be, that they exposed
them; Add to it, if you please, for this is still greater Power, that
they begat them for their Tables to fat and eat them: If this proves
a right to do so, we may, by the same Argument, justifie Adultery,
Incest and Sodomy, for there are examples of these too, both Ancient
and Modern. (I, 59)

Not only do the scriptures have to be treated with greater discretion
as evidence (a theme of his own writings on the scriptures), Locke
also held Filmer's use of them to be inaccurate. Centrally, Locke
denied that Adam was granted a private property in the whole world.
Adam is not to be interpreted as the first absolute monarch, but as the
progenitor and symbol of the human race to whom dominion is granted
over the world's resources. All men are his heirs and, if the patriarchal
argument were to be taken seriously, every adult should be regarded as
the inheritor of the absolute patriarchal power of kingship. This is
absurd and merely points to the necessity of finding some other
explanation of the subordination of one of these sovereign individuals
to another.

Locke's explanation of the origin of property steers a course between
Filmer and Grotius.[26] He agrees with Filmer that property can only
be private and that the theory of Grotius that property arose from
consent is false. But he rejects the explanation of property as a donation
to Adam. Since Adam is to be identified with mankind as such, God's
gift of the world's resources was to mankind in common but to no
man in particular. Private property arose by each man mixing his
God-given property in his own labour with the non-human resources
of the world and thereby appropriating them. Appropriation employs
divinely given human faculties to achieve the divine purpose of preserving mankind. Consent to private property is, hence, superfluous and
Locke also evades Filmer's accusation that the institution of private
property contradicts any alleged earlier grant by God to the community
of man. Locke also significantly detaches the institution of private
property from the institution of government. Men gain a title to property
independently of government, which has to be instituted to give
greater protection to this title. Property is not dependent on government and merely vouchsafed by government to subjects as it is in
Filmer.

Locke is prepared to make one concession to patriarchalism which
he clearly thinks unimportant but the significance of which is a matter
of some dispute and will be touched on further.[27] He acknowledges
(105–10) that historically the first governments were monarchies and
that in all probability the first monarchs were fathers of families which
had come to live separately as distinct units.[28] Accustomed to the

affectionate direction of a father, members of families were all the more likely to look to him when their affairs needed more general direction, firstly as leader in times of war, and then permanently as ruler in times of peace, as their territory expanded and their properties required regulation. Locke does not, however, regard these as instances of a natural, paternal authority, but of acts of consent or choice recognising the fatherly rule as a *political* government. Hence, Locke describes men as 'pitching upon' monarchy (106, 107) as the most suitable constitution or 'frame of government' based on their limited experience. Locke, however, sets himself problems by conceding that this consent may be given almost insensibly. He even concedes that the trust which men had in their early paternal ruler, combined with their limited property – which would not be a standing temptation to a ruler's ambition – could lead them to accept monarchy, without surrounding it with the 'limitations' and 'restraints' which he elsewhere makes so central to civil government (110). It is not so much that individuals casually drift into political society scarcely conscious of the inconveniences of the state of nature.[29] Rather, they are sufficiently aware of the inconveniences of anarchy to set up government, but not experienced enough to foresee any dangers in accepting, as a political power, the only form of leadership with which they are familiar. Locke emphasises here (111) as he does repeatedly elsewhere, that constraints on government arise when men discover that their trust has been misplaced and that mere good will must be reinforced by law.[30]

Locke therefore determines, to his own satisfaction if not to that of his critics, that this almost insensible transition from family life in the state of nature to primitive monarchy is to be understood as involving an act of consent on the part of the individuals concerned. Early monarchy in the hands of a father or a clan chief is thus not a case of the exercise of the natural authority of the father, but the exercise of the artificial authority of a political government. Having answered or, perhaps, evaded Filmer's point, Locke can then move on to the task of refuting Filmer's paternalist view of the role of government – the claim that rulers not only originally acquired absolute paternal power, but had a continuing right to conduct government in the manner of a father controlling his children.

(b) *The critique of paternalism.* Locke's attack on paternalism is grounded on his view of man. Paternalism in government degrades men to little more than the level of animals. For a government to treat its subjects as though they were children and lacked sufficient reason to think and decide for themselves, is unwarranted arrogance. Paternalist thought rests on a total misconception of family life and, hence, involves an utterly mistaken analogy between the purpose of the family and the purpose of civil government. With this argument Locke gave added weight to a conception of the role of government in human affairs which was to be of the utmost significance in subsequent centuries. Men are all born equal in the sense of being equally lacking in knowledge at birth. There can therefore be no natural difference between men which can justify political authority or subordination. To this extent Locke's starting point is that of Hobbes and places both on the side opposed to Filmer. The problem of political authority arises once the assumption of natural equality is made. No government can claim any naturally superior knowledge which could permit it to decide on behalf of other men what is good for them, since by nature rulers are men like other men.

It is, however, true that family authority is natural. Children are naturally subject to the power of parents. What, then, differentiates this authority from political power? Locke's answer is that the difference lies in the situation of children and the consequent purpose of family authority.

But first of all Locke puts forward one argument which, in the end, he admits is largely a debating point. It is one which reflects something of Locke's view of family responsibilities. Locke suggests that if the analogy between government and family is to be taken seriously it cannot constitute a model for the absolute indivisible sovereignty of a monarch. In the family, authority is divided between the two parents (52–3; also I, 6, 11, 61–6). This would, therefore, more properly serve as a model for a division of powers at the political level. Locke accuses Filmer of consistently ignoring the fact that the Fifth Commandment, on which Filmer sets so much store, enjoins the child to honour the mother as much as the father. It would be more appropriate, then, to speak of parental power. Although Locke's point is entirely consistent with his view of the role of the mother in the family and his somewhat advanced views on the rights of women (e.g. 81–2; see Laslett's footnotes for further discussion), he is not concerned to press the argument further in this context. He accepts the over-riding authority of the husband resting on his superior power, an argument which Hobbes had also advanced and which Locke may possibly have adopted in order to be able to pass on to the real issue, which concerned the whole character of the family.

Locke argues that when one examines paternal authority one discovers that its purpose is completely opposite to that which the defenders of governmental paternalism wish to promote. Their own analogy undermines their case. The object of paternal authority is to look after children and bring them up in such a way that they can assume responsibility for themselves in adulthood. The duty of parents is to educate children so that they will be able to make decisions for themselves based on a proper understanding of what they are doing. The rights of parents over children arise from their duties under natural law to protect and educate them. Such rights do not constitute a supposed sovereignty arising, as Filmer supposed, from the act of procreation. Only God could claim any rights from the creative act, since only God's acts of creation were fully conscious. God has placed an obligation on parents which arises from the particular constitution God has framed for the human child. Unlike the young of other species, the child remains dependent for a long period. During this period the child has a right to be nourished and maintained (78).

Children are born capable of reason but not born with reason, nor with any knowledge of moral principles such as the law of nature. Education is a process of acquiring the knowledge of such principles and the ability to understand them and apply them. Only when this knowledge and ability have been acquired, can one speak of a person as a free, rational moral agent. Education is a means of printing the necessary knowledge on the blank sheet of the child's mind. But until the child has this understanding, he is in a lengthy state of natural dependence.[31] Without parental authority and guidance during this period, the child would be little better than a 'brute beast' and could never arrive at a condition of moral maturity. The parents must, therefore, take decisions in such a way that they help to guide the child to independence at the same time. It is an essential part of Locke's view of education that the child should be allowed to see the reasons behind decisions so that he can learn to make similar decisions himself. For this reason he disapproves of the mere learning by rote. Education should be an exercise in reasoning.

Locke's general plan is to control the child very strictly when young, when he is most dependent and least knowledgeable, but gradually to relax the reins as the child grows older and more experienced. The child should begin by regarding his parents with awe as absolute lords, but end by loving them as his best friends.[32] Someone has said that the aim of education is to get rid of children. In Locke's terms this is achieved when the child has attained the condition of reason, and, at this point, the parents may relinquish the burden placed upon them (58). At this moment parental power ceases: 'The subjection of a Minor places in the Father a temporary Government, which terminates with the minority of the Child . . .' (67). This temporary element is of the essence of paternal power and marks it off from civil government:

> The power of Commanding ends with Nonage; and though after that, *honour* and respect, support and defence, and whatsoever Gratitude can oblige a Man to for the highest benefits he is naturally capable of, be always due from a Son to his Parents; yet all this puts no Scepter into the Father's hand, no Sovereign Power of Commanding. (69)

The Fifth Commandment, to which Locke refers indirectly in this passage, is declared to have nothing to do with political sovereignty, but everything to do with the more private family virtues of respect and gratitude (also I, 64). These are owed to parents who exercise the gentle and tender authority belonging to that relationship, which is far from the unlimited right of coercion possessed by a sovereign government. Locke thus pulls away one of the major scriptural props of the paternalist case. Scriptural authority is not challenged. Scripture is interpreted in a 'reasonable' manner.

Once the child has reached the age of discretion he is a free man. He still is under a duty to 'honour' his parents, but he is not subject to their authority. As Locke puts it elsewhere, the reader will see

> some difference between the state of children and grown men, betwixt those under tutelage, and those who are free, and at their own disposal; and be inclined to think that those reasons which subject children in their nonage to the use of force, may not, nor do concern men at years of discretion.[33]

The aim of parents should not be to keep the child in a state of backwardness so that he is always in need of their rule, any more than it might be the aim of the doctor to keep his patient in sickness so that he can continue to attend him. Locke's case, however, is that paternalism in theory and practice commits government to just such an attitude towards its subjects. Paternalist regimes act towards subjects like parents towards children, treating them as dependants who need guidance and protection. They behave as though the subjects had not attained the condition of rational men, who are able to understand moral laws and help shape civil laws in their image. But there can be no grounds for supposing that rulers are more rational and mature than their subjects. The subjects in a political system are all adults who have consented for good reasons of their own to place themselves under government. Unlike paternal power, political power requires a 'voluntary subjection'. It is an artefact; the creation of men who have relinquished their subjection to parents and who are property owners in Locke's full sense of the term.

Such men are both able to care for their own property, and able to see for themselves the advantages that a system of political authority brings in providing security for their various property rights. Equally, they are able to recognise that these advantages do not warrant an unconditional surrender of their property rights to an absolute government. Knowing how to handle their property, they do not need any government to interfere with their 'disposal' of it. Being a responsible human agent consists in seeing to one's own affairs in a rational manner. Governments do not, therefore, have any business, let alone any duty, to look after the economic and moral welfare of subjects who are well able to look after themselves. Civil government exists to protect property from invasion by others, not to tell its subjects how to use their property. Matters of morals and the larger part of economic affairs belong to the private realm of the individual. The government's task is to ensure the legal order within which men can exercise their responsible judgements about the preservation, acquisition or transfer of their property rights.

Matters of faith

Locke's arguments for religious toleration are grounded on his views on human responsibility and maturity. For a government to assume responsibility for a subject's salvation is wrong in itself. It is an arrogant usurpation of a right which belongs to any rational man – a right which is necessary to the performance of the duty laid on every rational man to seek God as best he can. It is typical of a paternalist attitude which regarded men as children unable to look after their own religious well-being.

This had not always been Locke's position. In 1660 he had examined the right of the ruler to intervene in matters of religion from what might be described briefly, if somewhat misleadingly, as a quasi-Hobbesian standpoint. In these early unpublished works, first printed in 1967 as *Two Tracts on Government*,[34] Locke argued that the individuals must be supposed to have surrendered their natural liberty and entrusted the ruler with absolute power.[35] The absolute ruler acts with the authority of his subjects to ensure peace. This must extend to control over religious worship, not merely over the central points of dogma but also over the details of observance – 'things indifferent' as these were termed – and which might include points of dress or the manner of praying. Locke's argument was couched very much in prudential terms. Absolute authority was necessary for peace and security. Locke described himself as being aware of the storms of the world as soon as he was aware of himself, and pointed to the religious disturbances not only of England but of Germany and other European nations. Peace was thus a recent benefit to be jealously preserved.[36] Conflict could arise as much from religion as any other interest and be occasioned by some apparently trivial detail, such as the time and place of worship, or the dress of the worshipper, or the food consumed at a service. Moreover the government could not exclude religion from its ambit since every potential rebel would then claim that his resistance was dictated by religion or a 'tender' conscience.[37] Peace would become impossible. Nothing short of absolute authority could be accepted. Locke dismissed the fears he was himself later to express concerning the threat emanating from such an overwhelming power. The ruler could be trusted not to use coercion except when necessary to restrain the disorderly multitude.[38]

By 1667 Locke had changed his position radically. By this date he had become increasingly concerned with the question of how natural law might be known and, by extension, with the whole question of the extent and limits of human knowledge – the questions which are the concerns of the *Essay*. These problems had seriously raised the problem of certain knowledge in matters of religion.[39] Locke had also entered the household of Ashley who, out of conviction and political ambition, favoured a policy of limited toleration extending to Protestant sects. These two convergent influences appear to have led to his writing an unpublished *Essay concerning Toleration* which approximates much more closely with the position he expounded in the famous *Letter on Toleration* of 1689.[40]

Throughout all his writings on toleration Locke allows the ruler the right to intervene in matters of religion where the religion constitutes a threat to order. For this reason Locke will never allow toleration to Roman Catholics who, as Locke believes, owe allegiance to a foreign authority and who, when in power, will never similarly tolerate others. Nor will Locke allow toleration to even the mere profession of atheism. Not believing in God and divine retribution, atheists cannot feel themselves bound by the oaths and contracts which are the basis of civil society and of civil dealings between its members. Protestant sects can be tolerated because their conduct and worship do not constitute a threat to order. In many respects Locke's argument may seem to represent a rather precarious defence of toleration. Much still depends on the ruler's judgement as to whether a religion constitutes a danger to order. In 1667 Locke still considered it possible that the Quakers were such a threat, and wondered whether their distinctive dress might be banned as being a kind of uniform of a subversive 'army'. But it is difficult for Locke to do better than many of his successors who have found it impossible to lay down a rule declaring how far one may tolerate the intolerant, or liberally and democratically allow freedom to the illiberal and anti-democratic. So far Locke's argument remains prudential. To this extent the logic of Locke's argument has not changed greatly and, as Abrams has pointed out, Locke has not had to move a great deal in order to transform an argument against toleration into one favouring it. What has changed dramatically is Locke's assessment of the facts of the matter, of the dangers arising from toleration.

But something else has happened which has given Locke's later case more than the prudential character which Abrams still believes it possesses.[41] Firstly, Locke has more precisely defined the limited concern of civil government with issues of civil order and civil interests. Secondly, and perhaps more importantly, Locke has brought to the forefront of the argument his belief in the individual's fundamental responsibility for his own salvation and moral welfare, which is latent in the *Essays on the Law of Nature*, but which certainly does not find true expression in the *Two Tracts on Government*.

Locke's later view of toleration is founded on the individualist principle that 'no man, even if he would, can believe at another's dictation'.[42] Locke insists that just as the individual must know and seek truth for himself, so he must believe for himself. In matters of religion, belief is all that can be attained. 'This is the highest the nature of the thing will permit us to go . . .'[43] The ruler cannot therefore lay claim to certain knowledge. He may well be fully 'persuaded' about his religion but he cannot *know* it to be the true religion. He has no advantage over other men. It would, therefore, be absurd for men who are by nature lacking in knowledge and 'apt to be misled . . . by passion, lust, and other men' to choose from amongst themselves men like themselves to establish and enforce the 'true religion'.[44]

But even if *quia impossibile* it were possible for a civil government to establish the true religion, it would still be unjustifiable to enforce it on subjects. A religion must be voluntary if it is to have meaning for the believer. A church is by its nature a voluntary association.[45] Men form a church and are not born into one. Locke's Constitution for Carolina provided for freedom of religious association. Political power is defined partly in terms of its coercive nature, and is out of place in matters of faith. It would be both vicious and absurd for a government to employ coercion to impose conformity to a religion which cannot by its nature be known to be true. Locke speaks more passionately in these writings than in any other. In the *Second Letter* in particular, and also in the *Third*, polemic combines with logical argumentation, ridicule and wit with earnestness. The government may neither enforce conformity nor attempt to compel a subject to study religion adequately. For what would this mean? Would it imply requiring a peasant to turn to theology, and study Latin and Greek, and give up sowing his seed? And without some standard of truth there could be no point at which one could decide when the subject has been brought into line by penal action. It is 'as if you should whip a scholar to make him find out the square root of a number you do not know'.[46] Imposition of even a true religion could not serve to ensure salvation since this necessitates inner conviction:

> No way that I walk in against my conscience will ever lead me to the mansions of the blessed . . . Whatever in religion may be called in question, this at least is certain, that no religion which I do not believe to be true can be either true or profitable to me. In vain therefore does the magistrate force his subjects into his church on the plea of saving their souls . . .[47]

Like 'J. S. Mill later, Locke declared that sin is not the concern of the civil magistrate, nor is it the ruler's task to institute truth: 'For the truth would certainly do well enough if she were once left to shift for herself. She has not received, and never will receive, much assistance from the power of great men, who do not always recognize or welcome her.'[48]

The search for truth and the quest for religious conviction are likewise part of what it is to act as an adult moral agent. To take away or inhibit this activity is to derogate from a person's status as a moral being. Government can only be concerned where the religious life of one person or group threatens the security of the commonwealth, and thereby endangers the path others have taken to salvation. A civil government also exists to ensure that no person can be deprived of his civil rights by dint of his religion.[49] No person or group may punish a person in this life from an alleged concern to promote his well-being in a future life. Similarly churches, as voluntary associations, may expel members for breaking their own rules but may not use this expulsion to deprive them of any civil or natural rights, nor may they attempt to coerce non-members. Tolerance between churches must be on the same footing as tolerance between individuals and, in each case, the civil government has the duty to keep the peace between them without fear or favour, without imposing any preferred order upon them other than the need to respect mutual rights.

Paternalism and welfare

The implications of Locke's position do not stop at denying the government's right to intervene in matters of faith. The idea of self-reliance links Locke's epistemology with his view of religion and of the limited role of civil government. Not only is the individual responsible for his own religious salvation, he is also responsible for his social and economic salvation. It is the mark of a responsible individual that he takes care of matters of welfare himself. For a government to intervene in the running of a subject's legitimate economic affairs would be as much a usurpation of responsibility as would be interference in questions of religious faith. The government's job is to set rules to penalise individuals who, in pursuing their own private interests, collide with other individual subjects pursuing theirs. It must ensure that neither defrauds or does violence to the other. It is not to tell any subject how he should carry on his business – other than that it should be within the law. Nor should it force him to care for his well-being. If the subject fails to look after himself that is his own look-out, as it is if he does not care for his religious salvation. The analogy is drawn in the *Letter on Toleration* with a question asked in a significantly rhetorical manner:

> The care, therefore, of every man's soul belongs to himself, and is to be left to him. You will say: What if he neglect the care of his soul? I answer: What if he neglect the care of his health or of his

estate, things which more nearly concern the government of the magistrate? Shall the magistrate provide by an express law against such a man becoming poor or sick? Laws endeavour, as far as possible, to protect the goods and health of subjects from violence of others, or from fraud, not from the negligence or prodigality of the owners themselves. No man against his will can be forced to be healthy or rich.[50]

Locke then proceeds, mockingly, to suppose a government trying to force its subjects to be healthy by requiring them to consult only official state doctors, or get their medicine only from state chemists, analogously to obtaining their religion only from an established Roman Catholic or Calvinist Church. Clearly Locke would have regarded a national health or pensions scheme (if he could have envisaged such a thing) as outside the proper scope of government. It would be the task of the individual, not of the state, to see to his health or look to his future. What marks off an individual is this distinctive capacity of deliberating and re-evaluating present and future benefits. He does not need a father substitute in the state to do it for him. He minds his own business. Reversing the direction of the analogy, Locke asks that the state show the same toleration or, indeed, indifference to a man's religious views as it normally exhibits to his economic activities:

In domestic affairs, in the management of estates, in matters of bodily health, every man is entitled to consider what suits his own convenience, and follow whatever course he judges best. No man complains of the bad management of his neighbour's affairs. No man is angry with another for an error committed in sowing his land or marrying his daughter. Nobody corrects a spendthrift for consuming his substance in taverns. Let any man pull down, or build, or incur whatever expenses he pleases, nobody murmurs, nobody forbids him.[51]

Throughout his writings on toleration, and particularly in his *Third Letter*, Locke insists on the necessarily limited character of civil government. There is nothing paradoxical in limiting the potentially greater power of a civil government to the specific narrower end of preserving civil interests from injury. Everything else but this can be attained by 'men living in neighbourhood without the bounds of a commonwealth'.[52] In economic affairs Locke's position is well described by Seliger as an 'admixture of mercantilist and *laissez-faire* policies'.[53] As a rough guide it might be described as *laissez-faire* internally and mercantilist in its approach to international and imperial trade. It must be remembered that as in classical *laissez-faire*, so also in Locke, the doctrine does not imply a total absence of government involvement in the economic arena, but an opposition to arbitrariness and to the unnecessary substitution of public for private enterprise.

The key to Locke's view of the relationship of government to economics, as it is the key to Locke's whole conception of civil government, is the idea of the rule of law.[54] The prime task of government is to ensure that all subjects are treated equally in law and that each has the same legal opportunity to pursue his individual plan of life. This requires formal equality in economic as well as political institutions. Men in the state of nature are able to trade with one another, and it was in the state of nature that money was invented when men consented to put a value to gold, and especially to silver, as a standard for exchange. It was partly as a result of the increased tension occasioned by expanding trade that civil government became necessary. Force and fraud became more tempting to men and only the greater force of government could suppress this tendency. But government not only required a supremacy of force, it had also to be impartial. Government could neither have an interest of its own nor be a tool of an interest group.

Neutrality means that government must uphold the arrangements arrived at in the state of nature. In the first place this implies maintaining the stability of the currency. Locke believes that silver is the accepted standard for exchange throughout the world and that it possesses an intrinsic value.[55] Men trade in order to obtain an agreed quantity of silver in exchange for the goods they market. The value of official silver coinage should, therefore, correspond to the intrinsic value of the silver contained in the coin. Government is expected to prevent fraud by ensuring that the coin contains an agreed quantity of silver. The government's stamp on its coinage is a public guarantee of the equal quantity of silver contained in every coin of the same denomination, and assures subjects and foreign traders alike of the permanent value of the currency they are exchanging and holding. The authority of the silver coin is ensured by the known rules about minting and assaying it, enforced by government. The standard set for the coinage should therefore be 'inviolably and immutably kept to perpetuity'.[56] For the sake of justice it 'is of great concernment that it should remain invariable'.[57] In Locke's own day, however, the value of the English silver coinage had dropped below the market price of silver and it became advantageous to clip coins or melt them down altogether and export the result as bullion. Coin came to be in short supply for trade and financing exports. The shortage required government action and the appropriate policy occasioned a major debate from 1690 and, still more urgently, in 1695.[58] Two major solutions were offered. One was to call in the coinage and remint it at a devalued rate so that each denomination (e.g. each shilling) would contain less silver than previously. It would then cease to be profitable to melt down the coin. Locke's alternative solution triumphed. He published his early papers in 1692, and added *Further Considerations* in 1695. He rejected devaluation as a fraud on the public and a breach of public faith.[59] Subjects must always be able to expect that their coins should be equivalent to the natural, intrinsic value of silver. Devaluation would be unjust to those who had traded or given credit on the expectation of a fixed quantity of silver in the coin in return. Creditors would then receive back from debtors money of less intrinsic worth than had been lent, robbing Peter to pay Paul simply because Paul was a debtor. Locke's solution[60] was for a revaluation by reissuing coin with a value equal to that of the silver content. The government would thus play its neutral role of restoring the standing laws of society. The impartial maintenance of the rule of law can, however, have partial consequences. Whilst recoinage helped to establish the credit-worthiness of the English financial system, internally it produced deflation which, as is the usual effect, hit hardest the poorest sections of society. Creditors and landlords did better, since debts had to be repaid at the old established full rate even if the loan had been in clipped money. Justice was done by the restoration of the community's rules. Locke's object, as ever, was the impartial enforcement of the rule of law and a central part of this policy was to place the value of the coinage out of the reach of any group in society and above all of the government. If government could alter the value of the currency every subject's property would be dependent on government will – a definition of absolutism.[61]

The same concern pervades Locke's attitude to any attempt by government to fix the level of interest rates by law. Money – as distinct here from currency, which is his other concern – is a commodity which may be bought and sold.[62] The price of money is determined by demand and supply and is reflected in the interest rate charged to the borrower. The rate for money is established by necessity and not by laws.[63] Attempts to lower interest by law will merely result in credit being withheld and trade declining, or else ways being found to circumvent the law and rates returning to their natural level. Locke did recognise two exceptions. Firstly, government might set a rate to enable judges in civil court cases to establish an equitable level of damages when parties to a disputed contract had not agreed a rate in their contract. This is fully in accordance with the rule of law. The second exception is more paternalist in tone.[64] Government might set some upper limit to interest rates to prevent an effective monopoly of lenders exploiting the young and the inexperienced and utterly destroying profitability. Such dangers arose in part from the tendency of credit institutions to concentrate in the City of London – relatively a far greater political rival to seventeenth-century governments than to any modern British Labour government. Ideally, resources would be more evenly spread through the country, providing a plurality of sources of credit and balancing the power of London.[65] Beyond this, any attempt at enforcing a reduced rate would commit an unpardonable breach of the law by making void contracts already made under the old rate, 'and give to Richard what is Peter's due, for no other reason, but because one was borrower, and the other lender'.[66] The rule of law requires the law to represent justice blindfolded and impartial as between the moral claims of borrowers and creditors.

The inviolability of lawfully made contracts is central to the rule of law and is stoutly upheld by Locke. The precise nature of what is a lawful contract may be determined by each state, and is nowhere Locke's concern. The state will be expected to establish what counts as a valid contract to be upheld in the state's courts. The state may lay down whatever rules it may think expedient relating to such matters as contracts for the voluntary transfer of property, providing only that these rules do not arbitrarily exclude any subject from making such contracts.[67] Contracts to buy and sell are similarly inviolable. The just price is the market price, dictated by supply and demand on the open market.[68] Provided that the seller treats all effective buyers in a like manner and does not arbitrarily exclude some from bidding on equal terms, the seller can justly get as high a price for his goods as the market will allow. There is no place for government interference to establish a just price or just wage as was the practice of Tudor and Stuart paternalism.

One possible qualification requires some comment. In the notebook headed 'Venditio' and in the *Two Treatises* Locke suggests that where one man's pursuit of his property rights – including his entitlement to a market price for his property – would result in another person dying of famine, justice allies with charity. The property owner has a duty to assist the starving man who in turn has a *right* to part of the property owner's surplus (I, 42). There can be no doubt that Locke, both in theory and practice, believed in voluntary charity to the deserving and industrious poor. How far this implied a duty on government to preserve the poor and unfortunate is then the difficult issue. As Seliger points out, this argument could serve potentially as a justification for a much more interventionist welfare state than seems consistent with the interpretation of Locke offered here.[69] Presumably this support could only be achieved by a transfer of property from the better off to the poor by means of taxation, and would be justified on grounds of natural law. Clearly this did not extend beyond caring for the poor in the most extreme necessity. On the whole Locke may have believed that the problem was limited. As mentioned earlier,[70] he believed that industry and expanding individual property ownership would by raising productivity benefit all, thus making the poorest day-labourer as well off as a king in America. Certainly Locke's own suggestions for social policy were less concerned with charitable transfers than with providing the poor with every incentive to be industrious.[71] Locke would have enforced such arduous conditions for adults and children on relief that they would do all in their power to be economically subsistent – children over 3 years of age might be required to work from sunrise to sunset and some able-bodied men might be forced into service at sea. Locke tends to alternate between regarding poverty and unemployment as the inevitable lot of a large section of society, as something beyond its control, and regarding them as the consequence of a moral failure through lack of foresight and debauchery. The old distinction between the undeserving and idle poor and the deserving and industrious poor is not far distant.

Seliger may be correct in seeing a potential in Locke's argument for welfare politics. The potential would be even greater if Locke had inferred equality of substantive protection from his equality of natural rights.[72] As it is, however, Locke is consistently committed only to the most minimal, emergency provision. Anything beyond this would involve the state in those paternalist provisions which Locke rejects as an infringement of the individual's responsibility for his own life. Individuality requires the qualities of foresight. It requires the liberty to suspend judgement and reallocate values so as to bring to the forefront of the mind those matters which this particular individual finds most significant. Robert Nozick describes the characteristics of such an individual in a manner consonant with Locke and, indeed, partly derived from him:

> . . . a being able to formulate long-term plans for its life, able to consider and decide on the basis of abstract principles or consider-ations it formulates to itself . . . a being that limits its own behaviour in accordance with some principles or picture it has of what an appropriate life is for itself and others.[73]

For such a being, paternalist care, compulsorily provided, is inappro-priate. It involves being made part of a pattern of life imposed by other beings who are not inherently morally or intellectually superior. All such beings require is to be governed by certain rules which will equally constrain themselves and others, so as to prevent one individual's pursuit of his life plans from colliding with, and damaging, the plans of other similar individuals. What they require is a civil government.

Notes Chapter IV

1 *Essay*, IV, iii, 18.
2 S. Wolin, *Politics and Vision*, London, Allen & Unwin, 1961, p. 5.
3 See Bernard Crick, *In Defence of Politics*, London, Weidenfeld & Nicolson, 1962, p. 15 and *passim*.
4 See below, ch. VI.

5   *The Political Thought of John Locke*, p. 175, fn. 4. Dunn's whole dis-
    cussion of this issue, particularly pp. 171 *ff.*, is typically incisive and
    scholarly. Seliger's discussion of conquest and colonialism is also very
    informative: *The Liberal Politics of John Locke*, pp. 109–24.
6   On Hobbes's case, see G. Parry, 'Performative Utterances and Obligation
    in Hobbes', *Philosophical Quarterly*, XVII, 1967, pp. 246–54, especially
    p. 247. Also, somewhat differently stated, D. D. Raphael's *Hobbes* in this
    series, London, Allen & Unwin, 1977.
7   For an account of conquest theories in the seventeenth century both before
    and after Hobbes, see Q. Skinner, 'History and Ideology in the English
    Revolution', *The Historical Journal*, VIII, 2, 1965, pp. 151–78.
8   See M. P. Thompson, 'The Idea of Conquest in Controversies over the
    1688 Revolution', *Journal of the History of Ideas*, XXXVIII, 1, 1977,
    pp. 33–46; 'On Dating Chapter XVI of the *Second Treatise of Govern-
    ment*', *The Locke Newsletter*, no. 7, summer 1976, pp. 95–100. I am
    indebted to Dr Thompson for comments in correspondence on these points
    and also to Mr J. B. Sanderson, University of Strathclyde, for discussions
    on conquest theory during the Leveller period. See also M. Goldie,
    'Edmund Bohun and *Jus Gentium* in The Revolution Debate, 1689–93',
    The Historical Journal, XX, 3, 1977, pp. 569–86.
9   *Discourses concerning Government*, edition of London, 1751, republished
    Farnborough, Gregg, 1968, pp. 327–8.
10 See below, ch. VI, pp. 126, 140–2.
11 On the theory of the 'Norman Yoke', see the essay by Christopher Hill,
    Puritanism and Revolution, London, Secker & Warburg, 1958.
12 *Some Considerations, Works*, V, p. 13.
13 See Seliger, op. cit., pp. 114–18.
14 The best account of patriarchalism including its relations to Locke is to
    be found in Gordon J. Schochet, *Patriarchalism in Political Thought*,
    Oxford, Blackwell, 1975.
15 See Peter Laslett, *The World we have Lost*, London, Methuen, 2nd
    edition, 1971.
16 *Observations concerning the Originall of Government*, in P. Laslett (ed.),
    Patriarcha and other Political Works, Oxford, Blackwell, 1949, p. 239.
    Henceforth cited as *Political Works*.
17 See above, ch. I, p. 10.
18 *Patriarcha*, ch. V, *Political Works*, p. 60.
19 *Patriarcha, Political Works*, p. 65.
20 *Patriarcha*, chs XXII–XXVIII, Political Works, pp. 95–113.
21 The story of the dispute over the constitutional history is brilliantly told
    by J. G. A. Pocock, *The Ancient Constitution and the Feudal Law*,
    Cambridge, Cambridge University Press, 1957.
22 W. H. Greenleaf, *Order, Empiricism and Politics*.
23 *Patriarcha, Political Works*, p. 63.
24 See Schochet, op. cit., for the place of the Fifth Commandment in
    patriarchal thought.
25 For convenience of exposition I have distinguished between a patriarchal
    theory concerning the origin of government and a paternalist theory con-
    cerning the role of government. Whilst paternalism in general does not
    presuppose patriarchalism historically the two theories were fully integrated
    in Filmer and his fellow patriarchalists.
26 See also above, ch. III, p. 52.
27 See below, ch. V, pp. 101–2.
28 See Schochet, op. cit., especially pp. 256–67 for a perceptive account of
    Locke's concessions to patriarchalism.

29 As Schochet suggests, p. 257. Schochet's intriguing comparisons of
    Locke's account with the conjectural histories of early society favoured in
    the eighteenth century seem correct although the best comparison is, oddly,
    less with Rousseau than with Locke's arch-critic David Hume who
    similarly explains early government as the outcome of experience of war
    leadership – a view common, however, since Tacitus.
30 See below, ch. VI, pp. 126–8.
31 For Locke's educational ideas see the excellent edition by James Axtell,
    The Educational Writings of John Locke, Cambridge, Cambridge University
    Press, 1968.
32 *Education*, sect. 41.
33 *A Third Letter for Toleration, Works*, VI, p. 211.
34 Edited by P. Abrams, Cambridge University Press. See the Introduction
    by Abrams for an excellent analysis of the complex question of Locke's
    relation to Hobbes even in these early and seemingly most 'Hobbist'
    writings.
35 *First Tract*, p. 125.
36 See Preface to the *First Tract* and the opening few paragraphs of the
    Second Tract.
37 *First Tract*, p. 154 and p. 166.
38 *First Tract*, pp. 158–9.
39 See again the discussion by Abrams and also W. von Leyden's Introduc-
    tion to his edition of Locke's *Essays on the Law of Nature*.
40 For a version of this early essay see H. R. Fox Bourne, *Life of John
    Locke*, London, 1876, Vol. I, pp. 174–94.
41 Introduction, p. 105.
42 *A Letter on Toleration*, ed. R. Klibanky, trans. J. W. Gough, Oxford,
    Oxford University Press, 1968, p. 67. References will be to this version,
    cited as *Toleration*. The original and widely available translation by Popple
    reads well but some of the highly coloured language is Popple's rather
    than that of the more restrained Locke.
43 *A Third Letter for Toleration, Works*, VI, p. 144.
44 *A Third Letter for Toleration, Works*, VI, p. 178.
45 *Toleration*, p. 71.
46 *A Second Letter concerning Toleration, Works*, VI, p. 102.
47 *Toleration*, pp. 99–101.
48 *Toleration*, p. 123.
49 *Toleration*, p. 79.
50 *Toleration*, p. 91. Locke had already pursued the analogy in his un-
    published 1667 *Essay on Toleration*. See H. R. Fox Bourne, *Life of John
    Locke*, Vol. I, pp. 176–7.
51 *Toleration*, p. 89.
52 *A Third Letter for Toleration, Works*, VI, p. 212 and pp. 213–18.
53 M. Seliger, *The Liberal Politics of John Locke*, p. 174. Seliger interprets
    Locke as more interventionist. His discussion pp. 172–9 is well worth
    attention.
54 See below, ch. VI.
55 *Further Considerations concerning Raising the Value of Money, Works*,
    V, p. 139.
56 *Some Considerations, Works*, V, p. 103.
57 *Further Considerations, Works*, V, p. 143.
58 For a fuller discussion of this complex issue, which very ably relates
    Locke's views on money to his overall political and social philosophy,
    see J. O. Appleby, 'Locke, Liberalism and the Natural Law of Money',
    Past and Present, 71, May 1976, pp. 43–69. See also A. Feaveryear,

The Pound Sterling, Oxford, Oxford University Press, 2nd edition, 1963, ch. VI, and W. Letwin, *The Origins of Scientific Economics*, London, Methuen, 1963, ch. 6, as well as the further references in Appleby's article.

59   *Some Considerations, Works*, V, p. 89.
60   See P. Laslett, 'John Locke, the Great Recoinage, and the Origins of the Board of Trade, 1695–8', *William and Mary Quarterly*, XIV, 1957. Reprinted in J. Yolton (ed.), *Locke: Problems and Perspectives*, pp. 137–64.
61   See further Appleby, loc. cit., pp. 64–9.
62   *Some Considerations, Works*, V, p. 34.
63   *Some Considerations, Works*, V, p. 15.
64   It is noted by Seliger in support of his more interventionist interpretation of Locke's social and economic position. *The Liberal Politics of John Locke*, p. 174.
65   *Some Considerations, Works*, V, p. 64.
66   *Some Considerations, Works*, V, p. 11.
67   See further below, ch. VI.
68   See Locke's Commonplace book entry headed '*Venditio*' printed at the end of John Dunn, 'Justice and Locke's Political Theory', *Political Studies*, XVI, 1, 1968, pp. 68–87. Dunn finds aspects of Locke's argument incoherent (fn. 2 p. 72) but they seem to cohere with the formal requirement of open and impartial access to the market required by the rule of law.
69   See Seliger, *The Liberal Politics of John Locke*, p. 175. Certainly John Cary, whose work Locke admired, goes much further in this direction than does Locke. Also an advocate of revaluation, his declared objective was the Lockean one of defending those 'inestimable Jewels of Liberty and Property'. *An Essay on the State of England in Relation to its Trade, its Poor, and its Taxes*, Bristol, 1695.
70   Above, ch. III, pp. 55–6.
71   See M. Cranston, *John Locke*, pp. 424–5. Fox Bourne prints the text in *Life of John Locke*, Vol. II, pp. 377–91.
72   It may be significant that so much of Locke's active governmental involvement in economic affairs was concerned with foreign and colonial trade. Colonies were not treated as if they were independent civil governments but as contributors to the prosperity of the home country. Moreover Locke considered foreign trade from a mercantilist standpoint, estimating its total contribution to the country's prosperity rather than examining it from the individualist standpoint he reserved for internal economic affairs.
73   *Anarchy, State, and Utopia*, Oxford, Blackwell, 1974, p. 49.

Chapter V

The Origins of
Political Society

It has become customary to draw a contrast between society and community. The former is taken to describe a relationship between people which is basically contractual and rule-governed. A community is identified by a more intense sharing of values. In this sense Locke presents a theory of 'society'. Yet at the same time Lockean society is underpinned by a notion of 'community', albeit an unstable and faltering one. It must, however, be remembered that this distinction is a categorisation introduced by modern sociological theory and that at Locke's time, and in Locke's own usage, the words society and community were interchangeable. Both terms implied association under rules and a more intense sharing of values. All mankind possesses like faculties and thus shares in 'one Community of Nature' (6; also 128). The law of nature is a tie which binds men together. Those who break this tie show that they do not belong to the same community as mankind, and may be reformed or removed. Ideally the law of nature sets the standard for all human conduct outside or inside civil society. It is the duty and the right of every individual to see that the community of mankind is maintained. However, as we have seen, the tendency of all men since the Fall to depart, in some circumstances, from the law of nature makes the individual enforcement of this law unreliable and arbitrary. Only collective action to restore and uphold the moral community can have any hope of being successful.

Civil society and government are brought into existence to rectify the 'inconveniences' arising from the inherent tendency of men to overlook or ignore the requirements of community. In rectifying these inconveniences society and government may in no way over-ride natural law, nor may they employ any means other than those granted by that law. The municipal laws of countries are 'only so far right, as they are founded on the law of Nature, by which they are to be regulated and interpreted' (12). The authority of the laws of any state can only derive from the authority each individual has to maintain the ties which bind mankind into a community of rational beings. This authority is expressed by the individual's right in the state of nature to put into execution the law of nature. Since this authority is exercised equally, there can be no natural subordination amongst men. Against the feudal notion that men might be born to a particular station and its duties, Locke argues that duties can only be incurred by some act akin to a promise. Admittedly there are duties of rationality and devotion imposed by the very station of being a man in the divine scheme, but the narrower specification of such duties, or the means to perform them, can only derive from the employment of that rationality to create some promise or pact: 'Man being, as has been said, by Nature, all free, equal and independent, no one can be put out of this Estate, and subjected to the Political Power of another, without his own Consent' (95). It is fundamental to the political theory of individuality that the only way in which a person can come to be under an obligation is by himself agreeing to it. On this point Locke is in basic agreement with Hobbes, although in no manner is he ready to draw attention to this. Both are then ranked against Filmer, and it was this foundation for sovereign authority that Filmer found so unacceptable in Hobbes.

The idea of government by consent has come to have a history bound up with the development of democratic theory. It is therefore necessary to establish what Locke's notion of consent does and does not do.[1] Locke is attempting to establish the proper source of authority for any government. Just as Filmer had discovered the source of authority in God's grant of government to Adam, so Locke finds it in the consent of the subject. Locke does not distinguish between forms of government on the basis of consent. A democracy would not rest on consent to any greater degree than a monarchy or an aristocracy. An absolute arbitrary regime of any sort is another matter, and is not, in any case, a civil government. Locke is not, therefore, using consent in the way suggested, for instance, by Robert A. Dahl when he cites Locke as identifying democracy with majority consent.[2] Still less does Locke employ 'government by consent' to mean that specific government policies must receive the consent of the people, through such devices as elections or popular participation. Majority rule democracy is not what Locke has in mind, although it might, if suitably defined, be one of several forms of civil government consistent with Locke's account.[3]

The subtitle of Harold Lasswell's famous book *Politics*, 'Who gets what, when, how', contains a useful suggestion for approaching any concept in politics. To ask who is free to do what, when and how, or to ask who is equal to whom, in what respects and in what circumstances, can tell us a great deal about what is being claimed for some understanding of freedom or equality. Similarly with consent, we need to ask of a theory of consent who consents to what, when and how. In Locke's case it is in fact necessary to ask these questions of two categories of persons – those who originally agreed by 'compact' or contract to establish a political society, and those members of subsequent generations who are supposed to have consented to be subject to the rules of such a society.

The social contract

The first question to ask, therefore, is who contracts? In the state of nature each person is supposed to have had the right and duty to enforce the law of nature. Each is also presumed to have recognised that this is a very uncertain way of maintaining a just order, because of the lack of an impartial person or body to decide disputes, and because of the haphazard and uneven quality of the law enforcement – insufficient in some cases, vengeful and excessive in others. The cure, rational individuals recognise, could only come through acknowledging some persons as authoritative umpires and, with safeguards, subordinating individual judgements to these persons. Such acknowledgement must be an individual act. It is in the nature of promising and contracting that it cannot be performed on behalf of another unless by means of some previous promise or contract. Still less can another invade someone's rights and enforce subordination.

The answer to the original question is, therefore, that all who are to be original members of the political society and obligated by its rules must contract. Only those who commit themselves in this way can be described as having surrendered any part of their freedom to govern themselves in sovereign fashion. Those who do not wish to join remain in the state of nature. Their freedom, Locke claims, is unaffected. This is not, however, correct, as Robert Nozick has shown,[4] since any person wishing to remain outside the political society and to retain his property in its vicinity, or even in its midst, would find the inconveniences of the state of nature even greater. Those inside civil society would have surrendered their rights of law enforcement to the common authority. The independent individual would therefore, find that in any disputes between himself and a member of the society he would be required to deal only with the collectivity, and could enforce a judgement against a member with the permission of the collectivity. If the collectivity chose not to grant this permission, or chose to pursue a case against the independent, he would find the ordinary difficulties of executing the law of nature immeasurably increased by the greater force of the civil society. The disadvantages are, indeed, greater than any Nozick cares to suggest. Since the civil society may act like any individual in the state of nature, it may either unjustly (but with impunity) over-react like any other individual to what it interprets as a threat to itself, or to one of its members, or it may legitimately act with great ferocity to deter any future challenge to its rights. In either case the independent will properly fear for his life and the community's offer of protection may be one he will find it difficult to refuse. In effect he would be forced to 'choose' either to unite himself with the society, or to place himself under the protection of another society and/or physically move, without, of course, his land.

To what do they contract? Each, realising the problems to which his private law enforcement gives rise, agrees to surrender his executive right of the law of nature. The compact is one in which each possessor of an executive right agrees to transfer it to a fictional body which is created by the compact – variously called a 'community', a 'civil society', a 'body politic' or simply a 'people' – of which every individual is an equal member. This political society now possesses the totality of the executive right of the previously separate individuals. So long as the political society lasts, these individuals may not resume the executive right they once possessed. Their individual sovereignty is at an end. It is no longer their right and responsibility to protect their own property, or to determine whether the law of nature has been broken, or what punishment is due. All 'private judgement of every particular member' ceases (87). It is now the right of the community to settle disputes as to the property rights of the contracting parties and establish the appropriate penalties. Political society performs these duties by laying down rules applicable equally to every member – the task of legislation. It must also take up the other part of the original executive right by enforcing these laws impartially – the executive power (88). Effective enforcement is possible because the body politic may rightfully employ any or all of its members to carry out its judgments, since the judgments of the community are to be regarded as the judgements of the individual himself (88) – an argument previously employed by Hobbes among others, and later to be used by Rousseau to considerable effect. Additionally, the community calls upon the assistance of each individual to defend the collectivity by enforcing the executive right of the law of nature against any outsiders.

It might appear that the power of the collectivity over the individual is total and that all vestiges of Locke's liberalism and individualism have vanished.[5] This would be misleading. The formal authority of Locke's political society is, indeed, considerable but this is true of the most liberal of political societies. The manner of exercising these powers is, however, restricted and it is restricted by the very terms of the contract. Political society cannot acquire any rights not granted to it by the individuals contracting to join it. These individuals surrendered their right to enforce the law of nature and no other rights. In particular, they did not grant to the society any of their property in lives, liberties or estates. Even though, in order to be defended by the society, each individual must place his property, including land, under its jurisdiction, the society does not acquire the property. It remains the right of the individual. No individual in the state of nature had the right to seize the property of another or enslave him, without good cause. It follows that the community cannot acquire, create or exercise such a right over its own members. It cannot, on its own initiative, redistribute rights, since this implies invading the property of one person to grant it to another. Contract and liberal political society are integrated by Locke's formulation. As there were natural law limits to an individual's authority over others, so there must be limits to society's authority over its members, since no member could logically contract to grant more authority than he had to grant. Absolutism is thereby excluded.

So far, Locke has been discussing political society and not government. Contract created a political society and is the means whereby once-free individuals become subject to the new jurisdiction. Government is not established directly by contract. For some earlier political thinkers government, too, had been the product of contract. There was a pact of association whereby society was brought into being, and a pact of subjection in which the members of society placed themselves under government, imposing duties on the government but incurring obligations at the same time. In Hobbes association and subjection were combined in one act. In the great natural law theorist Pufendorf the two agreements were distinguished, with also an intervening stage establishing the form of government. Locke took a different line from these predecessors. The only contract is that of association, 'which is *all the Compact* that is, or needs be, between the Individuals, that enter into, or make up a *Common-wealth*' (99). Government is instituted by a distinct act of trust whereby the associated community transfers its executive right to a smaller body of persons for the more effective performance of society's duties.

Society may institute government more or less immediately or, it appears, there may be periods in which small, loosely organised societies carry out the legislative and executive powers themselves. Locke speaks of the Indian nations which only institute government during periods of war, when a leader is elected, but revert to what might be termed primitive democracy in the intervals. Only later does society find it necessary to establish more permanent arrangements for government by a monarch or council. In other cases, probably the majority, political societies entrust government to the care of fathers who become monarchs in a civil government. Later experience leads many of these communities to alter the constitution in order to set narrower limits to the considerable powers of these early 'nursing fathers'. Still other political societies may have begun on a more constitutionalist footing. But whatever the form of government instituted, the process of institution is notionally, if not historically, identical. By contracting together to establish a political society, each party must be supposed to agree to whatever decisions may be taken by a majority of the community in order to further its objectives. Locke makes some play with Newtonian notions of a body politic moving like other bodies whither the greater force impels it (96), but his main arguments for majority rule are rather more pragmatic. In accepting a community a person must agree to commit himself to some ruling. To retain an individual veto whenever faced with a community decision to which he was averse would be simply like remaining in the state of nature (97). Locke regards nothing short of a majority decision procedure as satisfactorily binding, although he is ready to acknowledge that it may be reasonable to require something greater. Since it is this majority which establishes the form of government for the society, it is perhaps surprising that Locke does not establish strict boundaries to what it may decide. There is nothing akin to the restrictions John Rawls has suggested, whereby contracting parties to a code of justice might ensure that in a future community the worst off would be at least as favourably placed as possible.[6] The majority is restricted only by the law of nature and by the consequent limits on its executive right, which can only be exercised for the protection of the lives, liberties and estates of members. It cannot, therefore, be at liberty, as Kendall implies,[7] to define the natural law at will, even though it does have some latitude in interpreting the law in particular disputes. Although political society is created because of the tendencies of mankind to partiality and excess, paradoxically Lockean individuals are prepared to trust the majority in a body politic to act consistently with the general interest in preserving property. At this stage of his argument Locke appears to recognise an underlying sociological trust, a community of interest and experience. All contracting members have an interest in protecting property. In contrast to Rawls's supposition of a 'veil of ignorance', Locke's contractors can rationally deduce this degree of information about one another. At this early stage of political society it is likely that most, and perhaps all, members will have a stake in land, but whether they own merely their lives and liberty or also own estates, they are property owners. No person or section has an interest in subverting property. A majoritarian procedure can then be presumed to bring more benefits than costs. No clash of interests between landed and landless is supposed – or at least explicitly recognised. Property is the expression of community not the symbol of class.

The majority must, therefore, be trusted to seek the interests of all. Government is instituted when the majority 'entrusts', in a quasi-legal sense, its executive right to a person or body of persons. This government is entrusted with the majority's power of adjudicating disputes by making rules by which all future disputes of a similar type are to be settled – legislation; and the power of enforcing these rules – execution. Later experience teaches most peoples that the political elite is rarely to be trusted and that narrower constraints have to be set to this trust. This is part of the history of constitutional change. Government, to repeat, is not instituted by the contract. It is the recipient of a power entrusted to it for the same purpose as it was originally wielded by the society itself – the preservation of property. Governmental authority is limited by this trust and is forfeited if the trust is broken.[8] In return, the government does not obtain any contractual rights over the people. It has instead the assurance, implicit in the transfer of the original executive right, that neither the people nor the several individuals will attempt to exercise the power of law enforcement so long as the system of government is in being and is conducting itself according to the purposes laid down in its foundation. Locke's enterprise must not be confused with modern political processes in which the majority of an electorate chooses a government and may reject it at the end of a term if it fails to satisfy majority expectations. Locke is discussing a procedure, probably hypothetical, by which the system of government itself is established. When Locke states that the majority surrenders its right to the government and may not resume it whilst that government remains in being, what he means is that as long as the system of government survives no individual or group can legitimately make or enforce the law. In modern terms the electorate, even at election time, does not become either law-maker or policeman. This is the monopoly of the state, and it is the source of this state authority which Locke is explaining.

To summarise so far: civil government is originally instituted at the end of a chain of transfers of the executive right of the law of nature. This right is granted to each individual in the state of nature to enforce the law and protect the property of self and others. By the original contract each transfers this right to the political society which is created by the contract. So long as this political society remains in being, the individuals may not regain the right of law enforcement. The majority in the political society may, for the better protection of the rights of all, entrust this right to a civil government. So long as this civil government acts with the trust placed in it and remains in being, the political society may not regain its collective right of law enforcement.

When and how do the members contract? As should be clear, Locke is discussing the contract which is supposed to have been the source of political authority. Locke dips into history and his reading of travel books to cite some examples of such contracts. Generally, however, Locke argues that these contracts are lost in the remotest antiquity and that the objection that there are few records of original contracts is, therefore, misplaced (101). The inconveniences of the state of nature were rapidly discovered and political societies were established in earliest times. The contract creates political society and not society itself and Locke thereby avoids, by anticipation as it were, the criticism

levelled by Hume against the illogicality of creating a society by such
a social act as a promise or contract. Even Locke's state of nature
knows of contractual relationships and the keeping of promises is a
natural virtue which is not the product of political society. An interest
in history is a product of civilisation, develops only after the most
basic needs of security are attended to, and begins when all ordinary
memory of origins is long since lost (101).

More fundamentally, the historicity of the contract is not necessary
to Locke's case. The habits of historical explanation die hard in the
seventeenth century, but Locke's defence of constitutionalism is a
rationalist one just as was Hobbes's defence of absolutism. His argument
against any other source of political authority – against patriarchalism
in particular – is conceptual. Whether the first form of government
was a paternal monarchy or not is, for Locke, strictly irrelevant. His
historical 'concessions' to patriarchalism he regards as beside the point.
The only way in which a civil government – a government of law –
could claim authority was from the people who entrusted it with
authority. The only way the people could claim authority was by the
consent of each individual sanctioned originally by contract, since the
only way anyone, other than God, could claim authority over another
was through voluntary recognition by the subordinate. The historical
argument is secondary. It is reason which tells us that all political
authority comes from the consent of the people (104). No other
argument would be consistent with freedom.

The consent of subsequent generations

A formidable problem for theorists of contract and consent is to
explain in what way subsequent generations are free and able to
consent as to whether to be part of a political society or not. Filmer
and, subsequently, David Hume attacked consent at this point. Even
if it could be agreed, argued Hume, that political society was originally
founded upon contract, it could not be said that later generations were
free to choose whether to be under the laws of their society or not.[9]
Instead, men were born into societies and into obligations. Again we
shall follow Locke as he attempts, not always satisfactorily, to reply to
this challenge and to answer the questions who consent, to what, when
and how?

It will, however, be more convenient here to begin with the question
'to what do men consent?', since this raises relatively fewer problems.
The answer is precisely the same as to the equivalent question concerning the original contract. Locke's basic assumption is that individuals
are born free in the sense that they are born capable of freedom as well
as of reason. They are, therefore, also born capable of exercising the
executive right of the law of nature. Childhood consists of a period of
care and education, directed by parents, intended to lead the child to

a point at which he will exercise this right. At this point of maturity the child, now adult, must decide whether to consent to join himself to the political society in which he has been living,[10] by surrendering the newly acquired executive right to the community. By doing so he acknowledges that he will not attempt to take the law into his own hands and attempt to enforce natural justice. He will accept the rulings of the community as his parents did before him. If a government has already been instituted his consent to join the body politic is also consent to place his trust in that government. Strictly speaking, therefore, consent is never given directly to government but only indirectly by consenting to be one of a people which has already entrusted its collective executive right to the system of government. It will not necessarily be the case that this system of government will be identical with that first instituted by the community. Experience may have taught the people that the form of government needed to be changed in order better to secure the fundamental objectives of political society. Those who consent in later generations thus surrender an identical executive right, and on the same general terms, as did the original contractors, but do not always place themselves under an identical government. The form in which the executive right is exercised is subject to revisions in the course of history which may amount to revolutionary change.[11]

Who, therefore, consents? The short answer is 'every adult person living within a territory incorporated into a body politic'. This short answer conceals, however, a number of complications and requires elaboration since the issue of who are consenting parties in Locke is a matter of some controversy. In a rightly celebrated study, C. B. Macpherson has claimed that Locke employs the doctrine of consent to distinguish between two classes of person in the society of Locke's day.[12] On the one hand is the landed class whose members, as a consequence of their landed property, held such political rights as the vote. On the other hand is the landless or working class without political rights. Macpherson suggests that Locke's theory of natural rights permitted him to distinguish between two categories of property owner which corresponded with the two broad classes of contemporaneous society. These two types of property owner consented in different ways to the obligations of political society. Those who held property in lives, liberties and estates gave express consent and thereby incorporated themselves as full land-owning members of political society carrying full political rights. Those who possessed property only in lives and liberties did not consent expressly but tacitly, by continuing to live under law. They were fully obligated by the law but did not possess political rights, which were attached to property in some form of estate. There seems little reason to doubt that Locke assumed that political rights in England should be distributed broadly along property

lines, as Macpherson suggests. The franchise in Locke's day, and for
another two hundred years to come, was based on some form of
property qualification. Property which carried a vote included not
merely land but certain offices in church, national or local government.
The exact lines of the franchise were, therefore, by no means neat and
tidy, and Locke suggested they should be rationalised but in no way
revolutionised (157). Nevertheless, it will be suggested that Locke did
not arrive at his position by the route Macpherson outlines. Paradoxically perhaps, it will also be suggested that Locke's own route is by
no means as straightforward or intellectually satisfactory as the one
Macpherson sketches for him. To show this, however, it is necessary
to couple the answer to 'who consents?' with the answers to the next
set of questions.

When and how is consent given? All consent to join a political
society at the fairly arbitrarily determined official age of discretion,
which might be, say, 21 or 18. Since no person may consent for another,
it follows that no parent may consent for his now adult child (116).
Nor may the consent of past generations collectively bind present
generations. Consistently with this Locke then contends that a child
is, therefore, not born a subject of any country (118). No child is born
a British, American or French subject. He can only become a subject
by exercising his natural right to consent once he becomes a free adult.
Locke distinguishes two forms of consent – express and tacit. Only
express consent can make a person a member of a society (i.e. a
citizen, and a subject of its government) (119). Locke suggests that
the great difficulty lies in explaining the nature of tacit consent. For
the modern reader, however, it is the circumstances of express consent
which appear the greater puzzle. It is not clear how express consent
is registered. Locke does give one instance of express consent which
is attached to the ownership and inheritance of property. Much of
Macpherson's interpretation hinges on regarding this as the only way
in which express consent is given. However, I share John Dunn's view
that Locke is here giving one, admittedly salient, way of recognising
express consent, but that it is only one way and that there are others
which Locke does not bother to specify.

That Locke should have placed particular emphasis on express
consent given on inheritance of land is scarcely surprising. His consent
theory could be particularly vulnerable at this point. If political
authority rested on individual consent how was the continuity of this
authority in time and extent to be explained? What could prevent an
individual seceding with his land? The continuity of authority was
satisfactorily explained in patriarchal doctrine. By contrast, consent
theory might appear remarkably anarchic. Locke solves this problem
by surrounding 'free' consent in this instance with some formidable
conditions. Although, as has been said, a father cannot oblige his son

to join the father's political society, if the son wishes to inherit his father's estate he must become a member of the community. The argument goes back to the very original contract (120). At that time each proprietor of an estate attached both himself and his estate to the community. This does not mean, as has been claimed, that the property is given to the community which then grants it back to the individual. Rather, it means that the estate is brought under the jurisdiction of the society. The individual cannot join a community and ask for its protection and services and, at the same time, claim that the community may not have rights over the land on which he lives. This would imply that if a crime were committed on his estate (by him or against him) the community's agents could not step on his land to enforce the law. Although there are in English law significant restrictions on the right of police and government agents to enter private premises, Locke is clearly correct in thinking that the individual cannot retain exclusive jurisdiction over his own property once inside a political society. Just as the individual is a member of a political society as long as that society remains in existence, so his land remains permanently under its jurisdiction. The land is not 'owned' by the society. It is owned by the individual proprietor but the society is entitled to set conditions to that ownership. One such condition is that the land may never be removed from the society's jurisdiction. No society, Locke boldly asserts, will permit its territory to be dismembered (117). Secession has remained a difficult right for the most liberal society to admit, particularly where individuals might attempt to remove land in the midst of a territory leaving 'holes', as it were, in a country's jurisdiction. It is certainly not clear that Locke's argument is consistent with individual natural right, even if it is consistent with the trend of modern states towards territorial integrity. If secession were permitted, those withdrawing would find themselves under considerable pressure living in a state of nature with the surrounding political society and might again recognise the need to rejoin Locke's argument, however, denies the right to such experimentation.

The son who wishes to inherit his father's estate must, therefore, inherit an estate which has been permanently attached to the jurisdiction of a political society since its original incorporation. By inheriting, he expressly consents to become a member of the political community. He becomes a British, American, or French subject, apparently in perpetuity (121), although Locke's recognition of a right of emigration seems to stand in some contradiction to this. Locke is perfectly happy to interpret this act of inheritance as express consent, even though he admits that most people do not recognise its political significance and indeed scarcely take notice of it (117). It meets Locke's criteria for consent because it is individually entered upon by the person inheriting and because it is a free commitment. The heir might

have chosen otherwise. He might have suspended judgement and
considered whether he wished to accept the political conditions attaching to the estate. He may find them objectionable and choose to
renounce his inheritance. To choose to inherit the estate is equally a
conscious acknowledgement of membership. The act is free although
there is a powerful incentive to allegiance. As Locke says it 'is no
small Tye on the Obedience of Children' (73). It is a force for social
and political continuity, ensuring influence for the father and allegiance
to the body politic. The continuity is a matter of individual calcula-
tion of benefit. There is no sense of sympathy with a nation's past
nor of obligation to the community for sustaining the estate which he
contemplates inheriting. Although Locke believes that honour and
respect may be due to parents, there is little suggestion of any such
sentiments towards the state, little of Burke's reverence and sense of
continuity.

It is clear, therefore, that inheritance of an estate is an act of
express consent which makes a man a member of the political community. It would, however, be strange if, as is Macpherson's inference,
this were the only way in which a man might become a subject or
even a citizen with political rights. This would imply that the landless
not only lacked political rights but were not even subjects. It would
also imply that a person did not become a subject and acquire citizen
status until he inherited his estate, which might not be until an
advanced age. Up to this point he would have no means of acquiring
a political standing. Some further modes of giving express consent thus
seem necessary to explain such gaps. Sadly these further modes are
nowhere specified. We may justifiably speculate, as John Dunn does,
that express consent might be shown by the various oaths of allegiance
which seventeenth-century office-holders were required to swear. Certainly Locke regards such oaths as of supreme importance. They are
the great bonds of society which governments should render sacred
and not permit to be abused by careless, over-frequent and uncon-
sidered use. Without them 'all must break in pieces, and run to
confusion'.[13] Atheists might not be tolerated because the fear of breaking a sacred oath could not influence them. Nevertheless, this is but
a reasonable speculation unsupported in the Second Treatise and such
oaths would, as Dunn also points out, rarely be sworn by the poorest
classes whose power, to cite Hobbes in a related context, is 'perhaps
not considerable'. Even so, in 1650 the entire adult male population had
been required to engage itself to the Commonwealth. It would be odd
to regard them as not subjects, even if it would not have been odd at
the time to regard them as without political rights. Locke's account
of express consent and of membership is, consequently, seriously
inadequate.

What, then, of tacit consent? Macpherson's case is that Locke employs tacit consent chiefly as a device whereby the landless may be deemed to consent to subjection without becoming members with political rights. Locke is certainly clear that tacit consent does not give rise to political rights but it is also clear, as Macpherson necessarily admits, that this form of consent may be given by some who own estates. A person tacitly consents to the rules of the community merely by living within its jurisdiction or walking along its roads. If consent implied moral approval of government, then Locke's notion of tacit consent would have, as is sometimes alleged, emptied consent of any meaning. Acquiescence would then imply consent. But this is not what Locke has in mind. Right up to his late critical comments on William Sherlock's *The Case of the Allegiance due to sovereign powers stated*, Locke insisted that only some clear act of consent could establish a legitimate civil society and that general submission was not to be construed as general consent (MS Locke, c. 28, fos 83-96). The only instance of tacit consent he supplies is that given by foreigners who settle in or visit a country. They make use of the community facilities. They may buy and sell land within its territory. They do not, however, become members of the body politic. At any time they may sell up and leave. By residing in the country they tacitly acknowledge the authority of the political community and its government. This acknowledgement is not necessarily approval. A person who visits or resides in a foreign country by way of business or pleasure does not, in doing so, necessarily commend the government of that country but, as Locke argues, recognises the right of that government to regulate his business activities, to punish him for offences, to tax his income or his purchases and the like. Whether his conduct in that country implies approval of the regime would depend on factors other than his mere presence in its territory – on his expressed views, on whether he resides there from choice. As long as he remains, however, the government exercises its jurisdiction over him by virtue of his dwelling in the territory and using it and not, as with its own subjects, by virtue of some personal allegiance (121).

To summarise the argument: express consent is given by all subjects of a government. It may be given upon inheritance of land but also in other ways which Locke does not fully specify. It is suggested that it is given both by those who possess such political rights as the franchise and by those who do not. It is given by landed and landless. The distinction between the political rights of landed and landless, which Macpherson so rightly stresses as part of Locke's political world, is not established by different modes of consent but by the fundamental constitutional act which establishes the form of government in a country and which may be subject to revision in the course of that country's history.[14] Tacit consent is the recognition of the legitimacy of a government, given implicitly by any person who is not a subject of that government when living within the territory under its jurisdiction.

In both its forms consent implies the recognition of the authority of the state, rather than approval of its laws or its form of government. Even the subject who expressly incorporates himself into a political community is not necessarily announcing his approval of its mode of government, but is acknowledging the right of the community to set legal conditions to the way in which he will henceforth exercise his rights. He recognises that the community will umpire his disputes and act as his policeman. He surrenders any claim to enforce his own rulings on his fellow members. Approval of the community's rules and government is strictly another matter. It is true, of course, that no rational man would attach himself to a political community which left him more open to danger and abuse than he would be in the state of nature. Moreover, to the extent that the free man could have chosen to remain outside political society or to have entered some other community, his consent may indicate that he finds something congenial in his particular choice. Nevertheless, even Locke openly regards inheritance as a powerful inducement to consent and Hume's satirical comments on the freedom of choice of the poor and illiterate further emphasise the pressures on 'free' consent.[15] A person may, therefore, consent to become a member of a political community for a number of reasons which do not necessarily imply strong approval of its particular form of government. His consent will, nevertheless, bind him to acknowledge the authority of that community and, hence, of the government in which that community has invested its conditional trust. The allegiance he owes to the government will depend, like the allegiance owed by the community at large, on the way in which that government discharges the trust placed in it.

Notes Chapter V

1 A brilliant corrective to some misconceptions of Locke's idea of consent is John Dunn, 'Consent in the Political Theory of John Locke', *The Historical Journal*, X, 2 (1967), pp. 153–82. The approach here is in basic agreement with that of Dunn.

2 *A Preface to Democratic Theory*, Chicago, University of Chicago Press, Phoenix Books edition, 1963, p. 34.

3 Willmoore Kendall's *John Locke and the Doctrine of Majority Rule* is an essay to be recommended to any student of democratic theory in general even if much in it is inconsistent with the historical intentions of Locke himself.

4 *Anarchy, State and Utopia*, Oxford, Blackwell, 1974, ch. 5. One of Locke's first critics argued that it implied 'banishment' for the dissenter. Charles Leslie, *Cassandra*, Num. I, 2nd edition, London, 1705, p. 6.

5   A view taken in their different ways by Leo Strauss, *Natural Right and History*, ch. V, Richard Cox, *Locke on War and Peace*, and Willmoore Kendall, op. cit.

6   *A Theory of Justice*, ch. II.

7   Kendall, op. cit., chs IV–VII.

8   See below, ch. VI, for further discussion of the terms of the trust.

9   'Of the Original Contract', in *Essays Moral, Political and Literary*, p. 455.

10 The exact nature of a child's obligation to the law is obscure in Locke, as it is in the writings of most political philosophers. This interesting question has been raised in discussions and in a paper by Graham Haydon at the University of Glasgow.

11 Political change does not therefore eradicate all traces of consent in Locke's sense of the term, as Hume appears to suppose. This is discussed further in ch. VI.

12 *The Political Theory of Possessive Individualism*, pp. 247*ff*.

13 *Some Considerations, Works*, V, 6.

14 The form of government and distribution of political rights will be discussed in ch. VI.

15 This is true even though Hume probably contributed powerfully to the misunderstanding of Locke's view, particularly of tacit consent. 'Of the Original Contract', in *Essays Moral, Political and Literary*, pp. 461–2. See also below, ch. VII.

Chapter VI

Civil Government

Civil government is a very ordinary matter. It is lacking in any 'indelible character, peculiar sanctity of the function, or a power immediately derived from Heaven'.[1] It differs from a church as earth differs from heaven. Political society is like any other association which is established for some specific purpose and whose government and laws are directed toward the achievement of this purpose. In this respect civil government does not differ from the governing body of a club or association. The object of political society is the preservation of property, understood in its widest sense. The task of government is to employ the resources of the body politic in the effective protection of the rights of its members against one another and against external attack. Although the *Second Treatise* is, of course, replete with expressions of the objective of civil government, perhaps Locke's most explicit statement is contained in the *Letter on Toleration*:

> The commonwealth seems to me to be a society of men constituted only for preserving and advancing their civil goods. What I call civil goods are life, liberty, bodily health and freedom from pain, and the possession of outward things, such as lands, money, furniture, and the like.[2]

There is therefore no grandeur about either state or government. It was against this sort of conception that Edmund Burke was to complain in *The Reflections on the Revolution in France*: 'The state ought not to be considered as nothing better than a partnership agreement in a trade of pepper and coffee, calico or tobacco, or some other such low concern, to be taken up for a little temporary interest, and to be dissolved by the fancy of the parties.' Whilst Burke asked that the state should be looked upon with 'other reverence', Locke was equally determined that what Hobbes had already called a 'mortal God' should be brought down to earth. The state is a voluntary society constituted for mutual protection. Everything else is 'attainable by men living in neighbourhood without the bounds of Commonwealth' and consequently this can be the only rational purpose in establishing political society and government.[3] Politics concerns authority and Locke is asserting that the authority of a civil government extends only so far as is predetermined by its original constitution. It may be the case that, in order to carry out its appointed tasks, a government may acquire power in excess of what is strictly required. Nevertheless, such power does not grant it any extra authority. There may be many things a civil society could do, just as there might be many things a family or an army or the East India Company could do, but this does not imply that the civil government has the authority to, for example, run a business any more than an army has the authority to propagate religion.[4]

It is, at the same time, clear that a political society cannot be precisely on the same level as other voluntary associations. Granting Locke's view against those like Filmer who do not regard the state as being in the first place a voluntary association, it is still the case that the state has a authority not possessed by other associations and that it pursues a different kind of objective. The authority of the state is inherently more general than that of other associations. Its authority extends over these other societies, just as it does over individuals. It has the authority to protect associations from one another in the same way as it protects individuals. Such protection and the way it is effected implies a different type of objective from that of other associations. A club of next-door neighbours may aim at providing social activities or baby-sitting, a commercial company at manufacturing goods profitably, a church at propagating its creed. But a civil society and its government, such as Locke describes, does not have a similar substantive goal. There is no one paramount direction in which it is moving. Its task is to enable each individual and association within its jurisdiction to pursue its particular goal in such a way that it does not injure others in the legitimate pursuit of their goals. This task is not, as politics is sometimes said to be, the 'adjustment of interests', since this tends to presuppose that the state is to determine which of the interests is to yield to the others. Instead, the state is established to lay down the ground rules which the individuals and groups must observe in their dealings with one another. A Lockean civil government does not determine that the adjustment of interests is best achieved by allowing the airport to obtain the farmer's land. Ideally, the government lays down the laws whereby these different interests may settle their disputes and sees that they observe the law in these disputes. The protection of property is therefore the specific objective of civil government but it is not a particular 'interest' which it promotes, as the chess club may promote the playing of chess. Civil government, as Locke understands it, is neutral or 'indifferent' as between interests or particular properties. It umpires between property holders when they dispute the boundaries of their rights. How this particular view of government, differing very greatly from much modern practice, emerges in Locke may be seen by going back to what was lacking in the state of nature, since the only function of political society is to remedy these lacks.

There are three things lacking in the state of nature (124–6). By tracing how these lacks may be rectified it is possible to arrive at the minimum framework of Locke's civil government.

The first missing factor is 'an *established*, settled, known *Law*, received and allowed by common consent to be the Standard of Right and Wrong, and the common measure to decide all Controversies between them'. It might be thought that in the state of nature there is such a law – the law of nature. But the law of nature is subject to biased interpretation. Although the law of nature is knowable, at least in its most general prescriptions, it is not known with sufficient exactitude to decide specific disputes over rights. There is too often sufficient imprecision for someone to claim that he is not guilty when accused of a breach of the law. There needs to be an authoritative ruling on the interpretation of the law in specific instances. Locke undoubtedly does come perilously near a Hobbesian position at this point. Government rescues men from the near anarchy of interpretations of the law of nature. Whilst the law of nature does set somewhat clearer limits to the conduct of a Lockean government than to those of a Hobbesian sovereign, the room for interpretation and clarification of crucial property rights is considerable.

The second missing factor in the state of nature is 'a *Known and indifferent Judge*, with Authority to determine all differences according to the established law'. The self-policing of the executive power of the law of nature is, as has been seen, partial, haphazard and inclined to turn the restoration of justice into the exaction of vengeance. The third lack is of a 'Power to back and support the Sentence when right, and to *give* it due *Execution*'.

A system of authoritative judgements and law enforcement would be sufficient to turn the state of nature from a condition of uncertain, unstable sociability into a political society exhibiting peace, order and predictability. Nothing further is needed. Everything else may be attained by men 'living in neighbourhood'. The Lockean state is an apparatus of law, and its institution may be compared with H. L. A. Hart's conjecture about the creation of a legal system in *The Concept of Law*.[5] Hart suggests that a legal system can be understood as a construct of 'primary' and 'secondary' rules. Primary rules lay down the basic rules of social existence, concerning murder, theft and fraud. Hart envisages a society which subscribes only to such primary rules. This might be likened to groups living in Locke's state of nature according to the laws of nature. A society might exist for some while in this manner, so long as men are reasonably clear as to the limits and application of the primary rules, as might be the case in a close, stable, agrarian economy not much exposed to change. Considerable drawbacks arise once the society experiences change and becomes less closely knit by custom. This may occur as a result of foreign pressure or be the effect of money in hastening trade and the growth of property (48). Social life becomes less simple and the boundaries of property may be thrown in doubt. Consequently, it is not so clear what counts as an invasion of one's land, or what is an instance of theft or fraud. There is, however, no person or text to turn to for an authoritative resolution of this uncertainty. The group may, therefore, be pictured establishing its laws by writing them down, inscribing them on tablets of stone or otherwise recording them authoritatively. In doing so they are, in Hart's terms, instituting a secondary rule of 'recognition' – a rule about how one will recognise a rule to be a rule of the group. This rule states, 'Consult the tablets' or 'Check the constitition'. In Locke's version a 'known, standing law' has to be established which all who consent to be members of the new political society will recognise as authoritative.

Social and economic change also reveals the static nature of primary rules and, whilst it is proper that Locke's law of nature should be eternal, it is also the case that its interpretation needs to be adapted to a changing world. Natural law theory is regularly on the horns of a dilemma. Either it is so universally stated as to be almost vacuous or it is so particular as to be confined within the specifics of a particular historical era and its social relationships. In the face of change the group requires a rule granting authority to some body to change the primary rules according to an agreed procedure. By such a 'rule of change' a legislature is instituted with the right to make laws for the community, backed by penalties in terms of deprivation of civil goods up to the penalty of death.

Finally, the group will need a further secondary rule laying down ways of settling disputes about whether primary rules have been broken. This secondary 'rule of adjudication' will establish, define and empower courts and judges. In Locke's terms the group must establish an umpire. At this point, however, the comparison between Hart's model and Locke's reveals a difference which is highly significant for Locke's conception of what constitutes a civil government. Locke regards the legislative as possessing the ultimate power of adjudication. The rule of adjudication and that of change both confer power on the legislative as the supreme body in the Lockean state. Locke reverts to an older notion of Parliament and of legislation in general which dates back to medieval times and which had still been significant in England earlier in the seventeenth century. According to this view, the legislature is in the first place a High Court where disputes of a general nature concerning the rules of the nation are settled. The legislature must umpire between claims by declaring and clarifying what the law is in such cases. Locke's idea of government betrays the mixture of medieval and 'modern' ideas of Parliament which still survived in the seventeenth century. Legislators both represented the community and brought forward to Parliament the various claims of their constituents as matters for decision by themselves as judges in the highest court of the land. These issues for debate were not mere interests to be reconciled but claims in law which required settlement. The decisions of the Lockean legislature are therefore judgements or sentences of a court. They may take the form of enactments which change the law, but these enactments are to be construed as the umpire's announcement of how future disputes of a similar character are henceforth to be settled. As Laslett has insisted,[6] Locke's conception of government is essentially judicial. Government exists in the first place to settle disputes by declaring and clarifying a law, which already exists in its essentials in the law of nature and in the ground rules of the political society which, ideally, should have been created in the image of natural law. Locke shows none of the concern that many of his Whig contemporaries felt for the independence of the judiciary, whom he regards as 'inferior magistrates' who pronounce sentence according to the laws made by others. They are part of the executive branch and Locke raises no questions about the terms of their appointment, whether 'during good behaviour' or 'during pleasure' of the executive, which were a major issue of his day.

To adapt another modern terminology, whereas Hobbes presented a system of 'constitutive rules', Locke's is a system of 'regulative rules'. For Hobbes the rules made by government constitute the activities they are to regulate. Property is not merely regulated by state legislation, it is brought into being by it. Property is, therefore, the creation of legislation and the distinction between mine and thine a consequence of state convenience. Property cannot, of course, be possible without some rules but for Locke such rules were to be found in the law of nature. If property is therefore natural, political society merely regulates by law an institution whose legitimate existence is not dependent on the body politic. Hobbes's model for government is the creative legislator, as is indicated by the image of creation in the Introduction to *Leviathan*. Locke's model is the umpire settling disputes.

Umpirage cannot nevertheless be an exact analogy for government, even assuming the ideal of impartiality to be attained. Locke's limited government does more than the umpire of a tennis match who decides disputes about line calls. Government has to take on the sort of tasks performed by the ruling bodies of tennis when, for instance, they decided to allow professional players to enter tournaments previously restricted to amateurs. This is umpirage only in a much more metaphorical sense, when a dispute about the rules of the game itself requires settlement in such a way as to settle future practices and establish guidelines for later judicial decisions. It is also at this point, when the ground rules and routines of a political society are being established or considerably modified, that the whole model of umpiring is often called into question and government appears the adjustor of interests or their tool. 'It is the duty of the civil magistrate, by impartially enacted equal laws, to preserve and secure for all the people in general and for everyone of his subjects in particular, the just things that belong to this life.'[7]

This passage encapsulates Locke's idea of a civil government. It incorporates the notions of judicial neutrality and the classical conception of justice as giving each man his due. A civil government is distinguished by its adherence to the rule of law. Locke repeatedly stresses that a political society must be governed by 'known, standing' or 'settled, standing' laws. The subject must be able to expect that he will be treated by the government according to principles understood in advance. The law must be applied without fear or favour. It must not discriminate between different groups or classes, but must provide 'one Rule for Rich and Poor, for the Favourite at Court, and the Country Man at Plough' (142). In contemporary idiom we might say that government and law must treat all alike, regardless of race, colour, sex or creed.

A civil government's obligation to secure each and every person in possession of his civil goods is the obligation of justice. It is important to recognise what this does and does not mean. It does not imply that a civil government exists to ensure the distribution of civil goods so that each is to receive a comfortable level of existence.

There are certainly ways in which such a conclusion might be derivable from Locke's original assumptions of the equality of human rights, but there is little evidence that Locke would have wished to draw such a radical conclusion. Indeed, critics might feel that he showed some ingenuity in avoiding it. Nevertheless, as Seliger has emphasised,[8] Locke did believe that there was a natural law obligation on government to relieve the most extreme necessity. Even such minimal provision does imply some deviation from the non-redistributive principles of government in order to ensure 'enough' for all.[9] With this exception – admittedly of potential significance for the future – to render each man his due means, for a Lockean government, that every subject must be guaranteed security in that which is rightfully his according to either natural law or the law of the land. Subjects do not look to government for substantive decisions about the management of their individual affairs. They look to it to ensure that they are not deprived of what is rightfully theirs by violence or fraud on the part of others, including the government itself. The government performs this function by laying down the rules according to which owners of rights – property in Locke's widest sense – may carry out transactions between one another. It does not interfere with the use of such rights, except in so far as one person's handling of his rights adversely affects another person in the legitimate pursuit of his rights. Note that government is concerned with rights not interests. Clearly, one person may adversely affect another's interests quite legitimately. A baker who raises his prices is normally[10] acting against the interests of his customer but would not be undermining the customer's legal rights. He would offend a customer's rights if he refused, for whatever reason, to sell him goods when the customer was ready to pay the same market price as every other customer. If the baker withdraws his goods from the market and allows his customers to starve in a famine unless a higher price is offered, he offends against the natural law of charity rather than the rules of civil justice. He could be regarded as guilty of murder.[11] One can only speculate on the baker's likely legal position in such a case. Possibly the government would in the face of famine be forced to intervene and fix a just price in order to fulfil its obligation to secure 'enough' for all. The baker would then fall foul of civil law as well as the law of charity. This seems a clearer instance of Seliger's suggestion concerning the limits of exploitation yet even here Locke is again not explicit concerning an exception to the pure rule of law which could be broadened significantly.

Ideally no legal system should permit incompatible rights since this implies an internal inconsistency of its rules. Where this never-theless occurs, as in conditions of change, the legislature will be required to change the law to determine which category of rights will prevail in like cases in the future. Such laws are, therefore, general in char-acter. They cannot refer to particular property holders or holdings. Laws do not assign object A to person X but establish rules from which, in conjunction with certain empirical information, one can infer that person A is the owner of X. It is, therefore, not strictly correct to claim that a civil government, such as Locke envisages, upholds a particular distribution of property along class lines. Civil government defends property right as such, and designates the modes of legitimate transfer of such rights from one person to another. It would, indeed, be a fundamental breach of the principles of such government if it attempted to redistribute property rights for egalitarian or inegali-tarian reasons. Property is the exclusive entitlement of the owner, and government has no right to interfere with it, unless by some criminal act the individual has forfeited his right, or has consented to a degree of intervention.

The exclusive property in goods and land arose originally when persons first 'mixed' their property in their own persons and in their labour with land or other natural objects. This established only an original right and the goods, the land, or its products could subsequently be bartered, sold, bequeathed or donated to others who gained a right to them, not because of any labour mixed directly with them but by virtue of the terms of the particular transaction. It is clear that in a comparatively short time the pattern of property holding will bear only a tenuous and indirect relationship to the distribution originating from labour, even though in each case it should be in principle possible to trace the genealogy of any property back to labour. One tract of land may be owned by the direct descendants of the original labourer. Another may be owned by the descendants of a particularly industrious early settler, or his heir, who bought out his neighbour. Another may be owned by a merchant who has recently bought it with the proceeds of his trade. Yet another may have been acquired by gift or by gambling. The role of government is to establish regular modes of transfer for property in place of the disparate, unsystematic and probably imprecise modes which would have occurred in the individual transfers of a state of nature. Fundamentally, this will imply a law of contract laying down the rules for bequests and inheritance, for sales and donations. Such law declares that transfers must take place in the prescribed manner if the government, in the name of the community, is to recognise the resultant entitlement and defend it against force and fraud, employing the combined force of the body politic to do so. This is what Locke means when he states that in political society 'the laws regulate the right of property, and the possession of land is determined by positive constitutions' (50).

Property in political society must, therefore, partake of both a natural and an artificial character. In so far as in principle a chain of entitlements may be traced from the original title in the labour of the first owner, any property right is natural, exclusive and beyond the reach of any government or private person. But in so far as the chain of entitlements is the consequence of the regulations of government, the distribution of property takes on an artificial aspect. This will be readily seen when one considers how far a system of regulations may shape the distribution of property, even when there is no declared intention of imposing a particular social and economic pattern on the society. The law of inheritance offers an instance. It is a function of civil government to settle the rules of inheritance, the terms on which a person may bequeath his property to his heir. It has already been seen that this is of some significance in Locke's explanation of political continuity. The society may settle on a system of primogeniture or one of equal partition among the younger members of a family, or some other scheme. Whatever system is adopted, it is the duty of civil government to uphold it impartially. If Locke does not quite say, with Hume, that the particular mode is 'frivolous', he is in agreement that it is the certainty, predictability and impartiality of the rule that is of the utmost significance. The social pattern that will emerge from a system of primogeniture is likely to be significantly different from that produced by partible inheritance. Persons and groups will be advantaged or disadvantaged, actually or potentially, by either. Yet in both cases the civil government can be interpreted as playing a purely neutral role. It exists to maintain and facilitate whichever rule system has been adopted as the foundation of the society. In either case the government will be supporting a system some way removed from the original labour right.

An existing distribution of property is not likely to reflect very closely the labour and industry invested by present owners. The lazy squire has the title to his estates by the law of the land and, sadly, a day-labourer may be industrious with little to show for it. One has benefited, the other not, by the impartially maintained rules of inheritance. Certainly Locke believed in the virtues of industry and hoped to see them rewarded, but he was far from believing, as John Dunn has pointed out,[12] that these virtues were actually displayed by the gentry of his day. Idleness and waste might bring disaster, and were worth frequent warnings, but industry brought no guarantee of a rise in the social scale. Locke's own attitude to primogeniture is interestingly ambivalent. A civil government is acting legitimately in maintaining it where it prevails. Locke does not suggest that primogeniture involves any invasion of property rights. Yet he is uneasy about it, which is understandable in that it may seem to contravene the law of nature. Where it is maintained by law and custom subjects tend to think, mistakenly, that it is part of natural right (I, 91). However, by nature, every child has an equal right to a share of the father's estate as being equally in need of maintenance as the firstborn (I, 93). This title of the children limits the exclusivity of the property right of the father (I, 88). It might, therefore, be expected that civil laws should reflect a natural law of equal partition. The fact that Locke does not draw this inference is further indication of the tension between the egalitarian premises contained in the law of nature and the conservatism of the political conclusions. At the same time, it is clear that Locke's notion of civil government could just as happily accommodate a law of equal inheritance.[13] There is an unresolved tension in Locke's theory of property between the owner's unrestricted right of disposal including that of bequest, the family's right to expect maintenance, and the community's right to lay down whatever rules it thinks fit for the transferring of property, provided they are certain, permanent and impartial. In practice, certain rights would have to yield to others and it was a matter of contemporary European debate as to which should yield on grounds of justice and social utility.

Civil government is charged with upholding the fundamental terms of the political association. These terms represent the condition of order within which each member of the association may live the life he chooses. But beyond a very minimal level, the government is not charged with guaranteeing substantive economic benefits such as a certain level of income or employment. These are the product of transactions between property-owning subjects, whether the property exchanged is land, merchandise or merely the worker's labour power. The government's prime duty in relation to such transactions is to referee them, to ensure that no party suffers violence or fraud. This is achieved not merely by policing individual transactions, but by laying down the rules according to which they should take place if the parties are to receive the benefit of state enforcement of their agreements. In a list of government actions which promote trade, Locke stresses the provision of such general conditions for individual enterprise as freedom of trade, freedom of religion, certainty of property, simplicity of law and the avoidance of arbitrary power of arrest and imprisonment (MS Locke, c. 30, f. 18). In this respect, one of civil government's major tasks is to maintain the value of the currency so that transactions between subjects may take place on a formally equal basis.[14] This has always been recognised as a major function by the most extreme advocates of the minimal or *laissez-faire* state. It has been regarded, as it is by Locke, as an entirely neutral function. Some may have more money than others but it is essential that the value of the currency they own must be established as identical at all times. Locke recognises the great advantage of money as being that it can be stored. If it does not waste, it can be used for unknown future transactions (47). This being the natural advantage of money in general, it is clear that government must see to it that the particular currency a community employs must retain this permanency. The good of the community demands it, since uncertainty as to a society's currency will seriously damage foreign trade. Justice demands it, because every contract is made in the expectation of some monetary return which, in Locke's view, is represented by the intrinsic value of the silver contained in the coin contracted for. To allow this silver content to change must defraud one or other of the parties who will either pay more or receive less than he bargained. Reducing the silver content of any denomination – the proposal under review by Locke – would be tantamount to compulsory public robbery.[15] It would mean that all creditors would be forced to receive less silver than they were legally due, even though they would receive what was described as the proper amount in coin. Denominations, however, are 'but empty sounds'. What the creditor contracted for, whether he was a private lender, a worker owed wages, a church or university owed rent, or even the king owed taxes, was in real silver value, not devalued coin. Such action would involve an arbitrary forced gift of 'one man's right and possession to another, without any fault on the suffering man's side' and would be 'a public failure of justice'.[16] The supposedly neutral policy of stabilising the currency has proved a persistently difficult undertaking. As recent experience has shown, both deflation and inflation may lead governments to surprisingly interventionist policies in the interests of the impartial stabilisation of money. Locke's own policy of upholding the value of the coinage was deflationary and partial in its impact, but was justified by him as restoring the ground rules of the community which lax government had permitted to lapse. His defence encapsulates the role of civil government in economic affairs: 'The public authority is guarantee for the performance of all legal contracts.'[17] Currency laws, like the law of contracts, are not infringements of liberty but confer powers on subjects by facilitating the exercise of property rights. In the words of the *Second Treatise*, such law 'in its true Notion, is not so much the Limitation *as the direction of a free and intelligent Agent* to his proper Interest' (57).

The substantive concern civil government has with economics is in foreign trade where government should attempt to ensure an export surplus. This mercantilist concern does not appear to have the *dirigiste* implications internally which often accompanied it. Locke appears to believe that such surplus is chiefly attained by a vigorous colonial trade policy, coupled with freedom for individual enterprise at home which necessarily implies a framework of known standing laws. It does not imply any action by government of a redistributive nature to determine 'whether the money be in Thomas, or Richard's hands'[18]. Civil government does not acquire any property right which it might freely redistribute.

The major instance of the legislative disposing of a subject's property, other than by way of punishment, is taxation. Government provides a service to the community which must be paid for and taxation is the means of covering these costs. Like Hobbes, Locke regards taxes as wages paid to government. Taxes cannot be used for redistributive purposes to equalise income or opportunities, except in so far as minimum provision may be enforced. Money is the property of individuals, and taxation involves the legally compulsory surrender of a specified amount of such property to the government. Property may only be taken from a subject with his own consent and consequently Locke regards it as one of the foundations of civil government that taxation requires the consent of subjects, given either directly or through representatives (142). This consent must, however, be over and above the consent given by every subject on joining the body politic.[19] Each individual consents to the community – and hence its legislative – upholding the principles of property by laying down rules for the holding and transfer of property. Such consent does not go so far as justifying the legislative in depriving a subject of any of his property. By contrast, Hobbes held that the general ends of government justified the means to them and, hence, no special consent for taxation was needed. Indeed he regarded such a doctrine as one of the worst diseases from which a state could suffer. For Locke, the surrender of property must be by the particular consent of the subject or by representatives elected with authority to consent on behalf of their electors. In this, Locke is expressing abstractly the constitutionalist view of taxation in Europe in general, even though in many countries the institutions of consent had atrophied so that, if consent had any bearing on taxation, the relationship was more Hobbesian than Lockean. Some form of independent representative body is, Locke argues, required if property is to be safeguarded from arbitrariness.

Civil government is, therefore, necessarily limited in character. Political society is an association of persons who have agreed to subscribe to a system of laws to regulate their transactions, and civil government is the body which will make and enforce the law. Apart from this commitment to be ruled by general laws, the members of a Lockean civil society have not agreed to any particular policy objective whether of an economic, moral or religious nature, and thus government itself can have none. Civil government, though limited, is by no means necessarily inactive or insignificant. It has no place in the self-chosen substantive activities of persons or groups. It is not itself a merchant and should not be a church. Nevertheless, it may enact laws for the regulation of any activity to the extent that the activity impinges on the rights of others. It does not trade, but it lays down rules defining and penalising fraudulent trading. It should not impose any worship, but it should legislate to prevent a church from harming the civil rights of its members, of former members or other churches. It may not prevent an heiress from marrying a spendthrift, but it may lay down the rules and forms of marriage. Government is concerned not with what is a 'good' marriage but with what is a 'proper' marriage. The recognition of subjects as equals under law is, moreover, no empty formality but may have significant social consequences. A Lockean civil government would not properly legislate on matters of race and would certainly not indulge in reverse discrimination to favour underprivileged minorities. It could, nevertheless, act against a person who refused to sell his house to another because of his race. Refusal would imply the non-recognition of the other's equal civil status. The law would not require the seller to like the buyer, but would require him to treat him as a fellow citizen with full rights in any legal and commercial transaction. Government would take similar action over political rights or the enjoyment of public facilities. The conduct of private clubs would raise borderline issues which might be the kind of dispute over rights to be decided by the umpirage of Parliament. For those who believe that government should promote fraternity and be pledged to certain common values, civil government will seem inadequate. But such government is designed to regulate those who are strangers as well as those who are friends, those who are physically remote from one another as well as colleagues or neighbours.[20] It is impartial, or to use Locke's own and better word, 'indifferent'.

More troublesome than any lack of commitment to community is the question of the degree of neutrality achievable by any civil government. Community as a substantive goal implies, after all, a clearly different vision of politics from that of Locke. Whether civil government can be truly indifferent raises issues about Locke's internal coherence. A government of laws and not of men had been one of the ideals of politics since the Greeks and yet has remained elusive. Governments may profess their impartiality, and even do much to act in accord with their professions. Much of government is regulative rather than creative, but regulation is not without significant effects. Rules become routines which are inherently conservative and, usually, routinely advantage or disadvantage sectors of society. Those who apply these routines may not themselves be the beneficiaries, except in so far as they are agents of the state and are paid for applying *any* routine. Ground rules, known standing laws, may be fairly applied and no one's civil rights may therefore be injured. Yet the outcome may be accumulation of power in the hands of some and a cycle of deprivation for others. No conspiracy or class-consciousness need necessarily be supposed. This would be a matter of particular investigation. An instance would be the rules of inheritance mentioned earlier. Inherited wealth is a major resource capable of creating further accumulations and frequently granting access to political power. A Lockean government, out of respect for individual property right, would not be permitted to use laws of inheritance in order to redistribute wealth for social purposes. Estate duty based on such objectives would contravene the exclusivity of property rights – although even liberals like J. S. Mill have felt that respect for individual property and acquisition does not entail the equal respect for the right of inheritance shown by Locke or Nozick. A civil government must be strictly impartial in its application of a law of primogeniture and be firmly indifferent as to the individual acts of bequest and inheritance. Such inheritance forms part of the routines of society. The resultant distribution of wealth and power is likely to be significantly different from that where a civil government with equivalent impartiality and indifference applied a rule of equal partition of inheritance amongst a family – itself a unit which might be variously defined to include greater or lesser degrees of kinship. Neither government would be involved in any redistribution of property for social purposes. Under both governments civil equality and freedom would be scrupulously observed. Nevertheless routines tend to foreclose options. Rules interact in complex manners which make it difficult to mount a challenge to them and sometimes difficult to envisage that a challenge might be made, so well-embedded are they in the minds of the population. Locke himself pointed out how primogeniture, and many other social customs, could come to be regarded as facts of nature rather than ultimately human conventions.[21]

There is a great deal to be said for the virtues of society under civil government, and it is indeed difficult to see how certain ideals of negative liberty can be approximated except under such government. The precise quality of life under such government would, however, depend greatly upon the ground rules of the society. Not even the minimal state can help shaping to a degree the patterns of life and of substantive advantages and disadvantages of those under its jurisdiction. Locke's seeming shift from a concern with substantive equality under the law of nature to the formal civil equality of political society is, therefore, of the utmost consequence if one wishes to envisage what it might be like to live in Lockean society, or in the Utopia of his contemporary sympathiser Robert Nozick. A historical theory of entitlement does not, as Nozick acknowledges, establish the justice of contemporaneous property holdings which may be the outcome of historical force and fraud.[22] It might encourage one to construct an alternative conjectural history and envisage what kind of society might have emerged if all had started with equal resources (and not merely equal legal rights) and, under the protection of minimal civil government, entered transactions with one another. What would then have justified departures from equality in the distribution of resources? Such questions necessarily arise from the radicalism of Locke's premises, and both Locke and Nozick appear to escape by fixing such a low base line for a comparison of the benefits of private over communal ownership that private appropriation must always guarantee equivalent rights for others.[23]

A capitalist market economy is undoubtedly that which is most congruent with Lockean civil society. Private enterprise would act freely within the bounds of law. It is equally certain that a totally state-run economy would be incompatible with civil government. The state exists to pass judgements concerning civil transactions and would be judging in its own case. There would, however, be no inherent contradiction between civil government and co-operative enterprise. Any individuals may associate together for a purpose which does not injure others and may freely pool their resources. Such associations – whether clubs, churches or guilds of craftsmen or traders – may own property and govern themselves as they think fit. Civil government would umpire between co-operatives according to the same principles as it did between individuals. There is no difficulty in principle in changing a primarily individualist society into a co-operative one. J. S. Mill was to make such an intellectual transition towards co-operative socialism. How simple such a transition might be in practice is quite a different matter. The problems for workers of accumulating the necessary resources to establish co-operatives are far greater than Nozick chooses to acknowledge.[24] No civil government could legitimately raise money by taxation to lend to such co-operatives and the prospects for private investment would depend on overturning assumptions about economic management built up by the operation of the system of private enterprise. The openness of civil society must be set alongside the inertia which any society displays.

The institutions of civil government

The political community is established by contract and continued by consent of its members. Civil government is established by a distinct act of trust whereby the people conditionally transfer their executive right to some amongst themselves who would act as umpires and rule-makers for the rest. This act of trust is the fundamental constitutional act of the political community which determines the way in which authority is institutionalised. It is the *'original* and supream act of the Society'* (157). It establishes the form of government, the mode of succession, the relations of legislative to executive. All the institutions of government owe their authority to the act of trust. Locke founds government only indirectly upon consent. It is trust which defines the terms of government.[25]

The people's executive right is entrusted to government conditionally. As in any legal trust, the authority of the trustee is delimited by the terms of the trust. If a trust fund is set up to administer the estate of a child, the trustees are not empowered to employ the money for any other purpose, however charitable it may be. Should the trustee seek to act beyond the terms of the trust, his authority ceases and he may be removed. Locke's government is likewise removable:

> For all *Power given with trust* for the attaining an *end*, being limited by that end, whenever that *end* is manifestly neglected, or opposed, the *trust* must necessarily be *forfeited*, and the Power devolve into the hands of those that gave it, who may place it anew where they shall think best for their safety and security. (149)

In a normal legal trust, there are three parties – trustor, trustee and beneficiary. Locke's political trust is a relationship between a trustee and the trustor who is also the beneficiary. The trustor is thus in a special position to assess the achievement of the trustee and determine the degree of discretion he is to be permitted. Without this modification to the notion of a trust, it could equally take on a paternalistic character where the trustee claimed a full discretionary power to act in the interests of the beneficiary. As Gough has shown, this broad conception of government as a trust from God was fully exploited by the Stuarts. Later, a similarly broad view of trusteeship was to be part of the Burkean idea of the independent representative. Locke is, by contrast, ready to employ the restricted term 'deputy' in place of trustee. Accountability is essential to his case, whether or not he adequately describes the requisite institutions for accounting. The ultimate objective of entrusting power is, of course, the defence of property in accordance with law. This is more narrowly defined in what is an abstract summary of traditional European constitutionalism (142). Four 'bounds' are set by society and nature to the governments of any civil state:

(i) to govern by settled laws;
(ii) that the laws should be for 'the good of the People', which implies the defence of rights;
(iii) that government may not raise taxes without the consent of the people or of their representatives;
(iv) that the legislative may not transfer the law-making power to any other body.

These bounds apply to the 'legislative Power of every Commonwealth, in all Forms of Government' and serve to emphasise that civil government refers to a manner of ruling. Just as it is compatible with more than one economic system, so it is also compatible with more than one form of government. Locke's treatment of the forms of government, which had exercised political thinkers since Aristotle, is, therefore, quite perfunctory, occupying only two paragraphs in length (132–3). The early *First Tract on Government* similarly discusses the legislative power as such, 'not considering the form of government or number of persons wherein it is placed'.[26] The important distinction for Locke was between civil government on the one hand and absolute arbitrary power on the other, whether despotic or paternal. The people (i.e. the majority) may institute itself as the legislative body, constituting a perfect democracy, or it may authorise a few (oligarchy), or one man (monarchy, which may be elective or hereditary). Alternatively it may establish any mixed form it pleases. David Hume was therefore strictly incorrect when he accused Locke of identifying civil government with the government of England.[27] That Locke believed that a somewhat rationalised version of the English constitution approached most closely the condition of civility is, however, correct and it is to this version of civil government that he devotes most of his attention.

The people may establish whatever form of government it thinks fit. So long as the supreme legislative power acts according to the trust placed in it the people may not resume any direct sovereignty. Where the legislative breaks its trust the people may act to change the form of government in a manner which will more effectively safeguard property rights. The original form of government is not necessarily sacrosanct. Unlike nearly all of his contemporaries, Locke displays no interest in a historical ancient constitution.[28] It is the act of trust which is fundamental and inviolable, yet which permits of a historical evolution as a society searches to achieve the best approximation to civility. Thus Locke is fully prepared to allow that the first forms of government may have been monarchy exercised by the patriarch. Men placed government with those whom they most trusted. Only later experience could show that political power might be abused and become a threat to the very rights it was supposed to secure. Government needed to be further civilised by being brought under law (110–11). The history of a particular country may, therefore, be one in which successive attempts have been made to modify the form of government in order better to promote the basic ends of political society as such. At the same time, each modification can be explained as a restoration of the true foundations of the body politic. Other Whigs saw English history replete with events which were reaffirmations of an original contract.[29] Locke's argument is at a much more abstract level but has similar implications. The English constitution could be interpreted on Lockean lines as the outcome of the ebb and flow of attempts to maintain the principles, not of an original contract, but of the trust originally invested in government, and 1688 could be viewed as the most recent restoration of the civil government to its true principles.

Among the procedures established by the fundamental act of consent is the franchise. This is decided by the people on whatever basis it may choose when investing the legislative with supreme power (157–8). The extent of the franchise is not determined, as Macpherson suggests, by any distinction between express and tacit consenters. Locke offers no explanation of why some might possess the vote and others do not. In this respect his account is less intellectually satisfactory than Macpherson's![30] One might speculate that lesser property owners might defer to the greater landowners whose interests as property owners were in Locke's scheme of things identical, but who could be presumed more experienced in the management of property in general, and better able to check threats and abuses by the political elite. Through them the whole nation would be represented (158). Such a theory of virtual representation was understood by Locke's contemporaries, including Shaftesbury, and was to find increasing favour in the next century. It is also consistent with a somewhat paternalist attitude. Moreover it has an affinity with the other pillar of Macpherson's case, namely, the imputation to Locke of a theory of differential rationality, where the poor are too engrossed in the burdens of subsistence to have the leisure to develop their minds sufficiently to judge on matters of state. These remarks, scattered through Locke's epistemological and theological writings, are somewhat inconclusive for politics. The poorest man is able to reason sufficiently to understand his own affairs, to devote his Sundays to the contemplation of his salvation and to make bargains for wages, sometimes even to his own advantage. The argument is not extended to the political sphere. This must, therefore, remain speculation since Locke nowhere explained why the people might 'pitch upon' a form of government in which some amongst themselves were excluded from directly expressing an equal voice in affairs of state. Historical and economic reasons are, of course, readily to hand but no philosophical justification is forthcoming. The gap was recognised by Charles Leslie, one of Locke's earliest critics:

> When did all the people of England (for example) choose the free-holders to be worth so much per annum?
> If they did not, then not only every individual had no vote, but much the major part of them had none. And they all had lives and liberties to dispose of, as well as the rest.[31]

Even if Locke's fundamental act of trust is understood in the evolutionary sense indicated above, Leslie's questions remain pertinent.

Disillusionment with early patriarchal monarchy set in when men discovered that, with the growing prosperity of the society, their property began to tempt the very leaders they had established to protect it. The argument was familiar in much natural-law thinking. Hooker had employed it briefly in the sections of Book I of *The Laws of the Ecclesiastical Polity*, which Locke liked to cite.[32] Locke translates the argument into his language of trust. Monarchs began to believe that their interests were distinct from those of their subjects (111), and employ their prerogative power to act beyond the limited trust which was implicit in their very first institution, but which men in their innocence had not thought it necessary to specify. Excesses made it necessary to re-examine the '*Original* and Rights of *Government*; and to find out ways to *restrain the Exorbitance*, and *prevent the Abuses* of that Power which they having intrusted in another's hands only for their own good, they found was made use of to hurt them' (111). It became clear that the political elite could not be trusted. Human nature is always a mixture of self-interest and sociability, but positions of power provide opportunities for the pursuit of private interests which too many find unable to resist. Men are apt to grasp after power. Political experience teaches an apparent paradox. Government must be entrusted to men whom one distrusts.[33] The paradox is resolved by placing government under such constraints that politicians find it extremely difficult to promote their own advantage except in such ways as will benefit their subjects. If men cannot be trusted in politics, institutions must be found which can be trusted. Locke turned for a remedy for absolutism to the traditional European constitutionalist ideas of the rule of law as embedded in English practice. But instead of producing a legalistic defence of English institutions backed by a form of historical scholarship, he attempted a rationalised version of constitutionalism, abridged and reduced to more general propositions.

The first proposition was that the legislative should be bound to rule by promulgated standing laws. Locke accepts that the supreme power in a state is the legislative, which is the first principle of modern sovereignty theory. Nevertheless, despite the ridicule of both Filmer and Hobbes, he affirms that this supreme power is, in the traditional phrase, 'below the law'. Supreme power is entrusted to the legislative conditionally on its governing according to law. Its power is 'political' and thus limited to the protection of property right. Being the supreme power it is the first which may be open to abuse. The danger is counteracted firstly by the nature of law itself which must be general in scope, dealing with categories of actions and rights and indifferent as between particular persons. The legislative cannot, therefore, pass a law which would exempt any particular individuals from its jurisdiction or from the operation of any other law. A government cannot rightfully declare by law members of its own party to be immune from any legislation.

The legislative power is also itself bound by the laws it makes. Members of the legislative have two capacities – their representative capacity and their private capacity. Outside the legislative assembly they are private men and, like all other private citizens, are subject to the law (138). Whilst in session Locke believed that members of a parliament were properly exempt from the ordinary operations of the law. They could not be imprisoned or pursued for debt and, to this day, they cannot in Britain be sued for libel or slander for utterances inside the debating chamber. Such exemption was an argument against maintaining a legislative in permanent session. When members of a parliament knew that, upon dissolution of the assembly, they would be subject to the full severity of the law, they would be dissuaded from any attempt to subvert property because it would equally subvert their own. This, as Locke says, is 'a new and near tie upon them, to take care, that they make them [laws] for the publick good' (143). The deterrent would not be effective if the interests of the ruling group were totally distinct from those of the ruled. In such a case the government might pass perfectly general laws which did not affect their own interests. Locke shows no concern for this possibility. Believing all members of society to be in the widest sense property owners, he could assume that any law affecting property owners affected all alike. Differences in the scale of property holding he did not regard as differences in kind. Defining property in the narrower sense, land was an interest which should unite government and governed. He did not need to guard against the destruction of the property system so much as the possibility of the political elite surrounding the Stuarts abusing power in such a way as to accumulate property and rights at the expense of 'the people'. Only with the extension of the franchise in the nineteenth century did British thinkers have to concern themselves with the danger of class legislation by a majority with no interest of their own in property in its narrower sense. Locke's defence was against absolutism not collectivism. Nevertheless, Locke does not admit majority legislative tyranny by the back door to the extent described by Willmoore Kendall.[34] Whilst it is correct that within its allotted sphere a majority vote of the legislative exercises undoubted supremacy, the limited character of what is political and the legal limitations on the legislative constitute significant restrictions incompatible with the absolutism Kendall attributes to Lockean government.

Having brought the legislative under law, Locke turns his attention to the executive power which is established by trust to remedy the lack of an enforcing authority in the state of nature. The executive power must also be subject to the ordinary law. It exists to administer in specific cases the general laws passed by the legislative. It is, therefore, normally subordinate to the legislative power. Whilst subordinate in function, it should ideally have a standing of its own distinct from that of the legislative. The separation of powers has, since the American Constitution, become one of the most celebrated devices for preventing civil government from degenerating into absolutism. Locke's own formulation is designed in the first place to stop members of the legislative exempting either themselves or their friends and associates from the application of the law. The rule of law has already prohibited them from passing a law which declares individuals or groups A and B to be exempt. Separation of powers is designed to prevent legislators from issuing orders to the police, the courts or the civil service, not to apply a perfectly general law to A and B. A legislative assembly could therefore neither legislate nor issue executive commands to stop a citizen taking the government, or a member of it, to court for an alleged crime, or prohibit the police from investigating some alleged corruption. Legislators cannot 'suit the Law, both in its making and execution, to their own private advantage' (143).

If the legislative may not assume executive power, neither may the executive usurp or absorb the superior legislative power. Either action would constitute the assumption of absolute power which could permit of no superior judgement. Locke does not, however, find mixed systems incompatible with the separation of powers. His discussion of constitutional forms is transparently based on the British system in which the executive, in the person of the monarch, plays a part in the legislative process through the need for royal assent. The matter is thus one of degree. Such an executive may share but not monopolise the law-making power (151). Locke is then put to some pains to explain in what sense such a monarch may be termed 'supreme', a term he had originally reserved for the legislative. Monarchical supremacy is said to consist in the combination of the legislative share and the ultimate executive authority. Even this executive authority arises from the law. Although oaths of allegiance are taken to the monarch, they are taken to him only in his capacity as supreme executor of the law. The monarch merely represents the law and where he acts outside the law he loses this representative character and becomes, in this respect, a private person who cannot command obedience.[35]

Although the executive is generally bound within the framework of law, Locke assigns it to a wide range of functions which accord with English practice of his day rather than pertain necessarily to the executive branch of any and every civil society. The text of Chapters XII and XIII is essentially a commentary on the English constitution designed to show how its several institutions owe their authority to the fundamental terms of the political society.

Whilst the legislative ought not to be in permanent session, the task of executing law is a continuing one. The executive also possesses the prerogative power which is a power to act for the public good outside the close confines of law and even, on occasion, against the letter of civil law (160). No constitutional writer of the seventeenth century could deny a legitimate place for the royal prerogative, however much, like Locke, he may have sought to insist upon the rule of law. In essence the prerogative was an emergency power to be used for *salus populi* and the aim of the constitutionalists was to make certain that its use was confined to emergencies. The danger in the Stuart use of prerogative, as in the Ship Money case, was that it threatened to turn a legitimate emergency power into part of the ordinary operations of government and thereby remove these from the supervision of law. Locke's solution is to argue that although prerogative lies beyond ordinary law – indeed that is its definition – its proper use is delimited less formally by trust – the supreme act of the political community.

Some aspects of prerogative power, such as the power of pardon, are relatively uncontroversial, although to grant a pardon to a servant or associate of the executive can raise genuine political issues, as has been recognised from Locke's day to the twentieth-century instance of a presidential pardon for former President Nixon. Locke would also permit a dispensing power to the executive which would allow it to set aside the law in particular cases. As in seventeenth-century law, the dispensing power was permitted on grounds of public interest, but whereas the common law sought to limit the power by court precedents, Locke defines its authority by reference to the less precise terms of the trust placed in the executive. This is typical of the relationship between Locke's abstract principles and the concrete detail of the English common law. Locke derives a great deal from English constitutional practices but translates these practices into ideals. The dispensing power is a further power open to abuse and suspect to constitutionalists who fear that the executive may decide on grounds of public interest to set aside the rule of law and, for instance, not prosecute offences alleged against a prominent politician who has wide popular support, or a member of the executive who might divulge damaging information or, a common modern example, a foreign terrorist whose conviction would lead to reprisals.

The two major powers Locke assigns to the prerogative place the executive in the midst of politics and, indeed, of crucial constitutional controversies of the seventeenth century, which have also had their counterparts in subsequent centuries. These are the powers to call the legislative and dissolve it, and to call elections and determine the form of election. The existence and powers of the legislative are established by the supreme act of trust. The frequency of parliaments and the length of their sessions are another matter. The legislatve power should not be in permanent session. It is, however, difficult to establish in advance the emergencies which may arise and require legislative attention. It therefore makes sense for the original constitution to place the duty of calling parliaments in the hands of the permanent executive power. This is part of the trust vested in the executive and is not to be regarded as a superior power which permits it to dispense with the legislative when it finds convenient. The continuity and permanence of Parliament as an institution by right was notoriously a central constitutional issue of seventeenth-century England. The Stuarts had secured the repeal of the Triennial Bill of 1641 which had required the calling of a Parliament every three years, and the executive was hence constitutionally at liberty to call or dissolve Parliament at will. Only the practical need to obtain money through Parliament preventing the monarch from ruling without it, as he succeeded in doing from 1681 to 1685. The establishment of regular parliaments, preferably on an annual basis, was a leading element in the Whig programme of Shaftesbury. That Locke should have left the status of parliaments on the shaky foundation of the prerogative is therefore somewhat surprising.[36] It is true that failure to call the legislative within an unspecified length of time would constitute a breach of trust and might warrant censure or even resistance. Locke, typically, appears to emphasise flexibility rather than the strictest legalism. Nevertheless, the alternative was obvious to him and he leaves it an open question (153, 156) whether the original constitution might lay down fixed terms for the legislative, and hence a right of assembly (the method adopted by the American Constitution), or allow the legislative to determine its own dissolution and reassembly, or establish some mixture of constitutional limit and executive prerogative (the ultimate British constitutional position and instituted in 1694).

The extent of the franchise and the distribution of electoral districts are instituted, in Locke's view, by the same constitutional act which established the legislative. This act entrusted power to the legislative on condition that it did not attempt to alter the terms of its own constitution, which would amount to the illegal transfer of supremacy to a 'different' body. Social and economic changes bring about considerable changes in the distribution of population, making the original electoral districts very unequal in size and some even totally unpopulated. There is, therefore, a clear need for a more equal redistribution (157). According to Locke's principles, reallocation cannot be undertaken by the legislative, which has an established interest in the existing distribution. The only power which can, therefore, restore the electoral system to its original equality is the executive, exercising its prerogative to over-ride the law for the sake of the supreme law of the good of the people, implicit in the original constitution (158). Locke was, however, on dangerous ground as he well knew. The Stuarts, recognising that in practice government without Parliament was an impossibility, set out on the obvious alternative policy of controlling parliaments. Both Charles II and James II attempted to achieve this objective by changing the electoral system so as to secure favourable parliamentary majorities. Campaigns were mounted to 'remodel' the boroughs by revoking the charters which frequently granted the franchise, and replacing them with new charters which would have the effect of enfranchising supporters of the monarchy. The policy was in itself effective and was only ruined from the royalist standpoint by the capacity of James II to alienate even his new Parliamentary supporters by his religious policy. It was a well-recognised tool for political absolutism and such misuse is listed by Locke as a prime sign of impending tyranny. A prerogative power entrusted to restore the true constitution is being used to enable the executive to set up as a distinct interest from the people and dominate the legislative, destroying the separation of powers.

Locke's dilemma is that on his principles he cannot place this power anywhere other than with the prerogative that he and his associates so much feared. Laslett is correct in saying that Locke is 'dealing with a problem of his own making' (footnote to 158). At the same time, the alternative raises problems which have troubled constitutionalists. To allow the legislative to alter the terms of its own election or re-election is also an invitation to corruption. After 1688 the Whigs attempted both to restore the old borough charters and in turn to purge them to ensure their own control. British and American readers may compare the modern experience of the revision of electoral districts by boundary commissions and by the Supreme Court's decision on equal apportionment. In Britain changes recommended by the commission must be enacted by Parliament, but governments have been notoriously reluctant to put through changes which would harm their own party at the next election. In the United States redistribution was enforced by the outside agency of the Court but similarly still requires legislative enactment. Thus Locke's reluctance to place the function of redistribution with the legislative is understandable and betrays again his concern for the rule of law, even if his solution is so problematic. Locke failed to take his constitutionalism so far as to incorporate within the basic constitutional act some impartial means for the revision of the constitution. It was not until the American Constitution that anything akin to this simple yet imaginatively significant step was to be taken.

Despite Locke's assertion of legislative supremacy, he is as anxious to prevent legislative as to prevent executive abuse. Civil government should not permit either to dominate to the exclusion of the basic law of the constitution. Legislative supremacy cannot imply unilateral action to eliminate or restrict powers originally vested in the executive. In this respect, Locke is less a Parliamentary man than many of his Whig colleagues, and his constitutional conservatism has more affinities with older common lawyers like Coke, despite Locke's abstract and non-legal language. The third branch of government, the 'federative power' dealing with the external affairs of the political society, is also separated from the legislative. Like the other powers, it derives from the executive right of the law of nature. It consists in the right to enforce the law of nature against those who are not in a civil relationship with the political society. The federative power, therefore, protects the society and its members against injuries from foreign states and individuals who are in a state of nature *vis-à-vis* the political community. No aggressive policy is thereby condoned since the federative power is governed by the principles of the law of nature which allow the use of force only for punishment and reparation. It would appear to follow that a particular state could employ this federative power for the general policing of the world community, coming to the assistance of another society whose natural rights were threatened. Nevertheless, Locke nowhere explores this, possibly sensing that this would be to place the preservation of the state in question. There is, however, little justification for supposing[37] that the principle of self-preservation permits an unrestrained policy of *raison d'état* in foreign relations. Political and economic agreements between states are binding under natural law as would be individual contracts in a state of nature. Locke does not assert the prior right of self-preservation or state preservation over the keeping of promises or contracts. Instead, he allows individual or state to take action against injury, i.e. breach of right, and, it may be presumed, particularly where such injury calls into question the right of subsistence. Whilst Cox is correct in pointing to the uncertainties of the state of nature between sovereign nations, the tendency to identify this with a state of war seems an exaggeration. Locke's discussion of the limits to the right of conquest can give little comfort to a true believer in *raison d'état*, whilst in his discussion of trade he simply dismisses the possibility that nations can any longer acquire wealth by conquest – a speculation clearly premature and which admittedly appears somewhat odd in the light of his own preoccupations with the colonies.[38] Peter Laslett has made the interesting suggestion that the federative power was indeed that exercised over colonies such as America.[39] This would certainly help to justify the interventionist economic policy in the colonies, in which Locke fully participated, and the extent to which a civil government might treat them as akin to estates for commercial exploitation in a manner incompatible with the civil conduct expected in home economic policy. The difficulty, as John Dunn has noted,[40] is to define in this case the extent to which colonials, or their governors, were also in a civil relationship with their home government. The discussion of the federative power is too limited to press the case, and the possibility of interpreting the American Revolution as centring on just this very confusion of status is, no doubt, as Laslett has stated, succumbing too readily to the temptations of hindsight.

Internally the distinct status of the control over external affairs reflects once more Locke's constitutional conservatism. The federative power will normally be wielded by the executive since both require a condition of permanent readiness. Yet the English monarch's traditional control over foreign affairs was one of the occasions for internal tension of which the raising of moneys by prerogative was merely one instance. Nevertheless, on practical grounds, Locke sees no need to bring foreign affairs under any stricter control than is laid down in the conditions of trust. Although exercised by the same person or body, the federative power is juridically quite distinct from the executive. The executive power is normally wielded in accordance with the 'antecedent, standing, positive laws, partly stemming from the constitution and partly supplemented by legislation. The federative power is much more flexible – from the need to react to the unanticipated conduct of outsiders – and it clearly cannot be wielded over those who are in a civil relationship with the government. How far this may be an abstract way around the problems of a Ship Money case is again a matter of speculation, but it is arguable that in a Lockean civil regime it could be contended that the raising of taxes for foreign defence would be a misuse of the federative power in the internal conduct of government.

Each branch of government holds power on trust, a notion which, as has been seen, implies both a certain discretionary power for the trustee as well as an implicit framework of ground rules to ensure that the trustee discharges his duties. It is this discretionary power which makes the role of Lockean government difficult to delimit exactly, but which also makes Locke's stance more persuasive than the more thorough-going individualism of Hobbes. Within the framework of law and trust the government may – as it cannot for Hobbes – require the individual to sacrifice himself for the public good as a soldier (129) or it may – as it can for Hobbes – order a subject's house to be pulled down to prevent a fire spreading. There needs be some assurance that the authority and flexibility which government requires is not abused. Ideally, the trustee should be so sincerely convinced of the legitimacy of these basic rules that he can be trusted, in the informal sense of the word, to carry out the functions assigned to him. Where, however, the political leaders, whether legislative, executive or federative, cannot be entirely trusted because of their tendency to grasp at power, attention must turn to how far political and social institutions can be trusted to restrain them.

Locke's array of limitations is considerable, beginning with the fundamental notion of the independence of the man of property whose rights may not be arbitrarily invaded. They range through the rule of law binding governments and subjects, high and low, to the separation of government powers. All belong to a recognisable, rather conservative, common law tradition, albeit transformed from a basis in citable precedent into the status of rational principles. They do not, however, comprise all the constraints against despotism which formed the repertoire of many of Locke's contemporaries. Although sometimes regarded as the archetypal Whig political theorist, he stands apart from the very significant tradition of thought which took its starting point from the writings of the republican works of Machiavelli and from Harrington.[41] The neo-Harringtonians saw the chief danger to liberty arising from a Court which was undermining an ancient, free and balanced constitution by governing through political corruption, whereby the executive controlled the legislative, bureaucracy and a standing army, all of which required to be financed by high taxation and debts which further threatened the independence of the propertied man. That Locke showed some of these preoccupations is not surprising. The neo-Harringtonian remedies were not, however, the same. They sought a balance of property which would be reflected in the balance of power between king, lords and commons, a subject in which Locke showed little interest, unless one sees it reflected in his passing comments on the unrepresentative franchise and on the concentration of economic power in London. Locke warned of the dangers of the executive influencing the election of the legislative and its debates but he did not make much use of the terminology of 'corruption' favoured by the neo-Harringtonians, although there is one relevant example at 222. Locke complains on many occasions of the laziness and frivolity of the country gentry and their insensitivity to their social, intellectual and political obligations, and urges them to recall their duty to themselves and to God to improve themselves. There is, however, no expectation of the emergence of the civic spirit which was so essential to the Harringtonians. Locke's political theory, far from being predicated on classical humanism, is designed to operate with men prone to error and partiality. He has more in common, in this respect, with Hume and Madison than with many of the eighteenth-century Whigs. Perhaps most significantly he displays no interest in their fears that a standing army under the command of the executive would be a continuing threat to liberty, or in their support for an independent citizen militia of country gentlemen who would defend their freedoms as they would their hearth and home. He ignores the question, even though politically it found expression in some of Shaftesbury's utterances and intellectually it might have lent support and conviction to his theory of resistance.

The ultimate restraint on government is the right of resistance. There is no form of government which can institutionally guarantee that the political leadership abide by law. To suggest, as has been done, that Locke offers more a theory of resistance than a theory of government, is an unfortunate exaggeration. Civil government is a distinctive government of law which, in Locke's version, permits a broad discretion to office-holders and which in stable times may be counted both politically reasonable and sensitive to the general character of law. In more troubled and distrustful times, however, this discretion may be regarded as an invitation to abuse and corruption. The late eighteenth-century era of the written constitution saw attempts by such as Bentham to write down law in such detail that governmental discretion would be eliminated – thereby endangering the liberty the constitution sought to protect. It is, however, extremely doubtful if any such measures can be sufficient to withstand determined corruption and, as Locke is keen to point out, a right of resistance in the case of necessity is acknowledged by many of the most authoritarian political thinkers.

Locke's theory of resistance must show in what general circumstances it is legitimate to resist government, and yet reassure readers that neither the act of resistance nor the explanation of its possible legitimacy is subversive of either political authority or private property. At the same time, by drawing his illustrative material from obviously English sources, Locke is able to hint at the legitimacy of past and more recent acts of resistance and at their stabilising consequences.

What can justify resistance? The answer in one word is 'tyranny'. It is one of those political terms, like 'despotism' or 'democracy' which once had a specific meaning but which became vague terms of political denigration or commendation. Locke gives it its fundamental meaning in a phrase which captures what civil government and the rule of law means for him: *'Where-ever Law ends, Tyranny begins,* if the Law be transgressed to another's harm' (202). The employment of force outside the bounds of law is an act of war. Although the greatest danger of acts of war arising occurs in the uncertain conditions of the state of nature, it is crucial to Locke's argument that such acts may occur also within a political society and be performed both by subjects and rulers. It is this logical and practical possibility which most marks off Locke's conception of a state of war from that of Hobbes. Tyranny and war are therefore defined by law, which in turn will be a combination of the original constitutional act of trust and of the positive laws which have been framed in accordance with that constitution. Government is a matter of authority which is delimited by law and trust. The rights of any ruler or subordinate official extend only so far as they are stipulated in law. Where either ruler or official steps beyond the law to the detriment of the rights of the subject, he loses authority and is reduced to the status of any private man.

> And whosoever in Authority exceeds the Power given him by the Law, and makes use of the Force he has under his Command, to compass that upon the Subject, which the Law allows not, ceases in that to be a Magistrate, and acting without Authority, may be opposed, as any other Man, who by force invades the Right of another. (202).

In support, Locke cites instances out of the common law of England which limit the authority of government even in the execution of acts which are not tyrannical but actually in the general interest. Thus an official might not in England break into a person's house in order to serve a writ, even though he might properly serve it on that person outside. There can be no authority to break the law in order to enforce another law (202, 206), nor can superior commands excuse an official from respecting law – 'against the laws there can be no Authority'. Modern counterparts are not hard to discover, as some of the incidents brought to light by the investigations of Watergate would indicate.

If such infringements may be cited as examples of tyranny, still more must be cases of government conduct which contravene the whole spirit of the fundamental trust placed in it. The private subject may summarily eject the official who breaks into his house but the people at large possesses a similar right when the government – or one of its component branches – displays such a consistent trend in the breach of trust that any reasonable man must conclude that there is a settled design to establish a tyranny (210). Such a design can be recognised in general terms where any executive power seeks to usurp entirely the function of the legislative, or ceases to enforce the law impartially, and when the legislative places itself above the law or subverts the executive by exempting itself from law. All such activities constitute a direct attack on property rights or a recognisable threat to them, and the people need not be expected to wait until its rights have been virtually destroyed before resisting (220, 235).

Any form of government is liable to tyrannical subversion whereby will replaces law (201). The precise means by which tyranny can be introduced can therefore only be examined in relation to the form of government established by the original constitution. Locke suggests that one can examine as an instance how tyranny may arise in a constitution where a single hereditary person has supreme executive power, combined with the power of convoking and dissolving the legislature, which in turn is composed of an assembly of hereditary nobility and an assembly of elected representatives (213). He writes as if the resemblance of this example to the English constitution might be considered by his readers as merely fortuitous! Locke then proceeds to describe how absolutism might arise in such a constitution and, in doing so, to list many of the charges which were levelled by the Whigs against the conduct of both Charles II and James II. At the same time, they are instances of breaches of the rule of law which, without too much stretching of the imagination, can be recognised as having their modern analogues.

Firstly, the executive may attempt to displace the legislative by making his mere will the law or, more subtly, by executing rules which were never passed as laws by the legislative. In effect, this is legislating under the pretence of administering (214). If one were to seek a modern counterpart, it might be in the penumbral region of delegated legislation and administrative discretion where official practice may deviate from the intention of the original legislation and where legal recourse is difficult. Secondly, the executive may fail to call the legislative at the proper time or may call it, but subject it to pressure intended to impede its freedom of debate. In this case a parliament is a mere façade unable to exercise its genuine powers (215). Locke probably has in mind the Parliament of 1681 called by Charles II at traditionally loyal Oxford where it would be more subject to royalist pressure. Again, the phenomenon of façade legislatives is too widespread for it to require emphasising that Locke's concern can be of wider relevance. Thirdly, the executive may tamper with the electoral machinery so as to produce a legislative sympathetic to its interests. This may be achieved by altering the franchise or electoral districts, as both Charles II and James II had done, or by bribing and intimidation of the electorate (216, 222). Fourthly, the executive may bribe the elected members of Parliament either in a direct monetary way or by providing them, their families or associates with well-paid government offices or contracts in return for their Parliamentary votes – the 'corruption' against which the neo-Harringtonians of the eighteenth century protested. Whether described as 'corruption', 'influence' or 'patronage' this has become a complaint renewed at many periods when executive power has appeared to predominate in civil governments which otherwise are predicated on some degree of balance. For Locke its effect is again to preserve the façade but to subvert the real independence of legislative debate by ensuring that issues will be prejudged (222). It is a conception of legislative activity which does not necessarily deny entirely the role of party but which distinctly requires sufficient financial independence from the executive to support political dissent from it where it is morally demanded.

Fifthly, the executive may subvert the legislative and the whole government if it hands over authority to a foreign power. This would be in breach of the original determination to establish an independent body politic (217). Although such a voluntary surrender of authority may appear unlikely, Locke expresses the fear that a ruler might, by adopting the Catholic religion, defer to the authority of the Pope who was himself a temporal ruler and a political ally of regimes associated in the Whig mind with absolutism. This is a clear reference to Charles II. Locke also regards the surreptitious introduction of Catholic practices into the official religion as one of the warning signs of absolutism (210). The limits of Locke's toleration are here apparent. Where a religion is inherently a threat to order or connected with the interests of a foreign power, it ceases to be purely private and enters the civil realm and may be subject to coercion. This is not, however, a general invitation to the suppression of religious sects. Indeed, Locke argues that this would do more to arouse resistance and unrest than could possibly arise from free religious rivalry.[42] Locke expresses here the kind of confidence that the peaceful battle of books would replace religious war, which was to be more typical of the eighteenth century, and contrasts sharply with his fears in the early *Tracts*. Whilst it is unconstitutional to surrender government to a foreign power, Locke saw in his 1694 revision that it was necessary to distinguish this very clearly from the case where a ruler of a foreign nation is called in, as William had been in 1688, to uphold the system of government (239). Locke has throughout emphasised the role of the executive in subversion, as having, in his view, the greatest opportunity under such a constitution since a legislative cannot act independently of executive assent. Nevertheless, to the extent that the legislative is an accomplice, it is equally guilty (218).

These, then, are the circumstances in which the original constitution of such a nation would have been broken. On what grounds would this justify resistance? Government, as has been seen, is a matter of trust. Power was entrusted by the people in the body politic conditional upon its being used for the better protection of property. So long as the legislative governs according to trust, the people cannot resume the power vested in it by the constituent individuals. The legislative is supreme. In what Hobbes would have regarded as a nonsensical manner, Locke reserves an ultimate supremacy to the people. Where power is misused by the government, it is forfeit and reverts, as in any trust, to the trustor. The people can never surrender this fundamental right of protecting private property when it is endangered by the very powers set up for its protection (243). The people may then remove power from the trustee and may decide to exercise legislative power itself, or may reconstitute the legislative along lines which will achieve more effectively the original objectives of the community. In a sense, therefore, resistance requires little or no justification, since the power belongs to the people, is exercised on trust and the very abuse justifies the restoration of authority to its source.

Clearly, however, this is not sufficient to remove the stigma of sin from the notion of political resistance. Critics of the Whigs, still arguing along patriarchal lines, sought to suggest that their political principles would call into question the legitimacy of property and of the entire social order. Charles Leslie, again showing a typically Filmerian mixture of oddity and shrewdness, argues that a father like a king may make concessions limiting his power, but that this does not allow me (his son) to eject him if he breaks his promises so that

> I may lawfully lay hands upon him, turn him out of doors, and seize upon his house and inheritance for myself. This priniciple would dissolve all relations, as 'twixt children and parents, so betwixt King and subjects, servants and masters, and in short, of whole mankind.[43]

If such writers believed in liberty and consent they would 'call a council of their wives, children, and servants' who would meet and set 'rules for the government of [the] family',[44] with implied disastrous effects on social hierarchy, since Leslie reasserts what Locke had denied, that a 'Kingdom . . . is but a great family'. Locke must clearly show that the right of resistance will neither undermine property nor dissolve the social tie, but instead will strengthen both. Locke, therefore, performs an intellectual manoeuvre common in political thought, whereby the vocabulary undergoes a shift. He divorces the notion of 'resistance' from that of 'rebellion', and seeks to attach the opprobrium of 'rebellion' to the action of government as much as to that of individuals, or factions.[45] Authority is once more the central concept. Rebellion is defined as opposition to 'Authority which is founded only in the Constitutions and laws of the Government' (226). Anyone who systematically acts in opposition to law and constituted authority is therefore a rebel. The term may describe not merely the leader of a lawless mob or faction, but any government or branch of government which sets out to subvert the very authority on which it rests. Indeed, history shows that those most frequently guilty of rebellion have been rulers who have sought to forget their office and establish themselves as a distinct interest in society. It is they, rather than the people, who have the power and greatest opportunity for rebellion (230).

Having designated rulers who are in breach of trust as rebels, Locke can describe popular resistance as intended to put down rebellion by government. Edmund Burke was to defend the American colonists in this way in their revolt against the 'rebellion' of the British government which had ruled America without regard to the traditional rights of British subjects. With this argument, Locke is calling on a traditional

English theory of constititutional resistance interpreted in rationalist terms and without needing to cite historical precedents, as other authors of the period did, whether of a supposed Anglo-Saxon constitution or of Magna Carta. Locke perceives English history as comprising a number of such acts of resistance or 'revolutions', most of which have been provoked by the misuse of executive prerogative but in some of which legislators have been allies and thus also guilty of rebellion. Resistance has been intended not to destroy prerogative but, upon its abuse, to define it more strictly in accordance with its original discretionary purpose. Rulers have only themselves to blame if this prerogative requires definition. In the hands of wise, law-abiding rulers the prerogative has been at its greatest and it is a paradox that it is under such rulers that liberty is most at risk when vigilance relaxes, thus allowing less able or less scrupulous successors to turn a discretionary emergency power for good into a routine part of absolutist government (166). There is nothing novel in this. Locke stands in a familiar tradition justifying resistance to 'save the King from the King', to preserve the office from the malpractices of its occupant.

All political resistance is to be understood as restoration. Rebellion breaks with constitution and law; resistance restores government to its founding principles, even if this can involve a change in the form of government in order to establish such principles more securely. Political change, when undertaken in an ordered manner, is compatible with an attitude to government which is not properly 'conservative', nor precisely 'reactionary', but is 'fundamentalist'. As such, it could be consistent with marked change in forms where it had been determined that rule had deviated considerably from the original trust. One possible example might be the occasion in a community's history when it was first found necessary to constrain the discretion of the early patriarchal monarchy by law. At other times the form of government may require little alteration, but a revolution may be required to replace the person of the ruler when he has sought to undermine forms basically satisfactory in themselves. Thus the 'many revolutions' in England have ultimately always 'brought us back again to our old Legislative of King, Lords and Commons' (223). The Preface to the *Two Treatises* places William III in this role of the 'Great Restorer'. Locke is using revolution in its accepted contemporaneous sense of a revolution back to the previous or the original constitution. It was the Restoration of Charles II which was described as a revolution overturning the rebellion of Cromwell, and its supporters were happy to call 1688 a 'Glorious Revolution' in the hope of presenting even an alteration in the royal succession as an act of restoration of the most basic constitutional forms. As John Western so neatly put it, 'the "glorious revolution" of 1688 was so called precisely because so much of it was not in the modern sense revolutionary'.[46] Locke stigmatises absolutism as a 'new' policy

(239). Whether it represents the paternalist or even the managerial attitude to society increasingly typical of Tudor, Stuart and continental absolutism, or the attitude of oriental despotism, it is a policy which no past era of European civil society has found truly acceptable. Novelty was not yet a term of praise in politics.

Resistance is not rebellion and it is not, therefore, inherently sinful. It is not a revolt against the principle of subordination, since in politics subordination rests on authority and where the rebellious ruler flouts authority he loses superiority. The resultant state of war is, therefore, between equals, with right on the side of the party who is defending the law (235). A rebellious king in breach of trust dethrones himself and may be treated like any commoner and even prosecuted: 'For wheresoever the Authority ceases, the King ceases too, and becomes like other Men who have no Authority' (239). Locke, however, does not spell out the appropriate procedure for determining the succession when a king has dethroned himself – the issue latent in the Exclusion Crisis and faced early in 1689 in the debate over the constitutional means whereby William might be declared to have succeeded James. As Whig propaganda for either occasion, it would have been very reticent, the reader being left to infer that since the ultimate trustor of the constitution is the people, it may determine the succession through its legislative representatives or, if they too have proved allies in rebellion, by some directly constituent assembly.

To establish that resistance may be rightful does not, however, establish that there is a duty to resist upon every breach of authority. Nevertheless, Locke recognises that this inference may be made and he prepared to guard himself against charges of fomenting anarchy.

Resistance is the reassertion by the people of the authority granted to it, by the very institution of the body politic, to determine the appropriate procedures for the defence of property. An act of resistance is, therefore, an act taken in the name of the body politic to rectify its own government. It follows that to dissolve government is not to dissolve the social, or even the political, bond (211). Overturning government will, without doubt, introduce considerable uncertainty and danger. Where it is only the person of the executive who is to be changed, as in 1688, the degree of disorder can be limited since the people can express its will for change through its representatives in the legislative which maintains, throughout, its umpiring function. Nevertheless, during this period of change, the execution of the law is in doubt and the legislative, in reforming the executive, is not interfering with the separation of powers, but is to be supposed to represent the people's right to appoint an executive. This was an issue which concerned the 1689 English legislative when it debated its authority to determine the succession and even its own extra-parliamentary status, since it had not been called by the executive.

The situation is more complex where the legislative has itself rebelled, since this is a body whose laws umpire society's disputes. Remove the legislative and what remains? Hobbes's answer was straightforward – the anarchy of the state of war. But for Locke the removal of a rebellious legislative is a step towards ending a war waged by such a legislative. The underlying political community remains. Nevertheless, Locke does not make it clear in what way this community manifests itself, how 'the people' is to be identified or how it is to act when in dispute with its own legislative. That it is the ultimate judge in such a dispute is certain (241–3) and it is also clear that the ultimate means of decision may be force. He does not, as some of his fellow Whigs did, pursue the implications of the right of resistance to the extent of recognising that the power of resisting might require the right to bear arms, and the existence of a citizen militia as a countervailing force and potential rallying point for popular defence. If it were to come to what Locke euphemistically called an 'appeal to Heaven', the advocates of an independent militia would at least be ready for it.

Locke showed rather less concern for such eventualities because, whilst fully aware of the possibility of a clash between legislative and people, he concentrated his attention on conflicts between executive and people where the people would be represented by their legislative. This legislative would be the umpire and also the rallying point for resistance, being composed of the country's leaders and financially independent. So long as the legislative survives as an effective body there remains a court of appeal for society's disputes and the people's complaints of injustice. In conflicts between executive and legislative where the fundamental law is obscure, the ultimate judge will be the legislative, as the body entrusted with the authority of umpirage by expounding and amplifying the rules by which the society will be governed. Popular resistance is only fully justified where the executive has refused to acknowledge the umpirage of the legislative (242), or shows, by its policy of subverting the legislative, that it will not submit to any political judgement. It is the actual or impending destruction of the means of legal arbitration which justifies resistance. Both individuals and people are to be expected to use the means of legal redress until these are either exhausted, or in clear and present danger of being subverted (207). It is when there is no effective appeal to law that the state of war occurs and resistance becomes rightful.

When Locke declares that his theory is not a recipe for instant revolution, he is not merely stating that men are of a conservative disposition and normally unwilling to remedy injustice by force. This is certainly part of his argument. Men will put up with minor and often even major injustices. They will make allowances for mistakes by government as things normal to any human institution (225). They become accustomed to inconvenient laws and forms and are seldom eager for change (223). However, the true reason for delay in resisting is that it is not such mistakes which justify action, but subversion of the processes of arbitration, which generally reveals itself through 'a long train of Abuses, Prevarications and Artifices, all tending the same way' (225).[47] It is when the people recognises a settled 'design' against its procedures for umpirage that it justifiably arouses itself from its acquiescent mood and resists such a breach of the trust it has reposed in its governors.

The right of resistance resides with the people rather than with individuals. The right of individuals to attend to the general policing of society was irrevocably surrendered to the people for as long as the political community survives. Particular individual grievances do not in themselves justify an attempt to mount a general revolt, and the people will not normally base its revolt on the complaints of an individual or a small group (230). This is not to say that Locke is dismissive of injustice to individuals. Every person is entitled to pursue his rights in any court of the realm open to him and if his case is arbitrarily interfered with, he has been done a severe injustice by the authorities. If he has been denied the right to put his case at law, he has been denied the umpirage for which he entered political society. He is then entitled to resist this arbitrary oppression. However, this right is not likely to shake government since, unless the people interests itself in his case, he faces the concerted opposition of the state (208). It is as if an individual who had been the victim of severe injustice in a dispute over the building of a motorway through his land, and had been denied his rights in law, attempted to overturn the government. Locke suggests that the appropriate reaction of the people at large might be sympathy with his dilemma but a determined refusal to believe it justified the chaos of revolution. Equally, the individual should ask himself whether the rectification of injustice in his own case is worth the general disturbance of revolutionary action. It is difficult to find in this a general principle of majority will such as Willmoore Kendall suggests, but rather caution in the face of extreme political danger. Certainly there is no quasi-Hobbesian denial by the majority of the justice of the individual's claim. If such a case were one of many exhibiting a disregard for the fundamental laws, it might be interpreted by the people as clear evidence of a shift to arbitrary government and might precipitate legitimate resistance (209).

No government and no political theory has ever rendered rebellion by subjects impossible. There have always been over-mighty subjects and 'turbulent' spirits ready to pursue mischief and challenge government for their own ends. But such rebels can obtain no justification, Locke asserts, from his doctrine, which condemns all rebels high and low. Legitimate resistance occurs only when the appeal to law is being generally denied. In a constituted government, operating according to the rule of law, it is the simplest matter for government to avoid resistance by adhering strictly to the constitutional forms. In governments where the legislative umpirage has not achieved proper independence from the executive, and which are consequently closer to absolutism and further from civility, the chances of legitimate resistance are presumably greater since the opportunities for legal redress are fewer.[48] In pure absolutism, of course, there is a continuing state of war and right to resist, such as is available to the Christian Greeks under the Turks. A civil government need but observe the constraints of law to make resistance superfluous. The search for political stability can come to an end where government acknowledges law.

Locke's ultimate defence of his theory against the charge of anarchism is perhaps the most cunning in its self-justification. To proclaim the right of resistance and set down with precision the circumstances for its proper exercise is a service to public order. Rebellion is the fundamental crime. The theory of resistance informs those contemplating rebellion that their conduct will meet with resistance. Thus even if the Lockean doctrine of civil government fails to move the consciences of rulers, it may appeal to their sense of self-interest by making them aware of the consequences of arbitrary behaviour on their part. Anticipating the reactions of their subjects, legislative or executive rebels should then desist, bring their conduct into conformity with the law and thus render any actual resistance otiose. The argument is analogous to that sometimes produced in defence of modern elections, that the threat that they will not be re-elected makes governments avoid policies they would otherwise have contemplated introducing. The argument has been termed by C. J. Friedrich the 'rule of anticipated reactions'.[49] Locke's case is thus that his doctrine is the 'best fence against Rebellion' and, at the same time, the doctrine that is in fact the best assurance that resistance should not be required (226). The clear implication is that the defenders of the right of resistance do not deserve the fate of Algernon Sidney, hanged for writing yet unpublished works in similar vein. They should be regarded as truer defenders of order than either a Hobbes or a Filmer, even if they have to defend resistance so that order may be restored. Order, properly understood, is provided by the rule of law, by civil government. It is the defenders of civil government who are the true patriots.

Notes Chapter VI

1 Cited in P. King, *The Life of John Locke*, London, 1830, Vol. 2, p. 89.
2 *Toleration*, pp. 65–7.
3 *A Third Letter for Toleration, Works*, VI, p. 212.
4 *A Second Letter concerning Toleration, Works*, VI, pp. 117–18.
5 Oxford, Oxford University Press, 1961, ch. V.

6 Introduction to his edition of the *Two Treatises*, e.g. p. 118.

7 *Toleration,* p. 67.

8 *The Liberal Politics of John Locke*, pp. 173–6, in part correcting an earlier too extreme interpretation by myself. Seliger also suggests that Locke advocates political constraints against exploitation by property holders, but Locke's case appears to be that property cannot be the ground of political authority any more than can force. I, 42–3.

9 *Some Considerations, Works*, V, p. 11.

10 Much virtue in that 'normally' since the analysis of 'interests' is full of pitfalls which I hope to avoid exploring on this occasion.

11 See the paper 'Venditio' printed by John Dunn, 'Justice and Locke's Political Theory', *Political Studies*, XVII, 1968, pp. 68–87.

12 *The Political Thought of John Locke*, e.g. p. 217.

13 For a brief discussion of the attitudes to primogeniture up to Locke's day, see Joan Thirsk, 'The European Debate on customs of inheritance, 1500–1700', in J. Goody, J. Thirsk and E. P. Thompson (eds), *Family and Inheritance: Rural Society in Western Europe, 1200–1800*, Cambridge, Cambridge University Press, 1976, pp. 177–91.

14 See above, ch. IV.

15 *Further Considerations, Works*, V, p. 146.

16 *Further Considerations, Works*, V, p. 145.

17 *Further Considerations, Works*, V, p. 144.

18 *Some Considerations, Works*, V, p. 62.

19 This point has been noted by Aldo Tassi, 'Two Notions of Consent in Locke's *Second Treatise*', *The Locke Newsletter*, no. 3, spring 1972, pp. 26–31.

20 See D. J. Manning, *The Mind of Jeremy Bentham*, London, Longmans, 1968, ch. 1 for a discussion of strangers and politics.

21 For a discussion of routines see G. Parry and P. Morriss, 'When is a decision not a decision?', in I. Crewe (ed.), *British Political Sociology Yearbook*, Vol. 1, London, Croom Helm, 19774, pp. 317–36. This discussion was itself set off by the work of P. Bachrach and M. Baratz, *Power and Poverty*, New York, Oxford University Press, 1970. See also S. Lukes, *Power*, London, Macmillan, 1974. An article which examines property and inheritance from a similar standpoint is E. P. Thompson, 'The grid of inheritance: a comment', in Goody, Thirsk and Thompson (eds), *Family and Inheritance*, pp. 328–60.

22 *Anarchy, State and Utopia*, p. 152.

23 See above, ch. III, pp. 55–6; *Anarchy, State and Utopia*, p. 181.

24 *Anarchy, State and Utopia*, pp. 250–3.

25 For an excellent discussion of trust in Locke see the chapter in J. W. Gough, *John Locke's Political Philosophy*.

26 *Two Tracts on Government* (ed. Abrams), p. 125.

27 'Of the Original Contract', *Essays*, p. 473.

28 See the classic study by J. G. A. Pocock, *The Ancient Constitution and the Feudal Law*.

29 See Martyn Thompson, 'A Note on "Reason" and "History" in Late Seventeenth-Century Political Thought', *Political Theory*, Vol. 4, no. 4, 1976, pp. 491–504.

30 See above ch. V, pp. 103–8.

31 *The New Association of those called Moderate Church-Men, with the Modern-Whigs and Fanaticks, to Under-Mine and Blow-Up the Present Church and Government*, Part II, London, 1703, p. 5 (italics removed). One can sympathise with Leslie's contemptuous 'Forsooth!' at the end of this diatribe.

32 Hooker, Book I, 10, London, 1594; Scolar Press reprint, Menston, 1969.
33 For a further discussion of this paradox in political theory and con-
    temporary political science, see G. Parry, 'Trust, Distrust and Consensus',
    British Journal of Political Science, 6, April 1976, pp. 129–42 and
    references therein. In an interesting and scholarly article, Richard Ashcraft
    suggests that paternal monarchy represents a second stage of the state of
    nature which is brought to an end by a collective decision to re-examine
    the 'original' of government and institute civil government. 'Locke's State
    of Nature: Historical Fact or Moral Fiction', *American Political Science
    Review*, 62, 1968, pp. 898–914. The present suggestion is that early
    paternal monarchy is already collectively instituted, in what it supposes a
    civil manner, by an over-trusting people. This seems to be the implication
    of § 110 of the *Second Treatise*.
34 *John Locke and the Doctrine of Majority Rule*, especially chs VI and
    VII.
35 Laslett shrewdly notes how Locke uses 'representative' here in an anti-
    thetical sense to Hobbes where the sovereign represents the will of the state
    which can have no existence independent of him.
36 Dunn, *Political Thought of John Locke*, pp. 54–7, also discusses Locke's
    deviation from the policy of Shaftesbury's Whigs on this point.
37 As does Richard Cox, *Locke on War and Peace*, ch. V.
38 *Some Considerations, Works*, V, p. 13.
39 'John Locke, the great recoinage, and the origins of the Board of Trade:
    1695–8', in J. W. Yolton (ed.), *John Locke: Problems and Perspectives*,
    pp. 137–64, especially pp. 158–60.
40 *Political Thought of John Locke*, p. 162, fn. 2.
41 See J. G. A. Pocock's now classic article, 'Machiavelli, Harrington and
    English Eighteenth-Century Ideologies', in his *Politics, Language and
    Time*, London, Methuen, 1972. Also Caroline Robbins, *The Eighteenth-
    Century Commonwealthman*, New York, Atheneum edition, 1968.
42 *Toleration*, pp. 139–41.
43 *Cassandra*, Num. I, 2nd edition, 1705, p. 30.
44 *The New Association etc.*, Part II, pp. 6–7.
45 See the discussion by M. Seliger, 'Locke's Theory of Revolutionary
    Action', *Western Political Quarterly*, XVI, 3, 1963, and *The Liberal
    Politics of John Locke*, pp. 315–20. Seliger, however, finds the limitation
    on the legislative directly in natural law rather than in the original trust.
46 *Monarchy and Revolution*, London, Blandford, 1972, p. 1.
47 The similarity between such passages and the American Declaration of
    Independence has frequently been remarked upon. See Laslett's note to
    225.
48 See also on this point John Dunn, *Political Thought of John Locke*, p.
    182.
49 C. J. Friedrich, *Man and his Government*, New York, McGraw-Hill,
    1963, ch. 11.

Chapter VII

Locke and His Legacies

Intellectual legacies have many characteristics in common with monetary legacies. Once bequeathed they become the property of their new owners who may in general do what they will. Reckless owners may use their new wealth in ways quite removed from the intentions of its original creator. In the world of ideas it is even less possible to control the subsequent career of a person's creation, as the owner of wealth might set conditions to the use of his inheritance by way of a trust. In this respect, Locke's ideas have undergone an experience common to those of such other philosophers as Plato, Aristotle or Rousseau. They have become public knowledge but by being, in an appropriately Lockean manner, also transformed into the private property of subsequent thinkers who have mixed their intellectual labour with them, they have been subject to many reformulations. A series of understandings and misunderstandings have resulted in versions of Locke's ideas to which the adjective 'Lockean' can be applied only if it is recognised as referring not to Locke's original meaning,[1] but at best to some line of intellectual transmission. Yet these legacies are themselves 'facts' of intellectual history as much as the original meaning of the author. Locke's political thought must be explicable in terms of the social forms out of which it has grown, and the intellectual and political problems which Locke saw himself as facing.[2] At the same time, the explanation of the various legacies Locke has been supposed to have left is a different historical and philosophical enterprise which has its own distinct justification, showing how, in other social, intellectual and political circumstances, Locke's 'heirs' or their critics have shaped their inheritance, dispensing with parts of it – such as the theological underpinnings – transmuting others and adding still others.

This process of transformation by both admirers and critics started within Locke's lifetime. It was, however, the *Essay concerning Human Understanding* and the *Reasonableness of Christianity* rather than the anonymous *Two Treatises of Government* which were the subject of interpretative comment. Just as it was from discussing problems of religion and morality that Locke's epistemology first arose, so it was in these spheres that the implications of the *Essay* first caused consternation. John W. Yolton has shown that the *Essay* gave rise to very mixed reactions among theologians.[3] Some amongst the orthodox recognised Locke as achieving his declared purpose of establishing the revealed Christian religion on firmer principles. Others, however, saw, in his epistemology and religion, principles which could only have deistic conclusions. Locke assured his vehement critic, the Bishop of Worcester, that his account of knowledge and certainty left faith untouched and that 'faith still stands upon its own basis, which is not at all altered by it; and every article of that has just the same unmoved foundation, and the very same credibility that it had before'.[4] But this assurance left his critics unmoved, particularly when defenders of natural religion and deism supported their own position on this same basis, and when some amongst them acknowledged their indebtedness to Locke and, like Anthony Collins and, to a much lesser extent, the notorious John Toland, were acquaintances in Locke's late years. Locke's attempts to dissociate himself from deism, in its guise of Socinianism, could not prevent this pursuit of what others found intimated in his own ideas.

Locke's subsequent reputation as, along with his friend Newton, the intellectual founder of the Enlightenment, was also in the course of being established within his lifetime. Again, it was the *Essay* on which this reputation was built and it was through the *Essay* that Locke made his impact on the social and political assumptions of European intellectuals.[5] Outside the English-speaking world the *Two Treatises* made little impact. Here again, it is uncertain how far Locke himself would have acknowledged the purposes to which his ideas were to be put in the name of natural religion and anti-authoritarianism. The elements are there to be found in Locke's own work. The tension in Enlightenment ideas between man as a rational being and as a being capable of reason has been felt by scholars of later ages to underlie Locke's alleged theory of differential rationality, or to 'explain' his ability to draw conservative political conclusions from apparently uncompromising egalitarian premises.

The story of the reception of Locke's political works, including their nineteenth- and twentieth-century careers, has not yet been fully told. The important, pioneering work of John Dunn and of Martyn Thompson[6] has shown that in both America and England the reception of the *Treatises* was altogether more halting than has been frequently supposed. The clear echoes of Locke's language in the Declaration of Independence represent a high point in the Americans' ideological use of the *Treatises*, but the best read of the revolutionaries could call on much else in the European intellectual tradition of republicanism and also in their indigenous political experience to justify their resistance. In England an appeal to historical, constitutional right, however spurious, or simply to prudential considerations of protection, was considered to be more effective justification of the events of 1688 than Locke's references to general principles, which might be indeterminate in their applications. By 1740, however, Hume is able to declare that contractualism 'has become the foundation of our fashionable system of politics, and is in a manner the creed of a party among us'.[7] In the celebrated Essay 'Of the Original Contract', he identifies Locke as the 'most noted of the partisans' of this erroneous doctrine and, by implication, as one of the 'philosophers who have embraced a party (if that be not a contradiction in terms)'.[8] In doing so, Hume, however, has already made the subtle reinterpretation of Locke's thought which has dominated modern readings of Locke.[9] Hume represents Locke's philosophy as an individualist theory of political obligation based on an unsubstantiated and superfluous act of either express or tacit consent. His argument that such a position is illogical and remote from the ordinary practice of mankind is brilliant but, as has already been suggested, it is not precisely the position Locke adopted. Certainly, however, it still strikes home against Locke's criteria for an individual's act of affiliation to a society, even if Locke did not, as Hume supposed, advance a contractual account of the individual's obligation to his ruler. Hume's further suggestion that Locke's idea of civil government is incompatible with the actual practice of human governments is, however, only effective if one rejects Locke's normative attempt to distinguish civil government as a distinct manner of ruling, and instead sides with Hume in believing that political language must emerge from the actual usages of politicians and subjects. The issue may be appreciated in contemporary terms if one asks if the Soviet Union or the present regime in Chile would be in Lockean terms a 'civil government', whether or not either is a state.[10]

Hume had identified Locke as the supreme philosopher of Whiggism but, as he knew, even at this date Lockeanism had its strong rivals in the ideology of the Commonwealthman. Locke was additionally bolstered by his philosophical reputation. He became a figure of respectability to whom radicals of the French Revolutionary era could appeal, quite understandably claiming only the extension of political rights which appeared to follow from the Lockean premises of human equality. The tendency was apparently sufficient to warrant an edition in 1798 by Elrington with commentaries warning readers against interpreting Locke's arguments in a radical, individualist direction.[11] The labour theory of value, the germ of which is to be found in chapter V of the Second Treatise, was, via Ricardo and Marx, to make a singular impact on socialist thought. Most explicitly, early nineteenth-century radicals, like Thomas Hodgskin, were to appeal directly to Locke's natural right of property in defence of the right of every labourer to the product of his labour. Hodgskin perceives this as the logical consequence of the Lockean account of individuality and of personal identity. Cynically, he suggests that every writer since Locke has accepted this as the natural foundation of property and, at the same time, by defending the existing property system, has also denied its egalitarian implications.[12] Ultimately, however, Hodgskin was also defeated in securing the balance between liberty and equality, and his anarcho-liberalism turned into an unmoderated defence of *laissez-faire* and competition.

Locke's respectability was such that by the end of the nineteenth century Sir James Stephen could regard his philosophy as a whole, including the works on toleration and government, as the utterance of the 'commonplaces' of the literature, as the doctrine which one heard all one's life.[13] Nevertheless, these commonplaces are still subject to sundry interpretations, described as the commonplaces of analytical individualism, or of majoritarian democracy, or of bourgeois market assumptions. In some cases, these are interpretations of Locke's supposed historical position. In other cases, as in discussion of Locke as a theorist of majoritarian democracy,[14] the account can only be of some inherent logic in Locke's argument, which would point in this direction if certain historical assumptions are dropped (concerning the identity of 'the people' for instance) and the theory applied to a democratic age unfamiliar to Locke himself. This is a common and sometimes illuminating device of philosophical discussion. Intellectual dangers only arise when, as does occur, this enterprise is confused with the historical inquiry into Locke's own meaning.

Yet the picture of Locke as the theorist of consent and of popular, liberal and democratic government must be regarded as one of his legacies, even if it is one which he could not have intended to bequeath in quite this form. Every considerable philosopher has undergone such a posthumous experience. Whether, as historians are prone to believe, such transformations are totally regrettable is open to question philosophically. It may be, rather, a reflection of the fruitfulness of the original. Is it always 'wrong' to play Shakespeare in the costume of another age? In the face of so many and varied Lockean 'legacies' it may be excusable to concentrate finally on just one of them which, it is arguable, has more affinities with Locke's aims as these have been described here. This is the legacy of civil government and the rule of law.

Intellectuals in politics have a sullied reputation. Ever since Plato's philosopher–kings they have been widely regarded as visionaries seeking to impose an abstract, rigid pattern upon the variety of human life. Hobbes's analogy between the state and a geometrical theorem is a paradigm example, but even Machiavelli, so often viewed as the most practical of political thinkers, has been accused by one of his shrewdest commentators, Herbert Butterfield, of producing a 'Machiavellianism of the Study'. No better instance of an intellectual in politics could be provided than John Locke, yet he does not consciously succumb to the temptation to enforce on others a detailed pattern of life of his own preference. The place of politics amongst the rest of human activities is not, for him, a determining one but is regulatory. In his reflections on politics, Locke resists those theories which hold that order can only occur as a consequence of the imposition of one particular pattern of conformity. The logical conclusion of such a philosophy, he pointed out in his 1667 *Essay on Toleration*, would be to put to death all who persisted in dissent.[15] Instead, the exercise of political power should aim at ensuring how the variety of human endeavours may be accepted and rendered compatible with order.

Locke's starting point is with individuals who recognise themselves as self-determining agents and who regard their capacity for intelligent choice not only as the defining characteristic of human beings, but as something to be cultivated and enjoyed. In Locke's view of the world the cultivation of self-direction and autonomy is both a right and a duty to God, who has purposely endowed men with such capacity. Later thinkers were to abandon these theological foundations and emphasise the pursuit of individuality as a right, or as essential to the equal respect for persons or, with J. S. Mill, as an element in 'utility in its largest sense, grounded in the permanent interests of man as a progressive being'. The idea of individuality became secularised. The doctrine of natural law was increasingly a doctrine of the rights which were inherent in the mutual recognition of men as sharing and enjoying the power of self-determination, without regard to the source of such power. J. S. Mill's account of the rights and duties of the individual is not far removed from that of Locke in its seriousness and intensity. Yet its justification is altogether different, grounded on an eclectic fusion of Aristotelian ideas of human autonomy with Romantic ideas of the development of personal capacities and with a generous utilitarianism according to which each individual's distinct experience can enhance the knowledge of society at large, which can return it, with interest, to the individual, thus furthering his development. Nothing of theology remains. The moral force of Locke's own writing can, however, only be properly appreciated when the acts of reflection and of choice are understood as also imposing the most profound obligation on men. In Locke are to be found those twin themes of freedom and individuality in modern political experience – as right to be enjoyed and as burden to be borne. The problem for a political theory of individuality is to find a form of association under civil government where individuals join together by acknowledging the authority of general rules governing their several activities, but which do not impose on them any single substantive purpose, other than that of mutual protection.

The particular form which civil government took in Locke's thought is clearly derived from the English constitutionalist tradition, represented in detail by the work of Sir Edward Coke, but in general terms familiar to any gentleman at all active in the politics of seventeenth-century England – as a modern Member of Parliament or civil servant would be familiar with the outlines of modern constitutional practice. It could be said that Locke contributed nothing that was new, that almost every item of his politics could be found separately elsewhere in the writings of the natural lawyers or the constitutional lawyers, or of fellow pamphleteers, particularly his friend Tyrrell's *Patriarcha non Monarcha* of 1681, or even in the works of Levellers like Overton. Nevertheless, Locke succeeded in, to use Oakeshott's phrase, 'abridging a tradition' and producing ultimately the most acceptable reduction of English civil government to its underlying principles. For some, indeed, more may be lost than gained – it may be more satisfying to know that some specific property, say the tools of one's trade, is protected by legal precedent than to receive the assurance that the preservation of property in general is the chief end of government. Locke, however, is uttering more than conventional constitutional pieties. He is giving expression to a view of government which has had its adherents and its antagonists down to the present and which is currently expounded by such liberal–conservatives as F. A. Hayek[16] and conservatives like Michael Oakeshott,[17] and in a more self-consciously Lockean way by the liberal Robert Nozick.[18] Under such civil government an individual's liberty, represented by his private property in Locke's widest sense,[19] is protected by abstract neutral laws. To use Locke's terms such 'known, standing law' must be entirely 'indifferent' as between persons and actions. It must apply generally to unknown present and future persons and cases. Government and law cannot have a 'purpose' of its own which would involve the use of coercion to redistribute property in some particular direction, such as towards greater equality. Private property must be presupposed, and the just distribution is that which has been brought about as a result of transactions – sale, gift, bequest – which are fully in accordance with the law. The general terms of the law permit individuals and groups to infer the boundaries of the property and liberty of themselves and others, and to know what they may rightfully expect in dealings with one another and, therefore, what would normally constitute an encroachment on the rights of others. Boundary disputes are inevitable and are the province of an independent judiciary. Circumstance will also require adjustments in the general law, involving legislation which Hayek regards as the outcome of a dialogue concerning legitimate expectations issuing in laws, themselves experimental, subject to testing, but general and indifferent whilst in operation.[20] Such a 'dynamic order', as Hayek calls it, might well have been somewhat suspect to the fundamentalist

Locke who, like so many other writers before the mid-eighteenth century, would prefer law based on a more fundamental order of things, perhaps also suited to a political world less subject to fluctuation than that of today.[21] Since law must be indifferent to outcomes it does not, strictly speaking, maintain any particular distribution of property but only defends the legitimacy of whatever evolves from strict observance of the law. The law should be sufficiently open to allow a transition from private to group, corporate or community ownership and back again, if this were the choice of subjects. In fact, of course, law creates expectations and routines as well as regulates them, and the necessarily conservative character of a legal system will tend to preserve established patterns and render change difficult.[22] Firmly excluded, however, is any attempt to achieve the redistribution of rights by law. Such action is an attempt to establish justice according to an extraneous standard, such as 'merit', which cannot be objective, and could only be achieved by government subverting property and liberty and imposing its set of preferences arbitrarily over those of previously free individuals. In approximate Lockean terms neither despotism nor paternalism is permissible. Inherent in the argument is, of course, the further safeguard that the indifference of the law must mean that it applies to government and subject alike – to 'favourite at court' and the 'countryman at plough' – and should prevent government pursuing any separate interest.

This is a conception of government which has regularly been condemned by those, particularly socialists, who claim to see another dark side to the very virtues of indifference and neutrality it proclaims. Whilst defending private property as the basis of liberty, it necessarily defends not just individuality but aggressive individualism which puts property to anti-social uses. The legal freedom and equality it upholds are 'mere' formalities. It is, in another sense of the word, 'indifferent' to those who, for whatever reason, are unsuccessful in free social and economic competition and who have little private property to show. Sympathy, community, solidarity are virtues allegedly absent from this view of the world.

The logic of the idea of a civil association does not support the last charge, whether or not it is borne out historically by any of those who have held this view. Self-determining individuals may choose to join together for any legal purpose which may be for commerce, culture, sport or for the sheer enjoyment of association. Since many pursuits can only be in common, such a theory of government must expect lesser associations to arise as a matter of course. Nothing, therefore, prevents the search for community. Reverting to Locke himself, a theory of associational pluralism may readily be derived from his various writings, particularly on toleration, and he clearly recognises that one of the benefits of association is the feeling of fellowship itself. In religion he is more sympathetic to church than to private worship, believing that men ought to attest their faith together for mutual education and for the encouragement of others. In many churches, moreover, the rituals performed in common were inseparable from the creed. For the act of worship to have meaning for the believer, it must be performed in common with others, or through the office of others, or on certain days and in certain places. Other societies concern themselves with learning, business or amusement. All must be self-governing.[23] All may own property, just as an individual may; if, he cites, Jews may own houses then collectively they may own synagogues. As a matter of biography Locke was the most 'clubbable' of men, forming little learned societies at every turn. The only involvement of civil government with such communities is to ensure that they do not invade the rights of other communities, or other individuals, or of their own members. No society may, for example, by expelling or excommunicating a member, claim to deprive him of his civil rights. Civil government cannot consistently both umpire neutrally between communities and impose its own solidarist conception upon them all. Only in the sense of denying that the state itself may be a community is the philosophy of civil government unsympathetic to it as an ideal.

The degree of sympathy such a theory shows for the poor and the unsuccessful is more difficult to gauge. As a theory of limited government, built upon private property rights, it is necessarily close to ideas of *laissez-faire* in the common presumption in favour of individual and group action and against state action in matters of economics and welfare. But *laissez-faire* has never implied a total rejection of state intervention, and civil government implies that every activity is liable to regulation in so far as it has a civil aspect which touches upon the rights of others. It is agreed that government must legislate to provide the framework for predictable social and economic transactions – stable currency, the law of contracts and wills. These facilitate rather than coerce, offering legal recognition and enforcement for transactions performed in stipulated ways. Liberty, it is usually argued, is not infringed by such laws. In Locke's language they direct '*a free and intelligent Agent* to his proper interest' and hedge him from 'Bogs and Precipices' (57). J. S. Mill could later justify the state collection and dissemination of economic information in the same manner – such as Locke practised with regard to external trade. The regulation of conditions of work or of air pollution might also be justified as defending each individual's rights. Hayek has gone further in rejecting traditional *laissez-faire* (anyway a historical figment) in arguing that a community may provide welfare for the poor on grounds of charity or as an insurance, provided it is financed by taxation governed by uniform principles. This would be an act of humanity, or perhaps of prudence, rather than of justice. It would not constitute an illegitimate, specific act of redistribution, as would legislation to subsidise a particular trade or profession or to restrict entry into it in order to raise wages or to freeze rents for tenants. Such direct intervention in an individual's rights to pursue his way of life as he sees fit would appear similarly *ultra vires* to Locke's civil government. However, the care of the poor could be interpreted either as a matter of justice or of charity.[24] Even Locke's draconian measures for poor relief start from the assumption that 'every one must have meat, drink, clothing and firing'.[25] The object of the proposals was to ensure that the cost of this necessary support should be recovered by putting the poor to work and poor relief thereby made self-financing. The poor have a call upon others' excess to relieve absolute need, but not to equalise income as such, nor may the government adopt this as a policy on their behalf. Allied to this in Locke, as in Hayek and Nozick, is an empirical argument to show that the system of private property will in fact produce returns for even the lowest paid far beyond the rather low levels they regard as attainable by any other form of ownership and production – whether it be primitive communism, seigneurialism or modern socialism which is the presumed alternative.[26] Any detectable sympathy for the poor is thus moderated by an accompanying reflection that they are better off than they could otherwise be and that an open society, guaranteed by law, permits them opportunities for improvement not found elsewhere. Failure to take advantage of the open society is variously attributed to the character of the individual *manqué* who fears his own individuality, to the learnt cycle of deprivation and alienation, to the grinding daily round of subsistence living or to sheer debauchery – Locke alternating between the latter two explanations.

The theory of civil government – limited and conducting itself according to the rule of law – has had a long history as one of the main contributory strands in liberalism. Though describable as one of Locke's legacies, his was only one of very many contributions to its development and understanding.[27] Until a revival in recent years, it has been eclipsed by a different understanding of government to which the term liberalism also became attached.[28] Liberalism began, in the hands of such as Locke, as a theory aimed at discovering constitutional defences for rights of self-direction, said to be founded in nature, but civilised by being brought under general rules which all might acknowledge as authoritative. Individual autonomy was threatened by despotic and paternalist governments which for private, or for supposedly public, interests sought to displace general guarantees by arbitrary will. Liberty on this view is, as Locke so profoundly recognised, 'property' – the exclusive right to dispose of one's person and of what one has legitimately acquired as one thinks fit. Included in such right of disposal would be freedom of occupation, of expression and of association for purposes of religion, learning, commerce or pleasure. Integral to such liberty is that it is bounded by law, and that each individual's right receives the equal and impartial protection of the rules of society. As it is usually formulated, such liberty cannot imply anything about the extent to which individuals or groups actually can or do make use of the legal rights thus guaranteed.

In the late nineteenth century such liberalism yielded to a new understanding which pursued the implications of the equality of rights presupposed by all liberal doctrine. Arguing that legal rights had little meaning for those unable, through illness, poverty or other misfortune, to enjoy exploring them, the newer liberals advocated that the community, as represented by the state, must redistribute its resources to place the deprived in a position to cultivate their individuality. Each member of society should be guaranteed either employment or financial security when unemployed, should receive a basic education and medical attention. He must be guarded against entering the cycle of multi-deprivation – poverty, bad housing, alcoholism and unemployment. Liberals like T. H. Green, Muirhead, Hetherington and Haldane believed that society, backed by the state, should ensure the conditions for the development of what British nineteenth-century writers called 'character'.[29] They recognised, as K. B. Smellie succinctly put it, that there was no longer 'any reason to suppose that the market value of any individual's services in a system of complex division of labour will be sufficient to secure him the goods and services which his development as a citizen requires.'[30]

More significant still was the economics of Keynes in transforming liberal ideas of what a government could achieve, rather than ideas of what it ought to do – the enlightened absolutists of the eighteenth century were as ambitious as any modern interventionist government. It became possible to conceive that the poor need not necessarily always be with us, the underlying assumption in Locke or in a work like Burke's *Thoughts on Scarcity*. Gradually such liberal ideas allied themselves with those of social democracy and the rights of individuals became substantive goods, such as full employment, which government was to achieve by means of both general rules and specific directions. The manner of governing is by this time very different from that identified as 'civil government'. The shift in underlying justification, moreover, can appear misleadingly slight, from guaranteeing the rights to develop character to guaranteeing the conditions for the exercise of those rights. A different threshold is crossed when social democrats make the further assertion that socialism is 'about equality' and see government's job as that of redistributing the resources 'of society' to obtain a more equal society, enjoying a greater community of culture.

The 1960s and 1970s have seen a growing reaction against this movement towards a liberal social democracy founded on some conception of redistributive, social justice. Increasing attention has been paid to those liberal and conservative political philosophers, like Hayek and Oakeshott, who had consistently rejected such notions of justice and government. The reaction has coincided with, and fed upon, disappointment with the welfare state's actual achievements in the very things it had proclaimed itself able to manage. This disappointment become more widespread when interventionist governments experienced increasing difficulty in dealing with inflation. Postwar success in raising the standard of living tended to be somewhat overlooked or declared to have occurred for reasons other than government activity, and even despite it. The welfare states and their political elites have been accused of arousing expectations they could not fulfil. The remedy must be to trim the state's activities back to something akin to those of Locke's civil government. In economics Hayek and Milton Friedman sought, like Locke, to neutralise and stabilise money, placing it beyond the arbitrary or paternalist reach of the will of political leaders. By and large, government was there to ensure by general rules the frame-work within which each individual can pursue what Locke called his 'civil interests'. In sociology Edward C. Banfield's grim analysis of urban problems in *The Unheavenly City*[31] draws analogous conclusions from a different standpoint which is again reminiscent of Locke. Policies aimed at ameliorating the problems of the inner city have misfired and actually exacerbate them. A mistaken paternalism, repre-sented by many welfare payments, encourages the deprived to become more dependent, less self-reliant and hence less able to escape the cycle of multi-deprivation. Banfield suggests that the population may be divided into classes identified not by their relation to the process of production but by personal characteristics of which the crucial one is the propensity to defer satisfactions, to invest not merely money but time and energy in obtaining education, training or job experience and to postpone other more immediate gratification. This power to suspend one's decision, to stop and consider the balance of the remoter absent good and present gratification is, for Locke, at the same time the differentiating characteristic of human agents, the most basic of human rights, and its proper exercise the fundamental moral obli-gation.[32] For both Locke and Banfield the danger of paternalism is that it renders it unnecessary for the individual to exercise this capacity for judgement, and yet it is only by its exercise that a man can learn to be self-reliant, develop his individuality and thereby both improve his own condition and contribute distinctively to the variety of his society. Paternalism must therefore be self-defeating. Help must be given in such a way as to encourage future-oriented propensities and individual judgement, in education, for example, by lowering the school-leaving age and offering loans to those who choose to invest effort in the hope of an improved future. For the incorrigibly inept and present-oriented, however, Banfield's proposals might also make one think of Locke's suggestions for poor relief, suitably moderated and humanised for the twentieth century.

The theory of individuality and its attendant conception of civil government can be readily made to appear harsh and uncompromising. For Locke himself, and for many of his immediate public, any such harshness, if perceived, would be mitigated by its forming part of a world superintended by a just and understanding God. With this protection removed, the attraction of the theory must be based on one's sympathy with its view of the individual agent and with one's estimation of the conditions in which each individual is likely to be able to develop the unique qualities attributed to him and lying latent. Even when taken in purely secular terms, Locke's own presentation shows that the harshness of the theory does not arise out of any inherent lack of sympathy with ideas of community or out of any necessary aggressive individualism. Lockean men are self-determining but by no means self-sufficient. They will choose more often than not to associate together for commerce, learning or leisure and find comfort as well as profit by it. Though expected to be critical of all intellectual authoritarianism and where possible to think for themselves, they will both acknowledge what they owe to the 'whole stock of human knowledge' and offer what they can to the 'variety and freedom of thinking'. Nothing in such a view hinders a dialectical development of individual and community. The impression of harshness arises instead out of the tension between the characteristic liberal assertion of the right to equal liberty and the substantive inequalities in society which make for differential exercise of equal liberty and which liberalism variously accepts, condones or applauds. Chapter V of the *Second Treatise* is a classic account of the move from equality of property right to inequality of property holdings. It is this, too, which for its critics undermines the theory's claim to incorporate a notion of community. Whilst civil government is ideally indifferent in its laws as to the distribution of property and treats all holdings as the contingent outcome of transactions in which any member of society may join, the routines of a society tend to shape and reinforce expectations in a conservative manner, and what is strictly contingent can take on an appearance of inevitability. One of the attractions of liberal ideas is, of course, the insistence on the sheer freedom to do as one wishes within the limits of respecting the like freedom of others. But another, as Mill, Tocqueville and, within his theological framework, Locke also insisted, was that liberty is justified by the moral purposes to which it is put. The right to equal liberty can then only be put to equally effective moral use if there is something approaching equal access to what may contingently be necessary to the development of individual character and social improvement. In the modern world, the individual's access to what is required to make some impact on the world by his exercise of judgement may be increasingly through association with others in corporate business, intellectual and leisure enterprises – as in Locke's world it would best come by patronage. A balanced plurality of enterprises (never yet remotely achieved) would do something to equalise access of participant members to the means of producing something worthwhile with the liberty with which they are endowed, which they wish to respect and enjoy and which a civil government could justly and impartially defend.

Locke's writings on epistemology and on religion, on toleration and on politics, disclose a consistent style and disposition of thought.[33] It is, moreover, a disposition not only disclosed in the writings but also reflected in the Lockean legacies to the Enlightenment and to liberalism. It is opposed not to authority, which it explains and upholds, but to authoritarianism. Locke's theory of civil government fundamentally defends the right which Kant recognised as that underlying the Enlightenment: to 'dare to know', to 'have the courage to use your own understanding'. This is, as Locke indicated, 'the end and use of our liberty'. The liberty belonged to all men as men and it was the task of civil society to secure it against encroachments from other individuals or from government itself. If Locke did not show how such equal rights were also to be equally enjoyed, in this he differs little from other liberals who have shared his view of liberty and have lived in later ages more sympathetic to this objective. For liberals, liberty should have some ethical purpose and Locke perceived it with unequalled clarity when he declared: 'Without liberty, the understanding would be to no purpose; and without understanding, liberty (if it could be) would signify nothing.'

Notes Chapter VII

1 A brilliant and much discussed article on the interpretation of meaning in intellectual history is Quentin Skinner's 'Meaning and Understanding in the History of Ideas', *History and Theory*, VIII, 1, 1969, pp. 4–53.

2 Richard Ashcraft, 'John Locke Belimed: the Case for Political Philosophy', *Political Studies*, XX, 2, 1972, pp. 190–4.

3 *John Locke and the way of Ideas*, ch. V.

4 *Mr Locke's Reply to the Rt Revd the Lord Bishop of Worcester's Answer to his Letter, Works*, IV, p. 147.

5 For a conventional assessment see Paul Hazard, *European Thought in the Eighteenth Century*, London, Hollis-Carter, 1954, pp. 41–3.

6 John Dunn, 'The politics of Locke in England and America in the eighteenth century', in J. W. Yolton (ed.), *John Locke: Problems and Perspectives*, pp. 45–80. Martyn Thompson, 'The Reception of Locke's *Two Treatises of Government* 1690–1705', *Political Studies*, XXIV, 2, 1976, pp. 184–91. H. Aarsleff, 'Locke's Reputation in Nineteenth-Century England', *The Monist*, 55, 1971, pp. 392–422, is devoted to the *Essay*.

7 *A Treatise of Human Nature*, Book III, Pt II, sect. VIII.

8   *Essays Moral, Political and Literary*, Oxford University Press edition, pp. 473 and 455.
9   See e.g. John Plamenatz, *Man and Society*, Vol. 1, pp. 220–41, and with greater subtlety and interest Hanna Pitkin, 'Obligation and Consent', *American Political Science Review*, Pt I, 59, 4, Dec. 1965, pp. 990–9 and Pt II, 60, 1, Mar. 1966, pp. 39–52.
10 Compare Bernard Crick's somewhat comparable way of arguing that 'politics', as he calls it, is incompatible with totalitarianism. *In Defence of Politics*, ch. 2.
11 Elrington's comments are reproduced in Laslett's footnotes to his own edition.
12 *The Natural and Artificial Right of Property Contrasted*, London 1832. See particularly the second 'Letter'.
13 *Horae Sabbaticae*, second series, p. 106. Nevertheless, Aarsleff has shown the extent of criticism of Locke in the nineteenth century, loc. cit., *passim*.
14 E.g. Robert A. Dahl, *A Preface to Democratic Theory*, pp. 34–5.
15 H. R. Fox Bourne, *Life of John Locke*, Vol. I, p. 193.
16 See e.g. *The Constitution of Liberty*, London, Routledge & Kegan Paul, 1960; *Law, Legislation and Liberty*, London, Routledge & Kegan Paul, Vol. 1, 1973. This view of 'juridical liberty' is summarised by Franz Neumann in a typically brilliant essay, 'The Concept of Political Freedom', in *The Democratic and the Authoritarian State*, ed. H. Marcuse, London, Collier-Macmillan Free Press edition, 1964, pp. 160–200.
17 See e.g. *Rationalism in Politics*, London, Methuen, 1962, especially 'On being conservative'; *On Human Conduct*, especially essays II and III. No suggestion of Lockean 'influence' is of course intended.
18 *Anarchy, State and Utopia*, Oxford, Blackwell, 1974.
19 Compare Hayek, *Law, Legislation and Liberty*, Vol. 1, p. 107.
20 *Law, Legislation and Liberty*, Vol. 1, pp. 101–6.
21 Hayek is in fact critical of the permanent 'standing' character of Locke's formulation of law, ibid., p. 118.
22 See above, ch. VI.
23 *Toleration*, p. 73.
24 See Seliger, *Liberal Politics of John Locke*, p. 175; also above, ch. VI, pp. 115–16.
25 H. R. Fox Bourne, *Life of John Locke*, Vol. II, p. 382.
26 See above, ch. III, pp. 55–6.
27 See Oakeshott's 'The Character of a Modern European State', in *Of Human Conduct*, Oxford, Oxford University Press, 1975.
28 On the accommodating character of liberalism as an ideology see D. J. Manning, *Liberalism*, London, Dent, 1976.
29 See e.g. H. Hetherington and J. H. Muirhead, *Social Purpose: A Contribution to a Philosophy of Civil Society*, London, Allen & Unwin, 1918; J. Maccunn, *Ethics of Citizenship*, Glasgow, Maclehose, 1894. The inspiration was T. H. Green's work, e.g. the lecture 'Liberal legislation and Freedom of Contract' of 1881. For a participant's commentary on the attitudes of the school, see J. H. Muirhead, *Reflections by a Journeyman in Philosophy*, London, Allen & Unwin, 1945.
30 *A Hundred Years of English Government*, London, Duckworth, 1950, p. 94.
31 Boston, Little, Brown, 1970.
32 See above, ch. II.
33 A phrase borrowed from Oakeshott's prefatory remarks to his essays in *Rationalism in Politics*. Despite some noted tensions between the several works, one might add of them what Oakeshott also says of his own essays – that though each was written for a different occasion, they 'go together well enough to be put together'.

Notes on Reading

A complete bibliography of works on Locke's political thought would be inappropriate in the present introductory study and would be an immense undertaking. The following bibliography, therefore, contains some notes to students on further reading, followed by a list of works cited in the text, which cannot indicate many other studies used and found useful. Very full bibliographies can be found in the edition by Laslett and in the studies by Dunn, Cox and Seliger. A bibliography of Locke was commenced by Roland Hall and R. S. Woolhouse in *Philosophical Quarterly*, vol. 20 (1970) and is continued in the invaluable *Locke Newsletter* published by R. Hall, Department of Philosophy, University of York.

Locke's life and intellectual development are described comprehensively and most readably by Maurice Cranston, *John Locke: A Biography*, London, Longmans, 1957. Cranston uses sources not available to earlier biographers but H. R. Fox Bourne, *Life of John Locke*, London, 1876, cites extensively from writings by Locke only otherwise accessible in their originals, as does Lord King, *Life and Letters of John Locke*, London, 1829, though his transcriptions are not always accurate. Excellent modern editions of Locke's writings on government, law of nature, education and toleration are available with important interpretative essays by their editors. Peter Laslett's edition of *The Two Treatises of Government*, Cambridge University Press and in paperback from Mentor, is indispensable for the scholarly construction of the text and for the introduction with its revolutionary revision of the circumstances of authorship and its broad-ranging interpretation. There is scarcely a footnote which is not in some way illuminating. Also from Cambridge are Philip Abrams's edition of the early unpublished *Two Tracts on Government* with an important essay on the development of Locke's thoughts on toleration, the law of nature and religion, and James L. Axtell's edition of the *Educational Writings*, setting Locke in his historical context. Wolfgang von Leyden's edition of the early *Essays on the Law of Nature*, Oxford, Oxford University Press, contains an outstanding essay on the intellectual context of Locke's treatment of the law of nature and on his ethical writings in general. A useful compilation for students of selections from various texts is J. Yolton (ed.), *The Locke Reader*, Cambridge University Press, 1977.

As suggested in the Introduction, interpretations of Locke's political thought have shown considerable diversity. John Dunn, *The Political Thought of John Locke: An Historical Account of the Argument of the Two Treatises of Government*, Cambridge University Press, 1969, is a brilliant and scholarly study which rightly establishes the theological perspective from which Locke examined the world of politics. Dunn finds the key to Locke's view of human conduct in the Calvinist notion of a 'calling' and consequently the emphasis of his interpretation is on Locke's notion of duty. Locke's politics are of course not Calvinist – Locke detested Geneva's authoritarianism – and Dunn suggests, again rightly, that Locke's stress on individual judgement allowed him to combine an austere sense of moral obligation and social order with the voluntarism characteristic of his views of the state and church. Dunn writes from a clearly stated conception of intellectual history and is severely critical of other commentaries. The book should be read in conjunction with Dunn's articles listed below. Martin Seliger, *The Liberal Politics of John Locke*, London, Allen & Unwin, 1968, is a well-documented and careful study which regards Locke as offering a more positive view of the role of government than that suggested in the present study. Chapters on property and on resistance are also particularly rewarding. Dunn and Seliger are in their different ways both critical of the account of Locke given in C. B. Macpherson, *The Political Theory of Possessive Individualism*, Oxford University Press, 1962. Macpherson's analysis of chapter V of the *Treatises* nevertheless remains one of the finest examples of a Marxist textual interpretation. Although his conclusion that Locke's is a class state is in certain senses acceptable, the present study has tried to indicate where I believe Macpherson's argument is unsupported by the text. Raymond Polin, *La Politique Morale de John Locke*, Paris, Presses Universitaires de France, 1960, builds a coherent liberal doctrine on the foundations of an account of the Lockean individual moral agent which is an anticipation of Kant. It is a remarkable and valuable study which, however, fails to appreciate fully the theological component. Leo Strauss, *Natural Right and History*, University of Chicago Press, 1953, and Richard H. Cox, *Locke on War and Peace*, Oxford University Press, 1960, both discover Hobbesian notions of self-preservation to be fundamental to Locke and regard him as instrumental in the transformation of natural law from a theory of duty to a theory of rights. Locke's own argument and language as a result suffer frequent and unnecessary distortion. In opposition, the present study suggests that Locke's notion of individuality permitted considerable flexibility in the exercise of rights within a genuinely felt framework of duties. An impressive 'heretical' interpretation of Locke is Willmoore Kendall, *John Locke and the Doctrine of Majority Rule*, Illinois Studies in the Social Sciences, Vol. 26, no. 2, republished Urbana, 1965. Kendall sees in Locke a defence of the collective will of the majority. It is a brilliant essay on the fallacies of majoritarianism but does not fully take into account the limited character of what Locke understands by 'political power' and 'civil government'. J. W. Gough, *John Locke's Political Philosophy: Eight Studies*, Oxford University Press, 2nd edition, 1973, is a balanced study which takes Locke's defence of constitutional government as its main theme. The studies of natural law and toleration are interesting and the chapter on trusteeship is particularly noteworthy. John W. Yolton (ed.), *Locke: Problems and Perspectives*, Cambridge University Press, 1969, contains essays by the leading Locke scholars of the day, mostly bearing on his political thought.

General surveys of Locke's achievement can be found in Richard Aaron, *John Locke*, Oxford University Press, 3rd edition, 1972, and J. D. Mabbott, *John Locke*, Philosophers in Perspective Series, London, Macmillan, 1973. There are numerous histories covering the period of Locke's political interests and activities. Two which relate political thinking to political and constitutional developments are J. H. Plumb, *The Growth of Political Stability in England, 1675–1725*, London, Macmillan, 1967, Penguin Books, 1973; and J. R. Western, *Monarchy and Revolution: The English State in the 1680s*, London, Blandford, 1972.

Bibliography

R. Aaron, *John Locke*, Oxford, Oxford University Press, 2nd edition, 1955; 3rd edition, 1971.

H. Aarsleff, 'The State of Nature and the Nature of Man in Locke', in J. Yolton (ed.), *John Locke: Problems and Perspectives*, pp. 99–136.

H. Aarsleff, 'Some Observations on Recent Locke Scholarship', in J. Yolton (ed.), *John Locke: Problems and Perspectives*, pp. 262–71.

H. Aarsleff, 'Locke's Reputation in Nineteenth-Century England', *The Monist*, 55, 1971, pp. 392–422.

J. O. Appleby, 'Locke, Liberalism and the Natural Law of Money', *Past and Present*, 71, May 1976, pp. 43–69.

H. Arendt, *The Human Condition*, Chicago, University of Chicago Press, 1958.

R. Ashcraft, 'Locke's State of Nature: Historical Fact or Moral Fiction', *American Political Science Review*, 62, 1968, pp. 898–914.

R. Ashcraft, 'Faith and Knowledge in Locke's Philosophy', in J. Yolton (ed.), *John Locke: Problems and Perspectives*, pp. 194–223.

R. Ashcraft, 'John Locke Belimed: the Case for Political Philosophy', *Political Studies*, XX, 2, 1972, pp. 190–4.

P. Bachrach and M. Baratz, *Power and Poverty*, New York, Oxford University Press, 1970.

E. C. Banfield, *The Unheavenly City*, Boston, Little, Brown, 1970.

J. Cary, *An Essay on the State of England in Relation to its Trade, its Poor, and its Taxes*, Bristol, 1695.

M. Cranston, *John Locke, a Biography*, London, Longmans, 1957.

B. Crick, *In Defence of Politics*, London, Weidenfeld & Nicolson, 1962.

R. H. Cox, *Locke on War and Peace*, Oxford, Oxford University Press, 1960.

R. A. Dahl, *A Preface to Democratic Theory*, Chicago, University of Chicago Press, Phoenix Books edition, 1963.

J. P. Day, 'Locke on Property', *Philosophical Quarterly*, XVI, 64, 1966, pp. 207–20.

E. S. de Beer, 'Locke and English liberalism: the *Second Treatise of Government* in its contemporary setting', in J. Yolton (ed.), *John Locke: Problems and Perspectives*, pp. 34–44.

J. Dunn, 'Justice and Locke's Political Theory', *Political Studies*, XVI, 1, 1968, pp. 68–87.

J. Dunn, 'Consent in the Political Theory of John Locke', *The Historical Journal*, X, 2, 1967, pp. 153–82.

J. Dunn, *The Political Thought of John Locke: An Historical Account of the Argument of the Two Treatises of Government*, Cambridge, Cambridge University Press, 1969.

J. Dunn, 'The Politics of Locke in England and America in the Eighteenth Century', in J. Yolton (ed.), *John Locke: Problems and Perspectives*, pp. 45–80.

A. Feaveryear, *The Pound Sterling*, Oxford, Oxford University Press, 2nd edition, 1963.

R. Filmer, *Political Works* (ed. P. Laslett), Oxford, Blackwell, 1949.

H. R. Fox Bourne, *Life of John Locke*, London, 1876.

C. J. Friedrich, *Man and his Government*, New York, McGraw-Hill, 1963.

O. W. Furley, 'The Whig Exclusionists: Pamphlet Literature in the Exclusion Campaign, 1679–81', *Cambridge Historical Journal*, XIII, 1, 1957, pp. 19–36.

M. Goldie, 'Edmund Bohun and Jus Gentium in the Revolution Debate, 1689–93', *The Historical Journal*, XX, 3, 1977, pp. 569–86.

J. W. Gough, *John Locke's Political Philosophy*, Oxford, Oxford University Press, 2nd edition, 1973.

W. H. Greenleaf, *Order, Empiricism and Politics*, London, 1964.

J. Halliday, *John Stuart Mill*, London, Allen & Unwin, 1976.

I. Hampsher-Monk, 'The Political Theory of the Levellers: Putney, Property and Professor Macpherson', *Political Studies*, XXI, 4, 1976, pp. 397–422.

H. L. A. Hart, *The Concept of Law*, Oxford, Oxford University Press, 1961.

F. A. Hayek, *The Constitution of Liberty*, London, Routledge & Kegan Paul, 1960.

F. A. Hayek, *Law, Legislation and Liberty*, London, Routledge & Kegan Paul, Vol. 1, 1973.

P. Hazard, *European Thought in the Eighteenth Century*, London, Hollis-Carter, 1954.

H. Hetherington and J. H. Muirhead, *Social Purpose: A Contribution to a Philosophy of Civil Society*, London, Allen & Unwin, 1918.

C. Hill, 'The Norman Yoke', in *Puritanism and Revolution*, London, Secker & Warburg, 1958.

R. W. K. Hinton, 'A Note on the Dating of Locke's *Second Treatise*', *Political Studies*, XXII, 4, 1974, pp. 471–8.

T. Hobbes, *Leviathan*, ed. Oakeshott, Oxford, Blackwell, 1955.

T. Hodgskin, *The Natural and Artificial Right of Property Contrasted*, London, 1832.

R. Hooker, *Of the Laws of Ecclesiastical Polity*, London, 1594; Scolar Press reprint, Menston, 1969.

D. Hume, *Treatise of Human Nature*, ed. Selby-Bigge, Oxford, Oxford University Press, 1958.

D. Hume, *Essays Moral, Political and Literary*, Oxford, Oxford University Press, 1963.

W. Kendall, *John Locke and the Doctrine of Majority Rule*, Illinois Studies in the Social Sciences, Vol. 26, no. 2, 1941; republished Urbana, University of Illinois Press, 1965.

Lord King, *Life of John Locke*, London, 1830.

P. Laslett, 'John Locke, the Great Recoinage, and the Origins of the Board of Trade 1695–1698', in J. Yolton (ed.), *Locke: Problems and Perspectives*, pp. 137–64.

P. Laslett, *The World We Have Lost*, London, Methuen, 2nd edition, 1971.

C. Leslie, *The New Association of those called Moderate Church-Men, with the Modern-Whigs and Fanaticks, to Under-Mine and Blow-Up the Present Church and Government*, Part II, London, 1703.

C. Leslie, *Cassandra (But I Hope Not) Telling what will come of it*, Num. I, 2nd edition, 1705.

W. Letwin, *The Origins of Scientific Economics*, London, Methuen, 1963.

A. O. Lovejoy, *The Great Chain of Being*, Cambridge, Mass. Harvard University Press, 1936.

S. Lukes, *Power*, London, Macmillan, 1974.

J. MacCunn, *Ethics of Citizenship*, Glasgow, Maclehose, 1894.

C. B. Macpherson, *The Political Theory of Possessive Individualism*, Oxford, Oxford University Press, 1962.

D. J. Manning, *The Mind of Jeremy Bentham*, London, Longmans, 1968.

D. J. Manning, *Liberalism*, London, Dent, 1976.

J. H. Muirhead, *Reflections by a Journeyman in Philosophy*, London, Allen & Unwin, 1945.

F. Neumann, 'the Concept of Political Freedom', in *The Democratic and the Authoritarian State*, ed. H. Marcuse, London, Collier-Macmillan, Free Press edition, 1964.

166 JOHN LOCKE

R. Nozick, *Anarchy, State and Utopia*, Oxford, Blackwell, 1974.
M. Oakeshott, *Rationalism in Politics*, London, Methuen, 1962.
M. Oakeshott, *On Human Conduct*, Oxford, Oxford University Press, 1975.
K. Olivecrona, 'A Note on Locke and Filmer', *Locke Newsletter*, no. 7, summer 1976, pp. 83–93.
G. Parry, 'Individuality, Politics and the Critique of Paternalism in John Locke', *Political Studies*, XII, 2, 1964, pp. 163–77.
G. Parry, 'Performative Utterances and Obligation in Hobbes', *Philosophical Quarterly*, XVII, 1967, pp. 246–54.
G. Parry, 'Trust, Distrust and Consensus', *British Journal of Political Science*, 6, April 1976, pp. 129–42.
G. Parry and P. Morriss, 'When is a decision not a decision?', in I. Crewe (ed.), *British Political Sociology Yearbook*, Vol. 1, London, Croom Helm, 1974, pp. 317–36.
H. Pitkin, 'Obligation and Consent', *American Political Science Review*, Pt I, 59, 4, Dec. 1965, pp. 990–9 and Pt II, 60, 1, Mar. 1966, pp. 39–52.
J. Plamenatz, *Man and Society*, London, Longmans, 1963.
J. G. A. Pocock, *The Ancient Constitution and the Feudal Law*, Cambridge, Cambridge University Press, 1957.
J. G. A. Pocock, 'Machiavelli, Harrington and English Eighteenth-Century Ideologies', in *Politics, Language and Time*, London, Methuen, 1972.
A. Pope, *Essay on Man, Works*, Twickenham edition, Vol. III (i), ed. Mack, London, Methuen, 1950.
D. D. Raphael, *Hobbes*, London, Allen & Unwin, 1977.
J. Rawls, *A Theory of Justice*, Cambridge, Mass., Harvard University Press, 1971.
C. Robbins, *The Eighteenth-Century Commonwealthman*, New York, Atheneum edition, 1968.
J.-J. Rousseau, *Social Contract* and *Discourse on the Origin of Inequality*, ed. G. D. H. Cole, London, Dent, 1952.
G. H. Sabine, *A History of Political Theory*, London, Harrap, 3rd edition, 1963.
G. J. Schochet, *Patriarchalism in Political Thought*, Oxford, Blackwell, 1975.
M. Seliger, 'Locke's Theory of Revolutionary Action', *Western Political Quarterly*, XVI, 3, 1963, pp. 548–68.
M. Seliger, *The Liberal Politics of John Locke*, London, Allen & Unwin, 1968.
A. Sidney, *Discourses concerning Government*, London, 1751; reprinted Farnborough, Gregg, 1968.
Q. Skinner, 'Meaning and Understanding in the History of Ideas', *History and Theory*, VIII, 1, 1963, pp. 4–53.
Q. Skinner, 'History and Ideology in the English Revolution', *The Historical Journal*, VIII, 2, 1965, pp. 151–78.
K. B. Smellie, *A Hundred Years of English Government*, London, Duckworth, 1950.
J. Stephen, *Horae Sabbaticae*, London, Macmillan, 1892.
L. Strauss, *Natural Right and History*, Chicago, University of Chicago Press, 1953.
A. Tassi, 'Two Notions of Consent in Locke's *Second Treatise*', *The Locke Newsletter*, no. 3, spring 1972, pp. 26–31.
J. Thirsk, 'The European debate on customs of inheritance, 1500–1700', in J. Goody, J. Thirsk and E. P. Thompson (eds), *Family and Inheritance: Rural Society in Western Europe 1200–1800*, Cambridge, Cambridge University Press, 1976, pp. 177–91.
E. P. Thompson, 'The grid of inheritance: a comment', in J. Goody, J. Thirsk

and E. P. Thompson (eds), *Family and Inheritance*, Cambridge, Cambridge University Press, 1976, pp. 328–60.

M. P. Thompson, 'The Idea of Conquest in Controversies over the 1688 Revolution', *Journal of the History of Ideas*, XXXVIII, 1, 1977, pp. 33–46.

M. P. Thompson, 'On Dating Chapter XVI of the *Second Treatise of Government*', *The Locke Newsletter*, no. 7, summer 1976, pp. 95–100.

M. P. Thompson, 'A Note on "Reason" and "History" in Late Seventeenth-Century Political Thought', *Political Theory*, Vol. 4, no. 4, 1976, pp. 491–504.

M. P. Thompson, 'The Reception of Locke's *Two Treatises of Government* 1690–1705', *Political Studies*, XXIV, 2, 1976, pp. 184–91.

C. E. Vaughan, *Studies in the History of Political Philosophy before and after Rousseau*, Manchester, 1925.

J. R. Western, *Monarchy and Revolution*, London, Blandford, 1972.

S. Wolin, *Politics and Vision*, London, Allen & Unwin, 1961.

E. Wood, *Mind and Politics*, Berkeley, University of California Press, 1972.

J. W. Yolton, 'Locke on the Law of Nature', *The Philosophical Review*, LCII, 4, 1958, pp. 477–98.

J. W. Yolton, *Locke and the Compass of Human Understanding*, Cambridge, Cambridge University Press, 1970.

J. W. Yolton, *John Locke and the Way of Ideas*, Oxford, Oxford University Press, 1968.

J. W. Yolton (ed.), *John Locke: Problems and Perspectives*, Cambridge, Cambridge University Press, 1969.

INDEX